GRAPHIC
DESIGN
BEFORE
GRAPHIC
DESIGNERS

VINCENZO...

Altri Maestri: GIOACCHINO...
Maestro del Coro: EMILIO CASOLARI
Rammentatore: FRANCO PAQUITO
Direttore di scena: LEONARDO SETTIMIO - PIERO AQUINI
Scenotecnico: UMBERTO EMIDI - FERNANDO MAGNI

54 PROFESSORI D'ORCHESTRA - 46 VOCI DEL CORO
8 corifee - 60 comparse ecc.

PRO SPOLETO

SILENZI

ATTENZIONE
ALLE TRASMISSIONI

DAVID JURY

GRAPHIC DESIGN BEFORE GRAPHIC DESIGNERS

THE PRINTER AS DESIGNER AND CRAFTSMAN 1700–1914

779 illustrations, 560 in color

 Thames & Hudson

Copyright © 2012 Thames & Hudson Ltd, London
Written and designed by David Jury

First published in 2012 in hardcover in the United States
of America by Thames & Hudson Inc., 500 Fifth Avenue,
New York, New York 10110

thamesandhudsonusa.com

Library of Congress Catalog Card Number
2012932514

ISBN 978-0-500-51646-1

Printed and bound in China through Asia Pacific Offset Ltd

CONTENTS

Introduction

Graphic design truly began when the 'design' of printed matter became a viable commercial activity separate from printing. Once established, the graphic designer's function in relation to the printer has been described as analogous to that of the architect to the building industry.[1] Prior to this, designing and printing were one and the same thing, so much so that design was not itemized on the printer's bill. Although the term 'graphic design' was essentially coined in the twentieth century, the design service provided by the printing profession prior to this – stretching back to the invention of printing from movable type, around 1455 – was, undoubtedly, its equivalent. The responsibility for design fell to the compositor, whose role was just one of several interdependent activities undertaken within every printing office.

Johann Gutenberg invented movable type with one purpose: to print books. However, from the outset, printers were asked to put their presses to other uses. Such tasks, collectively called 'jobbing' work, increased in volume and commercial importance as industrial and business interests grew in variety and ambition, enabling many printers to specialize in this area. This book focuses on the printers who did this kind of work – effectually graphic design before graphic designers – their training and working environments, the products they designed, and the changing social and technological circumstances in which these were achieved.

The anonymity of the printer's contribution to graphic design prior to it becoming a profession in its own right seems at first curious. Because the history of printing has been written, understandably, by those from the book-printing fraternity, books and their typefaces have been the focus of attention. The work of the jobbing printer was either ignored or, if mentioned at all, used as an example of what happens when standards, moral and technical, are allowed to slip. Meanwhile, histories of graphic design generally start in the early twentieth century, when the designer began operating independently. To rationalize this development, references were chosen that demonstrated the 'chaos' perpetrated by the printer, to which the graphic designer brought order. This book aims to redress the balance.

Why has the jobbing printer been so vilified? First, before mechanization, uniformity, or precise repetition of a given form, was highly regarded because it demonstrated a craftsman's control of his materials. Variation from the norm was considered a mistake – surely the result of a printer's lack of skill or inadequate knowledge. Until the nineteenth century, the appearance of printed matter was also uniform because the type and equipment at the printer's disposal had been devised for the printing of books. Typefaces were a standard style and weight, sizes were rarely available up to, and never beyond, the equivalent of 72 point, while the word 'colour' was used to describe the text's greyness of tone. However, greyness was not, necessarily, the response required by a shopkeeper with a new competitor. For him it was differentiation that needed emphasizing, and it was the jobbing printer's responsibility to provide it.

Second, the purpose of jobbing printing was also a problem. That the printer of books was the 'preserver of all other arts' was often stated with pride. The jobbing printer, in contrast, dealt with the everyday, ephemeral activities of local businesses, entertainments and regional government offices. The nature of what was being communicated was not only superficial and mundane, but also sometimes morally questionable. As if to emphasize this, its useful and proper lifespan might be a mere second or two, requiring no more than a glance before being rendered redundant. The idea that print, in any form, could be disposable was anathema to the craftsman. Making things that had a long and useful life, passed down from one generation to the next, had been crucial to the craftsman's status in the community.

Of course, some kinds of jobbing printing survived better than others. A daily or weekly publication, with a fixed format and conspicuous amounts of content, encouraged the collection of newspapers and magazines from the start. But the endless variety of shape and size of other items, to say nothing of their perceived lack of information, beyond that pertinent to the moment, provided little incentive for their safe-keeping. For many, the spike on which the finance clerk impaled completed orders or bills was an appropriate end for such miscreant printed matter. In the process of compiling material for this book, the question was never why there was so little material, but why any survived at all.

Third, modesty and honesty were integral to the Guild of Printers' orthodoxy. Public outcry at the vulgarity of outlandish claims made by manufacturers in advertisements also implicated the printer. The jobbing printer's effort in making his client's message persuasive called into question his own honesty, while the necessity to create printed material that was brash enough to attract the eye was considered immodest. Good practice, historically demonstrated by quiet servitude, was now impossible and yet the jobbing printer attempted to reconcile the new business imperatives, necessitated by a burgeoning advertising industry, with the ideology of John Ruskin and the Arts and Crafts movement.

Over and above the antagonism of the printing profession itself, when the professional graphic designer – initially called a commercial or applied artist – finally emerged, great effort went into discrediting the jobbing printer. The incentives for doing this are clear: if the design of printed matter was to be a viable commercial activity in its own right, the business community had to be persuaded to effectively abandon the printer and begin a new business liaison with the advertising agencies or independent designers who would then deal with the printer on their behalf. This was no easy task. First of all, the fact that printed matter involved design at all often had to be explained. Persuading a customer that he should now pay for a service that the printer had apparently provided for free was achieved by explaining the irrelevance of the printer's outdated, craft-focused, workshop-bound experience to the needs of a modern, forward-looking business. Surely, the argument went, the modern businessman's media requirements could only be addressed by a new profession made up of university-trained communication strategists?

The images in this book have been chosen to demonstrate the jobbing printer's design solutions to normal, everyday communication problems. In this way, the function of the nineteenth-century jobbing printer can be more easily compared to that of the graphic designer today. Nevertheless, the symbiotic nature of print and message can sometimes make it difficult when choosing material to differentiate between sociological significance and design merit. The idea of the past being a 'foreign country' – to paraphrase L. P. Hartley's famous line – often came to mind during the process of editing and photographing these documents.

The ephemeral nature of these items means that, while examples might have been discovered in the office of a derelict printing works or even retrieved from a skip, it is equally possible that they survived because they belonged to an individual with a personal reason for keeping them. A ticket, an invitation and military call-up papers, for example, all carry huge potential for personal memories. It is helpful to be reminded that jobbing printed matter also has life-changing consequences in addition to more common, often utterly mundane purposes. In the words of Dr Jonathan Miller: 'It is in the negligible that the considerable is found.'[2]

CHAPTER ONE
ALTERNATIVE FUNCTIONS OF THE BLACK ART

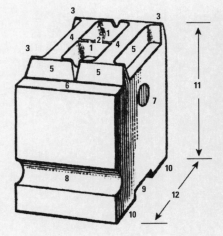

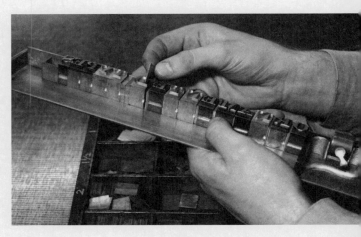

Left The anatomy of a typeface:
1 counter   7 pin mark
2 hairline   8 nick
3 serif   9 groove
4 face   10 feet
5 beard   11 type high
6 shoulder   12 body size

Right Composing letterpress type by hand. The type stick has an adjustable gauge (visible on the right), which is set to the length of line required. Spaces between characters are being adjusted.

This book begins in the eighteenth century, at a time when the printer was recognizing the need to reinvent the conventions laid down some 200 years earlier by the scholar-printers of the High Renaissance. It focuses on the nineteenth century, however, when printing processes underwent a technological revolution and the printer became integral to the expansion of industry and trade. Although slow to become industrialized, the print trade was quick to reap the rewards of an industrial society. The book draws to a close as the twentieth century gathers speed, the typical starting point for histories of graphic design.

Prior to the eighteenth century, the printer had, for the most part, been a maker of books, although it is inevitable that printing was also used from time to time to announce other information – the imminent publication of a new book, for instance. To the public, printing was a mysterious process, even magical, and commonly referred to as the 'black art'. Scholarly association, at a time when the majority of the public could not read, gave the printer a very special status. He was not only the master of a wondrous craft, but also the harbinger of culture and scientific knowledge.

The potential of print as a means of communicating government legislation or promoting local events, such as fairs or executions, increased substantially as towns and cities grew in size. While the town crier would remain a vital means of communicating information, a more dispersed method became increasingly necessary as urban development spread. Newspapers were just one of many solutions.

The eighteenth century is generally viewed as an age of elegance, taste and wit. It was also a period of commercial expansion. During the latter half of the century, road-surfacing enabled long-distance stage-coaching and, eventually, regular postal services. Previously isolated provincial towns

grew in prosperity and, by 1785, there were printing offices in settlements throughout Britain and Europe. In North America, large swathes of which were still British and French colonies, the population and printing expanded with the frontier. The movement of people and products brought the need for notices of coach times, tickets, bills and inn tallies, as well as advertising for events in neighbouring towns.

The use of print for the promotion of processed goods requiring labels or packaging remained relatively rare because production numbers were sufficiently low for labels to be written by hand. A grocer's stock was made up of locally grown produce displayed loose. However, before the end of the century, improved transport enabled wider distribution, and brand names such as Burgess, Keiller's, Lazenby, Twinings and Yardley were established. Bottled beers became available, as well as bottled hangover cures.

America imported most of the manufactured products required of a developing civilization from Europe. So eagerly anticipated was their arrival that, as early as the 1720s, newspapers devoted half their space to advertisements announcing deliveries and shipping notices. By the 1740s, the chain of activities that began with wholesale merchants at the ports was being extended as products were sold on to retail shopkeepers, or hawkers and pedlars carrying wares door to door.

As the business of commercial enterprise increased, so too did the demand for stationery, invoices, announcements, leaflets and other items that were needed to promote and record transactions. The notion that the printed word carried more authority than the hand-written equivalent was established in a commercial context from the very outset, and the ability to repeat a name or message precisely, consistently and, seemingly, ad infinitum had remarkable value. The means by which type and images might be reproduced –

Top left A 10 point letterpress character.

Top right Letterpress type and spacing material (furniture) locked into a chase. On completion, these combined elements are called a forme. Two metal quoins (pronounced coins) function like expandable

clamps, to ensure that all the elements are held when the forme is moved.

Bottom Letterpress type on the press and ready to receive the ink.

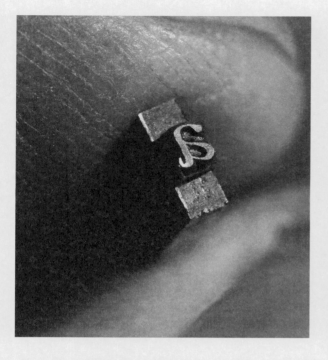

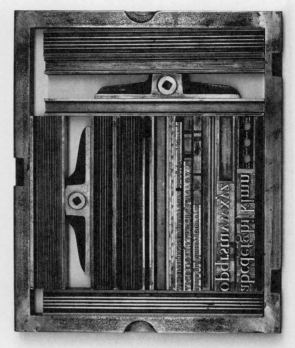

effectively limited to two print processes, letterpress (relief) and copperplate engraving (intaglio) – remained unchanged since their respective inventions in the 1430s and mid-1450s, but printing, as a trade, was evolving.

When discussing printing, there is an assumption that this means letterpress. Due to its meritorious association with 'the art of the book', the economic, cultural and technical history of letterpress has been documented in considerable detail. This is the process, invented by Johann Gutenberg between 1450 and 1455 in Mainz, Germany, that remained the predominant means of printing text-based books until the mid-twentieth century. However, when print was first used to promote goods and services, it was often the engraver who offered the preferred response. While letterpress was hindered by its limited ability to reproduce pictorial images, relying heavily on the skills of the wood engraver, engraving provided a versatile and generally more expressive means of delivering a printed message. But it was also time-consuming, both to engrave the artwork and to print. Engraving a small, single plate required a great deal more time than it took a letterpress compositor to set dozens of pages of text. Engraving remained viable because labour was cheap and, initially, the required print runs were low.

Letterpress provides a constant point of focus, running throughout the entire technical and cultural development of printing. Of all the print technologies, it remained, commercially, the most efficient. Not only was it much quicker and cheaper than engraving – 'handbills at an hour's notice'[1] –

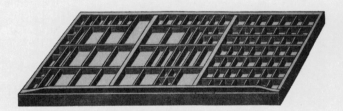

but also, in the hands of a printer with the ability and inclination to overcome its rather complex, systematic working process, it could become a creative means of communication. Yet it is also a process seemingly full of constraints, and this was especially true in the eighteenth century: a severely limited choice of typefaces, italic in some sizes but not in others, little or no variation in weight, few sizes outside the standard text range, and the perennial issue of missing or damaged characters. The resources of each printing office were uniquely restricted, so the compositor, over many years of using and reusing the same letters, would become familiar with the quirky characteristics of each and every one of the larger-sized characters at his disposal. Fortunately, customers' demands were, by and large, equally limited.

Letterpress printing and working conditions

Contemporary illustrations of eighteenth-century letterpress printing premises show no mechanical aids other than a heavy wooden press. Labour was cheap, but type was expensive and, in the later 1700s, as demand increased, often difficult to obtain. Moreover, the only types on the market were designed for book work and were generally limited to text sizes: 14 or, perhaps, 16 point normally being the largest available. A letterpress 'jobbing printer' – a term describing a printer of odd jobs or anything other than books, newspapers and journals – attempting to design a handbill (a leaflet handed to people in the street) with a distinctive appearance had little choice other than to make judicious use of text-sized capitals, lowercase and italic characters at his disposal. Alternative weights were not available, and so to provide emphasis a contrasting typeface had to be used.

Until around 1815, all printing companies, large or small, and regardless of whether they were printing books, newspapers or raffle tickets, used very similar presses. After 1815 (the year that *The Times* newspaper in London commissioned the installation of its first automated press), the increased capacity proffered by steam and, later, electric power enabled the larger printing companies to undertake higher print runs with increasing efficiency. However, the small printer with lower overheads could also be ambitious, not in volume, but by servicing the unique requirements of a growing number of small-business customers.

The printer purchased his metal type and most other equipment from a typefoundry. The once combined crafts of punch-cutting, typecasting and ink-making became separate trades during the eighteenth century. A font (originally fount) consisted of uppercase (capitals) and lowercase characters, numerals, punctuation, and a range of symbols such as

Below Engraving workshop, Italy, *c.* 1915. Female and child labour is much in evidence here. Although this photograph was taken in the early twentieth century, little would have changed in the previous hundred years.

asterisks, daggers and fists in one size only. If an italic version of the same typeface and size was required, and available, this had to be purchased separately. In addition, typefounders also supplied ornaments, or flowers, with which the compositor could set decorative borders and panels.

Each font was stored in a shallow drawer (case) that had a standard arrangement of compartments of varying sizes, each allocated to a character or spacing material. Fonts were sold by weight, so with a font of large-sized type the printer received fewer characters for his money. The size of text in books and newspapers was very small because 100 pages in 10 point type can be proportionally converted to 64 pages in 8 point – an important consideration when the printing press was manually operated and paper was a major expense. Interword spaces were made from cast metal in standard widths to enable the compositor to adjust the amount of space between words. Other spacing material – to be used between lines of type (leading, pronounced 'ledding'), for example, or in the margins around the text area – was made from wood and metal (furniture) and also came in standard sizes.

There were two quite distinct stages to letterpress printing. The first involved the compositor, who collected and assembled the individual letters to compose words and sentences together with spacing material, knowing how these elements would appear when printed. A good compositor also adjusted spacing between characters, words and lines to make textual matter easier to read and its appearance more harmonious. When complete, he secured this material with wedges into a metal frame[2] (see page 11) so that it could be carried to the press room for the second stage.

Working a handpress normally required two men. One was responsible for inking, achieved with the use of two leather daubers, which had to be rolled together to keep the ink evenly distributed over their surfaces during the application of ink to the type. The second, with ink-free hands, handled the dampened paper and 'pulled' the print. The process was speeded up with the assistance of a 'printer's devil' (effectively a casual labourer) who removed the sheets of paper from the press and hung them to dry.

There is some debate over the number of impressions a handpress printer could achieve in an hour.[3] Two hundred and fifty is the commonly quoted figure,[4] but it is difficult to imagine pressmen, regardless of level of strength and skill, being able to pull more than four impressions per minute and maintain this as an average throughout the working day. A more likely number is between 156 and 166 per hour.[5]

Income for a provincial printer could be meagre. However, the detailed day-books recording the business of John Ware, printer and bookseller of Whitehaven, UK, between August 1799 and August 1802[6] illustrate that provincial printing shops might also thrive. The breakdown of sales reveals that printing alone accounted for less than a quarter of Ware's total income of £399 8s 4½d, with the remainder coming from books, part-books, serials and almanacs, bindings, paper, other stationery and medicines. Listed separately under 'other sales', he also records his income from *The Pacquet*, a provincial weekly newspaper that carried advertising from London-based publishing houses. The income from the newspaper during the same period was £1,214 1s 1d, of which £581 12s 0d came from advertising.

Space in which to work, even in a large printing house, was generally in short supply as it was taken up with cases of type and racks of stored 'locked-up' type. A typical printing works would previously have been a private house, probably with strengthened floors to support the weight of a press and type. Contemporary descriptions suggest that conditions were

Top right A selection of punches by Giambattista Bodoni, *c*. 1790. This packet includes two ligatures (fi fl), punctuation, exclamation and question marks, and parenthesis (commonly called a bracket). The surface discolouration is caused by beeswax applied to protect the metal.

Bottom right The making of punches may originally have been undertaken by the printer himself or commissioned from a highly proficient metalworker. Working from the printed specimens of other printers' books or, perhaps, adapting the letterforms of handwritten manuscripts, the punch-cutter had to cut the letterform from the end of a metal rod using a variety of files (for the outer areas) and counter-punches (to create the inner spaces, or counters, of letters such as 'o', 'e' and 'd'). The punch, having been cut, was hardened. It could then be pressed into a softer metal to make a mould from which an infinite number of identical characters could be cast.

often squalid and hazardous, and made worse by poor lighting, little ventilation in summer and no heating in winter. In such works, stocked with paper, quantities of oil and turpentine, and with only candles (or, later, oil lamps) providing light, it is not surprising that fire was a constant fear.

There was also the danger of handling materials high in lead-metal content, a risk exacerbated by long working hours and insanitary conditions. Yet it is unlikely that printers' working conditions were worse than those of the average worker before 1800. In fact, working in the print trade had advantages. For an intelligent youngster looking to improve himself, the book-printing trade was a means of self-education.[7] Progress to the status of a master compositor in a noted book-printing establishment required an extensive knowledge of grammar, punctuation, and scientific and mathematical symbols, as well as a fair appreciation of foreign languages. This stands in stark contrast to the small, eighteenth-century jobbing printer, where working conditions might, at best, be utilitarian and opportunities for self-improvement limited.

The first manual of instruction for printers had been Joseph Moxon's *Mechanick Exercises, or the Doctrine of Handy-Works Applied to the Art of Printing*, which was published in sections between 1683 and 1684. Although Moxon only discussed printing in relation to books, his advice was tempered by the recognition that the requirements of print would surely change over time: 'Therefore, a Lasting Rule cannot be given for the ordering of [the title page]: only what has been said in general concerning Emphasis, and in particular, the humour of the eye, the compositor has a constant regard to.' The first printer's manual to address jobbing as well as book work was Martin Dominique Fertel's *La Science Pratique de l'Imprimerie*, published in France in 1723.

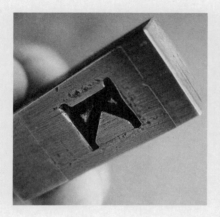

Training and aptitude

As far as the law was concerned, a person could not set himself up as a master of his craft without having served an apprenticeship, typically seven years, the idea being that the apprentice should learn about every facet of his chosen trade. For the print apprentice, this would include all aspects of type, typography, decorative borders, rule-cutting, imposition of pages, papers and their preparation, mixing and transference of ink to type, the working of the various presses, proofreading and correcting, all print-finishing procedures and the effective running of the workshop. An apprentice's experiences in a large printer-publishing house and a two-man jobbing print shop would be very different. Size, nature of output and geographic position all affected hierarchical status within the industry. Choosing where to undergo an apprenticeship determined the kind, as well as the quality, of training that would be received. This lack of consistency would later prove problematic.

Thus 'printer' as a generic term covered what, in fact, might be eight or nine quite specialized activities, all requiring different levels of skill. The master printer was famously protective of his trade secrets, and so it is understandable that to an outsider the various activities required to produce a book, newspaper or handbill were all the same: printing. Poor printing might be caused by uneven inking (the pressman's responsibility) or an unbalanced arrangement (the compositor's responsibility). In other words, no distinction was made between printing and typography; indeed, Johnson's dictionary (published 1755) defines 'printer' as 'typographer'. Not surprisingly, occupational hierarchies of status within a printing company were formed, the most crucial being the compositor, the man who established the appearance of the printed matter.

Master printers became members of the Printers' Guild. Guilds provided cohesion among producers of similar services or goods who, as a collective body, defended the privileges made possible by the monopoly of 'secret' skills. Guilds also jealously guarded the cultural traditions of their trade, and internal or corporate structures encouraged the maintenance of technical, commercial and social standards of its members.

In the eighteenth century there was a sense of community among the various master artisans of different crafts. All were recognized as being engaged in making products that required not only a high level of manual skill, but also trust from their customers. The diversity of these skills, whether it be baker, butcher, carpenter, cobbler, ironmonger or stonemason, did not, generally, decrease the mutual affinity between practitioners. Despite a formidable preparation for membership of different guilds, however, general levels of literacy were often poor. A study conducted in Mannheim, Germany, discovered that the majority of masters were not

Right Nettie Watson at the typecase of *The Elma Chronicle*, USA, *c.* 1900. Although women worked in printing establishments of every kind, their presence was tolerated only because their work was deemed unskilled. It was in the American newspaper industry that women first made real inroads into printing during the second half of the nineteenth century.

capable of completing their questionnaires.[8] In this respect, the master printer considered himself to be superior to his fellow master artisans.

Training in the print industry was undoubtedly hard. An apprentice was indentured (legally bound or tied) to a particular workshop for the duration of his apprenticeship, for which the parents paid the master an agreed sum. The apprentice lived in the master's family home, and received board and lodging for his efforts. In such circumstances, apprentices were both sons and strangers, workers and servants, at the same time.[9] The newly arrived apprentice would probably be about twelve years old and his inevitable naivety provided entertainment for the 'old hands'. Tasks such as finding the paper-stretcher or the box of dots for the lowercase 'i' were intended to remind the youngster of his complete ignorance – and requisite status – within the workshop. At some point, normally between the ages of eighteen and twenty-one, an apprentice completed his indenture and became a journeyman printer. The tradition was that the master gave the journeyman a suit of clothes – a symbol of reaching manhood – and a set of tools (more likely a type stick) in recognition of his formal entry into the trade.

Female apprentices were nonexistent. This is not to say that there were no women printers. There were, in all probability, thousands of them. In small jobbing printers, wives and daughters would regularly work in the print shop. Nonetheless, printing and its journeymen represented an entirely gendered occupation. There may have been many women in the trade, but none ever completed a printing apprenticeship and therefore could not progress to become journey(wo)men. Where they did find employment was as casual workers, doing supposedly unskilled work, typically cutting, folding and collating sheets in the finishing room.

Deprived of the opportunity to gain formal recognition for their skills, women lacked the credentials that defined a working person's virtue. However, this did not stop many a wife who inherited her husband's print shop from successfully running and maintaining the business.

During the nineteenth century, printing unions would become remarkably robust organizations that fought against the decline of formal apprenticeship by urging employers to consider their responsibilities to the future of both craft and industry, 'advocating also the desirability of teaching apprentices more ample details of their trade, not only for the boys' sake, but as a means of their becoming of greater utility to employers themselves'.[10] The apprentice was the future craftsman and a potential competitor for employment and, as such, it was argued that standards would be improved for employers. In return, the apprentice deserved 'the exclusive use and enjoyment of their art and trade'.[11]

Right *A Specimen of Printing Types* by Joseph Fry & Sons, London, 1785. See page 54.

The status of the early letterpress jobbing printer

Changes in printing during the eighteenth century reflected increasing levels of automation within industry generally. The growth of a new spirit of capitalism and individualism, and a more relaxed, *laissez-faire* attitude to the idea of progress were much in evidence. The concept of change as a positive rather than a negative phenomenon was becoming the norm. With an increase in the variety, number and size of business enterprises came the need for a regular method of conveying, exchanging and recording information. The printer became a major beneficiary of these new requirements, and by the second half of the 1700s there was a well-established demand for stationery, trade cards, price lists, handbills, window-bills, forms and legal documents.

Unlike book work, jobbing work was varied, unpredictable and ad hoc. The purpose of jobbing material was generally ephemeral – that is, it had few pretensions as its function was immediate and short-lived – and each assignment could usually be undertaken by a single compositor from start to finish. In theory, this gave him a certain amount of freedom for creative interpretation. The jobbing printer was more than a printer. Like many of his customers, to survive he had to be something of an entrepreneur. With a small, truly multi-skilled workforce, often numbering no more than three employees, changeable working patterns were the norm. A customer was often responding to an unforeseen opportunity and, therefore, a speedy solution was essential.

Many jobbing printers used their front office as a shop to sell stationery, newspapers, broadsheets, chapbooks, almanacs, and theatre, coach and lottery tickets. Some or perhaps all of these items would have been printed in-house. As in most small business establishments, there were few opportunities for employees to advance. On the other hand,

for many, the informality and varied experience offered by a small business might outweigh the benefits of working for a large employer. A jobbing establishment would certainly require that all employees were adaptable and skilled in every aspect of composition, printing and print finishing, as well as the general day-to-day running of the printworks and, probably, the shop.

The cultural influence and social status of the major book-printing houses remained dominant throughout the eighteenth and much of the nineteenth centuries. This is reflected, and indeed was established, in the written histories of print which, with few exceptions, have concentrated exclusively on 'the art of the book'. The perception of scholarly purpose coupled with a diligent defence of traditional standards and working methods provided the printer of books with a proud craft-consciousness. For the book-printing fraternity, the perceived lack of cultural gravitas in both the content and purpose of the jobbing printer's work, emphasized by its brief period of usefulness, represented the worst effects of the Industrial Revolution.

This dogged defence of traditional standards gave the book printer a heroic status that was often misplaced. The reality is that the work of the book, periodical or newspaper compositor was done to a house style: the choice of typeface, its size, line length and leading, as well as grammatical rules, spelling, abbreviation, punctuation and accents were largely preordained. At a time when standards of literacy were low, the ability to apply rule-based grammar and spelling was of great value to authors and society generally.[12]

The trade was well served by an excellent range of specialist journals whose primary contributors and editorial staff, as well as much of their readership, came from the book-printing and book-selling trades. The autobiographies of

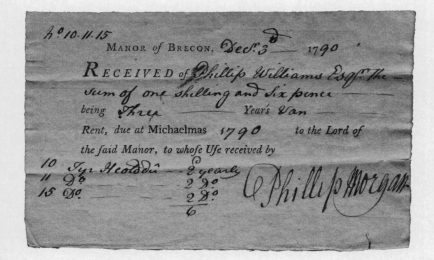

literary leaders and those in the upper echelons of major publishing houses, and numerous self-serving company histories have combined to celebrate the art of the book.

The status of the book, but also the limited resources available to the jobbing printer, ensured his efforts remained rather bookish in appearance. A window-bill, for example, looked very similar to the title page of a book. In fact, the title page did occasionally have a second function. In 1755 an additional 250 sheets were printed of the title page to Johnson's two-volume dictionary to act as posters to advertise the book in shop windows.[13]

Over time, it must have become clear to the jobbing printer that, in order to be effective, he had to provide an alternative visual language to that established for the book. To achieve this, he would have to break with the traditions that tied him to his profession's scriptorial past and reinvent his craft. Jobbing work was not convention-bound. A handbill had a very different function from a calling card, which differed from a label or a raffle ticket. The rules of the book printer, for whom similarity rather than individuality was the intended outcome, could not apply to jobbing work. To serve the needs of this new, brash, perhaps uncouth, or semi-literate clientele – in other words, the general public rather than the privileged and educated few – the jobbing printer had to design and print something non-standard.

The means at his disposal were, however, severely limited. Because letterpress fonts had been made specifically for book work, the jobbing printer had to adapt types to a purpose for which they were not designed. This must have been all the more apparent and frustrating for the jobbing printer with the burgeoning number of large, brightly coloured, hand-painted signs in and around towns and cities. The lack of constraints upon the sign-writer – not only in scale and

colour, but also in the freedom to draw letterforms without restriction – must surely have made the jobbing letterpress printer plainly aware of the limitations imposed on him by his equipment.

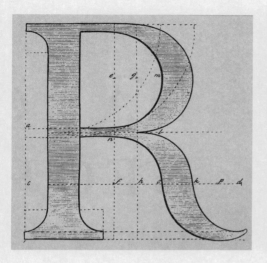

Far left George Bickham, from his book *Geometric Construction to Form the Twenty-four Letters of the Alphabet*, *c.* 1775. The letters were intended as models for large-scale use on buildings ('J' and 'U' are missing).

Left Wooden mould used for making a letterform on the surface of a brick, nineteenth century. Signage took on many forms in city centres. Where it could be presumed the function of a building was permanent, individual letters could be cut directly into the brickwork or cast individually as part of the brick-making process.

Below C. A. Carlssons Lithogr., lithograph, Stockholm, *c.* nineteenth century. It is assumed that sign-writing was an extension of the painter's and decorator's repertoire. Their skills in mimicking the surface of wood panelling or marble – much in demand during the eighteenth century – were utilized by shopkeepers requiring signage.

The sign-writer

The role of the sign-writer is closely associated with that of the interior painter and decorator. These were craftsmen who created the illusion of marble, cut stone, and other surfaces and architectural details such as elaborate cornices and dado-rails on flat, plain plaster walls, or made a cheap soft-wood door look like elaborate hard-wood panelling. Although the use of illusion inside buildings is as old as architecture itself, during the eighteenth century there was a growth in clients employing the decorative painter to embellish the rooms of country houses or their commercial establishments. Painters working on a retail interior would also paint or etch lettering onto glass windows, the façade and, no doubt, the shop sign.

Sign-writers had no formal connection with the world of printing. They had few concerns about the integrity or historic precedence of the letterpress printed word, and faced an entirely different set of practical problems compared with those of either the compositor or the punch-cutter. But with their knowledge of *trompe-l'œil* techniques, and their expertise at providing visual illusion, it seems only natural that they would experiment with basic letter shapes, devising additions, extensions and elaborations; such adaptations were integral to the interior decorative artist's repertoire.

The effect of shadow, for example, the most common aid in providing the illusion of three dimensions, must surely have been introduced to letterforms by these craftsmen. The weight and substance suggested by a drop shadow highlight the potential of the sign-writer's letterforms to express, extol and persuade. In this way, the skills of the sign-writer could be used not only to provide information, but also to design a distinctive visual presence that enhanced the nature of a business. With the sign-writer unhindered by elaborate processes or tools, new letterforms evolved with remarkable speed.[14]

The importance of the sign-writer's work in London was given prominence in April 1762 by a Grand Exhibition of the Society of Sign-Painters. Eighty-four signs and twenty-five carved figures were shown, some created specially for the exhibition, others borrowed from local tradesmen and from sign-painters' workshops.

As well as letterforms, simple pictographic symbols (such as a goat or cow for milk and cheese, or a chisel for a carpenter) had long been used. However, during the eighteenth century, signs were designed to enable customers to distinguish between shops offering similar commodities, goods or services. The concentration of trade, even within larger cities, meant that it was not uncommon to have ten guild-based but competing shops of the same kind in one street. And without a house-numbering system (introduced in Paris in 1761), its location on stationery would be described as 'at the sign of...'.[15]

Businesses had been careful to retain the image or symbol on their shop sign even if this no longer bore any relevance to the current trade or function. Symbols were passed on from father to son, or from previous businesses that had used the same premises. With no reason to renew the sign, it is easy to imagine how these might deteriorate into a dangerous condition. In June 1762, just two months after the Grand Exhibition, hanging signboards were suddenly banned by law, and, henceforth, owners either had to fix these flush against the wall of the premises or, more likely, have a new sign designed and fitted.

Businesses situated on wider roads often already had lettering on their fascias and façades. These were generally fixed above the door or running the length of the shop frontage, and made up of cut-out bas-relief letters or recessed letters creating cast-shadows with sun-, moon- or gaslight. Major public buildings had letters describing the function cut directly into the stone, their place and style being integral to the architectural design. Such letterforms were invariably roman in appearance and cut deep into the surface, their permanence providing an appropriately authoritative statement.[16]

It cannot be coincidental that when the ban on hanging signs was imposed, there was a significant growth in the use of print by businesses. Initially, this took the popular form of trade cards: a printed announcement on paper, sometimes approaching A4 in size. These often included an illustration of the painted sign that had previously been fixed outside the business premises. In this way the trade card has provided us with an invaluable record of the appearance of shop signs.[17]

These cards were invariably printed by the copperplate engraver. The engraver, drawing and cutting directly onto metal, had a similar freedom of expression (albeit limited to one colour) to that of the sign-writer. Indeed, during the eighteenth century, this was the medium of choice for the majority of tradesmen's cards and billheads. Together with that of the sign-writer, the engraver's work was to have a profound influence on the development of typeface design in the nineteenth century.

The jobbing engraver

Engraving responded to the need to apply words and decoration to metal surfaces such as clock faces and trophies. In contrast to the letterpress trade, the ability to draw was a prerequisite for the engraver since all the printed elements were incised by hand, typically into a copperplate. However, the printing of an engraved work was also slow compared to letterpress, making it impossible to reproduce large amounts of text. Printing from an engraved plate involved working the ink into the lines before cleaning off the surplus, leaving a polished plate with the ink retained in every line. The plate, with dampened paper on top and covered with a blanket, was wound, under pressure, between rollers to make the print.

The eighteenth century was the high point for the copperplate-engraved trade card. About 300 impressions of a typical trade card could be made in a working day. The printing of trade cards caused many business owners to recognize that the old sign, with its mix of obscure, often irrelevant symbols, was obsolete. The tendency, instead, was to depict a more immediate interpretation of business culture through illustrations of products, tradesmen at work, manufacturing processes and premises. The format was reduced, and heavier paper was used. Even chimneysweeps and nightmen (who emptied cesspits) carried elegant trade cards.

The process of engraving, especially its free, hand-drawn lines, made it particularly suitable for jobbing work. When letters were drawn by the engraver, the result was inevitably an extension of handwriting in appearance, rather than roman type. The jobbing work of the copperplate engraver was elegant, often elaborate and, for a considerable time, the height of sophistication. But in the 1800s, as the letterpress printer re-emerged with a new range of fonts, quite suddenly the calligraphic appearance of the engraver's work looked archaic. There are numerous examples from the first half of the nineteenth century in which the engraver mimics the appearance of letterpress, sometimes with disastrous results.

Historically, the services provided by the engraver and the letterpress printer were inextricably linked. Collaborations on book work and jobbing commissions were commonplace. Usually, the engraved work was printed in the engraver's workshop and then passed to the letterpress printer, who added it to the textual pages and gave the whole to the binder. Another common activity within the engraver's workshop was wood engraving. The wood block was cut to the same height as the metal type, allowing it to be relief-printed by the letterpress printer alongside, and at the same time as, the type. When speed was a prerequisite and the illustration required less detail, the plank-face of the wood would be used. For finer work, the design would be cut on the end-grain: the even, firmer texture of the wood allowed a more controlled image to be created.

During the last quarter of the eighteenth century, wood engraving became popular in large part due to the Englishman Thomas Bewick (1753–1828) who, by his ability to

Left The drawing of 1764 (*top*) is a
close copy of the engraving of the
previous year (*bottom*). The later version
may be the work of an alternative
engraver, asked to match the skills of
the original, or it may have been normal
practice to redraw the whole ticket when
showing the client the revised text.

Top right Watchpaper, engraving, UK,
eighteenth century. A disc of paper
originally used to protect the movements
of a pocket watch from dust later took on
the second function of a miniature trade
card. The ability to draw a range of
small-scale letters was a long-standing
skill of the engraver, and much admired.

Bottom right Writing master's sample
sheet, engraving, UK, date unknown.
Calligraphic skills meant that the engraver
might also be a writing master. Indeed,
books concerned with handwriting were
generally printed entirely from engraved
plates. This example shows a systematic
approach to handwriting.

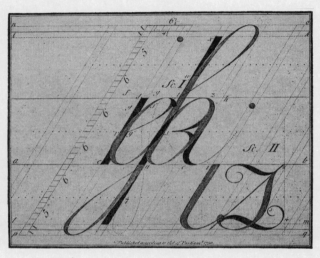

provide a rich tonal range from what had, formerly, been
associated with a simple, even crude linear form of image-
making, raised the craft of wood engraving to new levels.
Bewick's reputation was established with the publication of
his *General History of Quadrupeds* (1790) and *History of British
Birds* (1797–1804). However, while his work is closely associated with publishing, his influence spread into jobbing work.
Being a fine draughtsman, Bewick worked from his own
drawings, but jobbing wood engravers would also be asked to
replicate a pen and ink drawing or copperplate engraving.
Such demands, and the skills required to achieve suitable
results, would greatly influence the appearance of print in the
nineteenth century and, in conjunction with letterpress
printing, transform wood engraving into a veritable industry.

The engraved writing manual

The increasing volume of printed material in circulation
encouraged people to learn to read, and many of those who
did so also wanted to be able to write in a manner that displayed their newfound sophistication. In the eighteenth
century a writing master was likely to be a school teacher or
an independent master taking private pupils.[18] Some of these
sought to further their reputation (and income) by publishing their own writing manual.

The means of printing these books was intaglio. The free-
flowing line of the copperplate engraver – sometimes the
writing master himself – made this the perfect medium for
conveying calligraphic, florid curves, which were considered
the prerequisite of a cultured handwriting style. But many of
these manuals go beyond the requirements of a 'good hand'.
There is extravagance in the elaborate way that letters are
executed, wrapping and winding around themselves and
each other. In this way, the writing master demonstrated his
consummate skill and the imaginative potential of letters.

Explanations of how to write the letters also had to be
incorporated into the plates, and for this the engraver would
imitate roman letterpress-printed letterforms. However, the
tools at the engraver's disposal (as well as his creative inclination) encouraged him to reduce the serifs and thin strokes of
these letterforms to the finest lines, providing a far more dra-

The engraved frontispiece and title page

The letterpress printer's limited choice in terms of style, size and weight of type often led publishers to commission an engraver to design and print not only the frontispiece but also the title page. The frontispiece commonly illustrated a quote from classical literature to elaborate a theme from the book. Its intention was to establish authority by association for the book and its author. The letterforms of the quote, depicted as a stone-cut inscription or handwritten on scrolls, drapery or even stretched animal skins, were integral to the engraved image, while the illustration itself was often an imaginary piece of ceremonial architecture or folly.

The title page, meanwhile, acted as a temporary cover: the buyer was expected to have the book bound to his own liking. As such, it had to attract the eye of potential buyers (in the same way that a conventional book cover works today), as well as possibly function separately as a poster. In drawing these letterforms, the engraver might refer to standard roman letters but then broaden or narrow them, and add texture (large areas of solid black are difficult to achieve when printing from an engraved plate), variances in weight and fanciful embellishments. It must surely have been galling for the letterpress printer to see considerable sums of money going to an engraver to produce such a prestigious element of what was otherwise an entirely letterpress-printed book.

One of the earliest – and certainly the most important – pioneers in the design and cutting of letterpress-decorated letters was the French typefounder and printer Pierre Simon Fournier. His first ornamented types appeared around 1749, and by the time he published his *Manuel Typographique* (1764–66) he had cut nine different decorated and shaded letters in a variety of sizes, from 6 point up to 44 point. The embellishment of Fournier's decorated types is generally

matic contrast between the thinnest and thickest lines than the punch-cutter could achieve for the letterpress printer.

Although such books were called writing manuals (or, later, copy books), many also included examples of constructed letterforms, which used perspective to imitate shadows, giving them a distinctive, three-dimensional form. These inventions have nothing to do with handwriting and so it must be assumed that they were included for another purpose. The most likely reason is that these decorative letterforms were embellishments of examples seen on shop signs, designed to extend the potential readership to include the apprentice sign-writer.

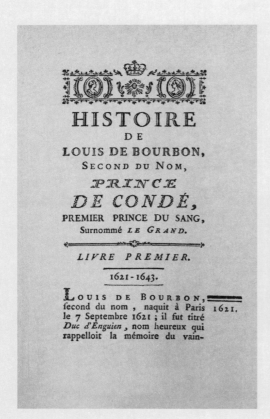

Left Opening page of *Histoire de Louis de Bourbon* by historiographer Joseph-Louis-Ripault Désormeaux, Paris, 1768. It shows the ornamented letterforms of Pierre Simon Fournier, which first appeared around 1749 and were designed to provide the letterpress printer with a response to the engraver's decorated offerings.

Bottom left Engraved title page (detail) with a variety of ornamented letterforms. One of the many compilations published by John Roach, London, *c.* 1795.

Right Decorative flowers from Pierre Simon Fournier's *Manuel Typographique*, Paris, 1764–66.

Opposite Bill of lading (detail), letterpress, UK, 1745. These bills, listing what had been loaded and where it was destined, became standardized in both content and design. However, many companies incorporated their own individual elements such as the 'S' in this example, using imagery appropriate to their activities.

restricted to inside the letterform. This was due to technical limitations of casting at that time. In fact, even in the casting of these relatively simple ornamental types, Fournier's type-foundry encountered many difficulties, among them the fragility of punches and the significant problem of getting molten lead into the finer, detailed recesses before it cooled during the casting process. It was not until the nineteenth century, when lead was forced into moulds under pressure, that the casting of ornamental types became a truly commercial, practical venture.

The influences on the appearance of eighteenth-century jobbing work, first by the sign-writer, then by the engraver, had been formidable. Fournier's decorated types aside, for the jobbing letterpress printer it had been impossible to emulate their refined hand-drawn images and decorative types. However, engraving and the intaglio printing process could not compete with letterpress on speed or price. What was so clearly required by the letterpress printer were types designed for jobbing work. They needed to have the attractiveness of Fournier's decorated types but be more robust and versatile. The essential break with tradition was finally achieved in London during the early 1800s.

Hipped in good Orde

Thos Elmer & ys Rest

In and upon the good   *Sloy*

whereof is Master [under Go

Williams   and now Ridin

and (by GOD's Grace) Bound

To Say, *len hov*

of Lumber on the

the Shippers and

Elmer

Being Marked and Numbred as

in the like good Order and wel

Barbadoes ___ [the Danger

only Excepted] unto *P.*

or to *his Affig*

In Witness whereof, the Master

Affirmed to *three* Bills

One of which *three*   Bills

stand Void. And so GOD send

Port in safety, AMEN. Date

Corrected proofs
Here is a situation every graphic designer
will be familiar with. Researched,
planned and designed printed matter
has been carefully produced using the
agreed information provided by the
client. A week later the proof is returned
creased and dog-eared, with sections
pasted over and covered with scrawled
alterations. The nature of graphic design
has changed little since this eighteenth-
century Italian printer took receipt of this
corrected proof.

Below Theatre ticket, printer's proof,
letterpress with wood engraving, Italy,
eighteenth century.

Hanging signs

Until the 1760s, a business promoted its presence primarily through a hanging sign. With no legal restrictions, signs grew ever larger as shops competed with each other for custom. But in 1762, perhaps due to a spate of accidents, hanging signs were banned and shopkeepers were limited to fixing their signs flat against the wall.

Printed on paper and considerably larger than the modern equivalent, early trade cards often carried the business sign. The necessity of an image meant that most trade cards were engraved rather than letterpress printed (*bottom left*).

The hanging sign reflected the nature of the business, but also, without a house numbering system, describing an exact location was complicated. 'At the sign of...' was the common first line of a business address. In the billhead below (*top right*), the original engraving predates the introduction of the house numbering system for London (1762); the number 85 was added later.

In the example bottom right, the shop number is incorporated into the design and the address itself is more concise. The hanging sign is no longer required and, instead, selected products are illustrated.

Top left Hanging sign, possibly originally signifying a goldsmith's business, Colchester, UK, date unknown.

Bottom left Trade card for a bell foundry, engraving, London, *c.* late eighteenth century.

Top right Billhead for a grocer, engraving, London, 1779.

Bottom right Billhead for a glassmaker, engraving, London, 1798.

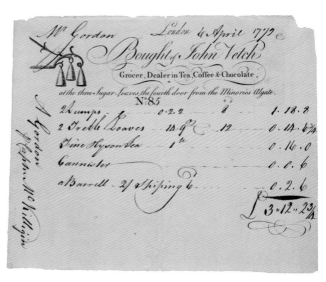

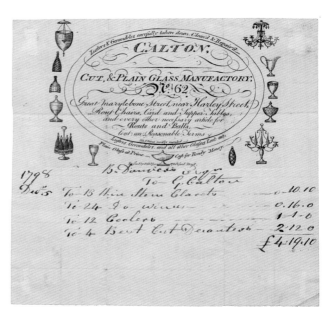

Official documents

The authority and gravitas associated with legal documents had a great influence on the appearance of early printed commercial material, not only because both were designed and produced by the jobbing printer but also because the client inevitably wanted to convey to his customers the perception of status and trustworthiness. The owner of the document below was in a hurry, quickly folding it before the ink had dried. The stain on the left is from the wax seal on the other side of the sheet.

The printed proclamation (*opposite, top left*) is a formal expression of the will of authority. It was from this document that the town crier would normally read before it was pinned on the public notice board. The style of presentation of such documents was remarkably similar throughout Europe. It was important that they had a broad international currency, regardless of the language.

In its necessary recording of activities and expenditure, the military has generated huge amounts of printed matter – from ancillary forms, manuscript notes and declarations to maps – and made a significant impact on the appearance of print. The recipient of the military call-up order (*opposite, bottom*) would avoid his fate if he could find someone to take his place or pay £15 in lieu of service.

Below Legal document, letterpress, Italy, 1610.

Top left Proclamation, letterpress, Italy, 1691.

Top right Electoral announcement, letterpress, Venice, 1786.

Bottom Military call-up paper, letterpress, London, 1817.

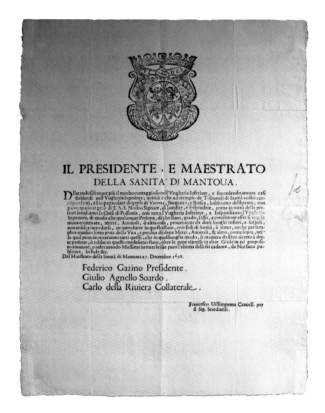

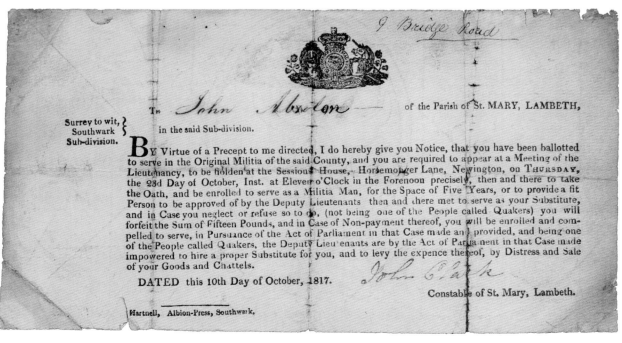

The title page and the poster

Books were often sold without a cover, the function of which was temporarily performed by the title page (*left*). During the eighteenth century many title pages became increasingly occupied with information concerning the precise nature of the text within. It is also known that additional prints of title pages were made specifically to be used as window posters (*right*).

Both of these items demonstrate the limitations imposed on the compositor who had to design such material. Display type, as such, did not exist, and so red lines were added to this poster by hand for extra attraction.

Left Title page of *The Apologies of Justin Martyr, Tertullian, and Minutius Felix*, letterpress, London, 1709.

Right Poster for the book *Exposition of the Creed*, letterpress with wood engraving, London, 1692.

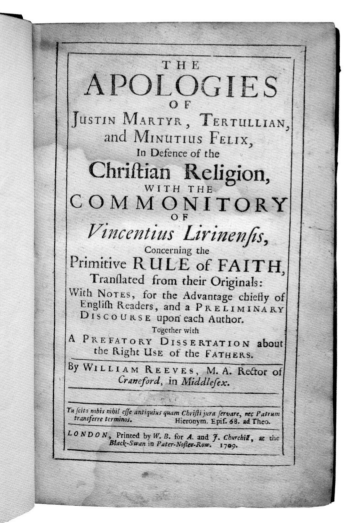

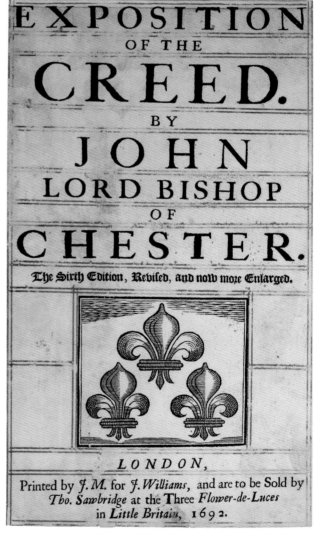

Public information

The size and proportion of the notice (*top left*) suggest it was designed for display in the window of local shops as well as the George and Dragon ale house. The compositor has provided a heading and given it additional emphasis by the use of a swelled rule, conventions common to the opening pages of a book. Emphasis within the text area has been limited to the use of small caps. This was a small commission, but one over which the printer has taken great care.

The advertisement (*bottom left*) was likely also designed to be displayed in shop windows. The choice of Blackletter to provide a distinctive heading was one of the few options available to the printer, and commonly used, while italics provide emphasis within the text. Question marks and colons have been used to fill out the two lines of flowers to the same measure as the text.

The poster (*right*) promotes a touring theatre troupe with thirty animal acts including a cannon-firing mountain stag.

Top left Notice, letterpress printed by Thomas Wright, Leeds, UK, 1799.

Bottom left Advertisement, letterpress, UK, *c.* eighteenth century.

Right Poster, letterpress with wood engraving, France, *c.* eighteenth century.

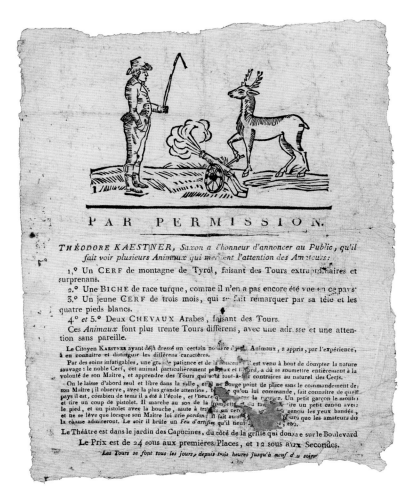

31

Engraved trade cards

William Pole's card (*left*) and the anonymous trade card (*top right*) exemplify the vogue for exuberant, asymmetrical rococo- (or Chippendale-) style mirror frames between the 1740s and 1760s. The absence of tradesmen's wares on the former suggests it belonged to a member of the landed gentry (Pole was, in fact, the owner of a large country estate in Ireland). The anonymous card, on the other hand, clearly belonged to an optician and includes an impressive range of instruments, all drawn in considerable detail.

The Thomas Heming trade card (*bottom right*) is less ornate and the frame is symmetrical, in keeping with the less exuberant baroque tastes that began to replace the excesses of the rococo style. Trade cards were often too large to fit into a pocket (note the fold across the middle).

Left Trade card, engraving, Ireland, *c.* 1760–70.

Top right Trade card (name probably trimmed off the bottom), engraving, eighteenth century.

Bottom right Trade card, engraving, London, 1769.

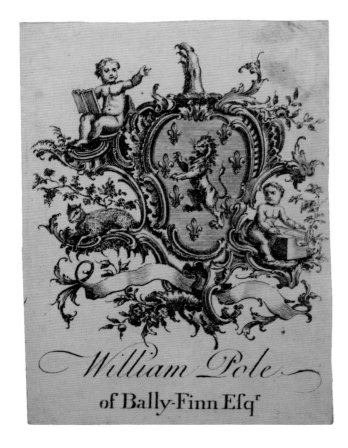

Legal documents

The contract and legal document (*top left* and *top right*) have been designed with spaces so that the required information can be filled in by hand. In the earlier document the spaces are too small, impeded further by the engraver's trailing descenders, while a much more generous allowance has been incorporated into the latter. More significantly, the later

example has been set by a compositor and printed letterpress, which not only provides more clearly defined spaces but also a distinctive contrast between the handwritten and the printed information.

Even in the design of forms, ingenuity is required. In the annuities document (*bottom right*) the elongated brace ({}) was fashioned by the compositor from a brass rule.

Top left Contract, engraving, UK, 1692.

Bottom left Wax seal, UK, date unknown.

Top right Legal document set in Latin, letterpress, UK, 1729.

Bottom right Annuities document, letterpress, UK, 1795.

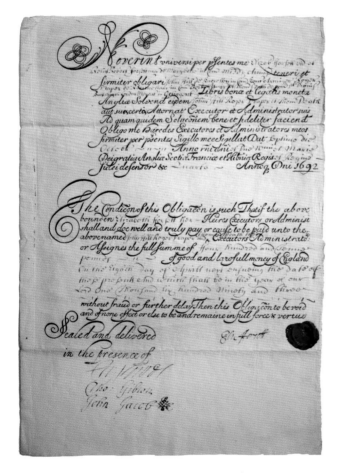

33

Shipping documents

A bill of lading is a statement recording the goods loaded for transportation by ship. In effect, it is a receipt by which the carrier takes responsibility for the goods listed. The wood-engraved illustration below depicts the infant Christ being transported by boat, the message being: no matter how precious the cargo, this shipping company can be trusted to deliver it safely.

Below Bill of lading, letterpress with wood-engraved monogram, Italy, 1786.

The need for distinction
The styles of the illuminated 'S' on the two documents below (*top left* and *bottom left*) are remarkably similar. Both documents were printed letterpress with a wood-engraved monogram. Although monograms such as these emphasize the nature of the trade – here, shipping – competition caused companies to recognize that it was the business name, not its activity, that had to be promoted.

The latest of the three documents (*centre right, with detail above*) was printed from an engraved plate. Typically, the text is cursive in style and the wording is reminiscent of the earlier documents. As it is a copperplate (rather than wood) engraving, the cutting of the monogram is more refined. More importantly, it has become a company emblem, incorporating the business name and activity.

Top left Shipping document, letterpress with wood-engraved monogram, issued in Malaga, printed in London by Robert Hayes, 1726.

Bottom left Shipping document, letterpress with wood-engraved monogram, London, 1745.

Top and centre right Shipping document, engraving, London, 1780.

Bottom right Detail of the monogram in the document of 1726.

Copperplate engraving
Unlike the letterpress apprentice, the novice engraver was required to achieve a high level of draughtsmanship. Learning to control the cutting tools used in copperplate engraving, although crucial, came second to drawing skill in the advancement of an apprentice to the status of master. During the nineteenth century these two activities became increasingly specialized.

The engraver cultivated a calligraphic style that was very much his own, but he was also required to draw typical seriffed book type. Letterforms interlocked within heraldic ornamentation were a mainstay of many engravers' work in the Victorian era (*opposite* and *top right*), but as the century progressed the early vine-like characteristics made way for a harder, more industrial appearance (*top left*).

Opposite Pencil drawings in a sketchbook of unknown date.

Top left Monogram or crest from a printer's catalogue of letter combinations, *c.* mid-nineteenth century.

Top right Detail of a two-colour printed coat of arms, *c.* mid-nineteenth century.

Bottom left Engraved personal card featuring a family coat of arms and motto, 1701.

Bottom right Personal bookplate, *c.* 1860s.

Drawing and engraving
The transitory nature of the design process, coupled with the unwillingness of the early craftsman to reveal the secrets of his trade, resulted in drawings such as the three monograms (*left*) – here arranged as they appeared in a scrapbook – being quite rare.

The drawing on the right, featuring the letters 'BMB' faintly sketched within a roundel, is from the same source. The purpose of this pencil drawing is not known, but it may have been for something other than print. Note the compass point and fold to aid in constructing its symmetry.

Left Three monograms, pen and ink drawings, date unknown.

Right Drawing, possibly for a personal card or bookplate, pencil, date unknown.

The lavish style of the drawing below (*left*), characterized by rich flourishes, suggests it was produced between 1720 and 1770 when rococo was at its height. The pencil drawing on the right (*top*), signed 'TGW', is very different, with delineated forms clearly described, indicating that this might have been a design intended for a metalsmith to produce.

The small drawings (*bottom right*) have the hallmarks of an apprentice's exercises. There is an element of delight in the abstraction of their design: 'EHE' ingeniously appears four times in the same monogram.

Left Monogram, pencil, pen and ink drawing, date unknown.

Top right Drawing, pencil, date unknown.

Bottom right Two monograms, possibly an apprentice's exercises, pencil, *c.* 1800.

The engraver's depiction of letterforms

Considered something of a genius in his own time, Thomas Wyon was appointed Chief Engraver to the Royal Mint in 1815 at the age of twenty-three. He was a highly influential proponent of the neoclassical style, demonstrated by the Greek relics casually strewn about in the engraving below (*top*). The plate, which is of a quality rarely seen among jobbing printers, is assumed to have been engraved by Wyon himself.

Visiting cards are thought to have originated in Europe, where it was common courtesy in certain circles to present a card with one's name written by hand. Printers probably had a small stock of various plates already made and printed the cards to order.

Subject matter generally bore no relation to the activities of the card bearer. Even commercial travellers, who might go to the considerable additional cost of having their names incorporated into the design, rarely indicated their line of business. Alluding to his role as a distinguished medallist, Wyon's card reflects social changes regarding commerce and professional occupation.

By the end of the eighteenth century, travel was becoming an important source

Top Personal card of Thomas Wyon, engraving, UK, *c.* 1800.

Bottom left Calling or visiting card, engraving, Italy, late eighteenth century.

Bottom right Trade card, engraving, France, date unknown.

of income for the jobbing printer. Developments in transport also led to printers in different towns, or even countries, comparing standards and stealing ideas. Trade cards in France, Germany and England were uncommonly similar in appearance.

The influence of Thomas Bewick (see page 48) is evident in all the cards below, bar the example top left, but is most pronounced in the Fitzroy Library card (*bottom left*), in which the engraver has ambitiously chosen an ornamental letter design.

Some larger trade cards may also have functioned as handbills. The example top right provides a great deal of information concerning the activities of a regional printer, John Fletcher, who describes himself first and foremost as a 'stationer', although the goods he is selling are those he has printed and bound. Note the words 'bill stamps' at the foot of this card. Their slab-like serifs and drop shadows are reminiscent of shop signage at this time, but here – and similarly on the label (*bottom right*) – is an early example of their use creeping into the printed word. The design of early labels was little more than an extension of the trade card.

Top left Trade card, engraving, Germany (for a British customer), *c.* early eighteenth century.

Centre left Trade card, engraved and printed by Harrison & Co., York, UK.

Bottom left Trade card, engraving, London, *c.* late eighteenth century.

Top right Trade card, engraving, *c.* 1760–70.

Bottom right Label, engraving, *c.* late eighteenth century.

Writing for business and pleasure

Writing was once the only way of communicating with someone other than by speech. Initially, postal services were organized by individuals under government licence. The Paris Petite Poste and London Penny Post systems, set up in 1653 and 1680 respectively, were typical private services designed to cover a city.

At first the price of sending a letter was calculated by the number of sheets used. For this reason it was not uncommon to write in two directions on a single sheet (*top right*). The use of envelopes, rather than folding the paper to form a secure package with a wax seal, became a popular option when letters began to be charged by weight alone (*top left*).

Keeping a personal scrapbook – the equivalent of a visual diary, complete with watercolour paintings recording events, flowers or images copied from books – was considered an appropriate pastime for a young person (*bottom*).

Top left Closed letter, Madrid, date unknown.

Top right Opened letter, London, 1838.

Bottom Personal scrapbook, UK, *c.* 1835.

From penmanship to engraving

Historically, there has been continual interaction between the penman's quill and the engraver's burin. Some engravers became master writers, and it was not uncommon for penmen to become expert engravers. Self-promotional items or even a whole book on penmanship were within the grasp of the penman willing to learn the skill of copperplate engraving. One such example is *Esemplari Moderni del Carattere Spagnuolo* by Ottavio Cupilli (*bottom*), a book of remarkable penmanship and engraving, although much of it is dedicated not to the art of writing as such, but to 'constructed' decorated letterforms – presumably intended for the aspiring sign-writer.

Top left An example of the calligrapher Louis Barbedor's penmanship, *L'Escriture Italienne Bastarde*, Paris, 1647.

Bottom Ottavio Cupilli's *Esemplari Moderni del Carattere Spagnuolo*, Italy, c. 1837.

Top centre and right Decorated letters, engravings, early nineteenth century.

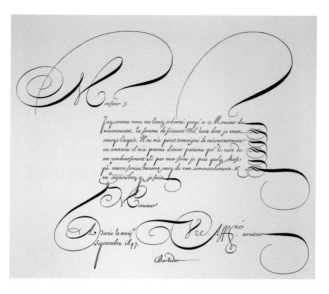

Commercial opportunities

As travel became more commonplace, entrepreneurs sought out new markets. The card below (*top left*) doubles as a 'traveller's guide', outlining distances from the hotel to various destinations. The swan is decorated with a complex, elegant arrangement of ornate swashes, while the prominent letters at the centre are in the style of the 'constructed' ornamental letters used by the sign-writer for commercial signage.

Swashes were in vogue for a time, especially in the United States, where newly trained penmen offered to embellish the customer's name with an angel, a bird or a whole menagerie, budget permitting. The two 'flourished' calling cards (*bottom left and right*) are original calligraphic works produced with a quill. The example in the centre (*left*) is engraved.

It became a standard professional trick for the itinerant penman to write the whole of the Lord's Prayer in the space of a small coin (*top right*). This card also features two examples of writing exercises demonstrating methods employed in teaching the subject.

Top left Trade card, engraving, UK, *c.* late eighteenth century.

Centre left Trade card, engraving, probably American, nineteenth century.

Top right Trade card or handbill, hand-coloured engraving, UK, nineteenth century.

Bottom left and right Two calling cards, original calligraphic works produced with a quill, probably American, *c.* nineteenth century.

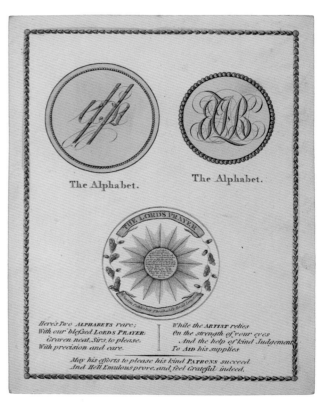

Trade cards and billheads

In the late eighteenth and early nineteenth centuries, shop window displays became a point of fascination for city-dwellers. At the same time, the design of trade cards evolved from depicting the shop sign to showing the whole building, often with people gazing into the window (*centre*).

The engraver tended to add scrolls to his calligraphic letterforms (*bottom left*). However, in France there was an interest in a simpler, more business-like approach to jobbing printing (*bottom right*). The carefully judged additional spaces between the characters give them a calm authority, while the inclusion of rules provides clarity of purpose for those receiving the document.

Top left Billhead for a painter and decorator, engraving, UK, 1783.

Centre Trade card for an ironmonger, engraving, UK, *c.* early 1800s.

Bottom left Billhead for a hatter, engraving, Ireland, 1787.

Bottom right Billhead for a perfumery, letterpress, France, 1813.

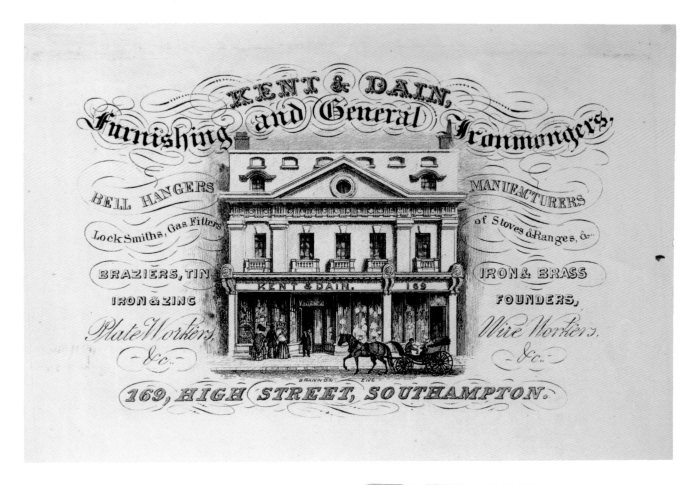

Popular printed matter

Selling for just one penny or less, chapbooks were at the height of their popularity in the late eighteenth and early nineteenth centuries. For this reason, they often carried religious or political content. They were made from a single sheet folded to make anything from 8 to 32 pages including a cover. The idea was that the owner would trim and sew the folded sheet to make a simple book, although it appears very few actually did. The chapbook below is a particularly fine example. More often than not they were indifferently printed, generally with worn type and old, battered wood engravings bearing little relevance to the story.

Periodicals such as those illustrated opposite were already commonplace,

Below Chapbook (cover and opened flat) entitled *The Life and History of the Famous Mother Shipton, and her Daughter Peggy*, consisting of 24 pages, letterpress printed by J. Davenport, London, 1797.

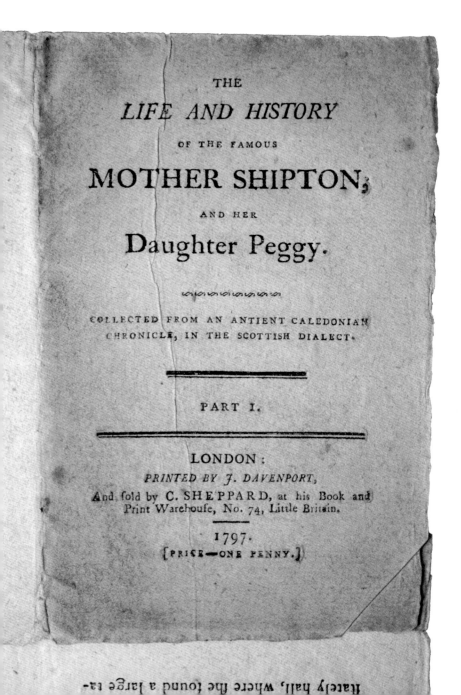

THE
LIFE AND HISTORY
OF THE FAMOUS
MOTHER SHIPTON,
AND HER
Daughter Peggy.

COLLECTED FROM AN ANTIENT CALEDONIAN
CHRONICLE, IN THE SCOTTISH DIALECT.

PART I.

LONDON:
PRINTED BY J. DAVENPORT,
And fold by C. SHEPPARD, at his Book and
Print Warehoufe, No. 74, Little Britain.

1797.
[PRICE—ONE PENNY.]

although most did not survive beyond the first few issues. The journal (*top left*) is distinguishable from the typical daily newspaper through the use of an illustrated cover. This convention, although not applied in every case, became a regular feature of journal design. However, the image often remained the same from one issue to the next.

Illustrated booklets designed as teaching aids were produced for use in the home (*top right*). The illustration is intended to reinforce the statement. However, in this instance, the illustration does not appear to bear any relation to the concept 'three times 5 are 15'.

Top left *The Reading Mercury, or Weekly Entertainer*, vol. 1, no. 1, letterpress printed by W. Parks and D. Kinnier, UK, 1723.

Bottom *The Ipswich-Journal, or, The Weekly-Mercury*, no. 504, 1730.

Top right Page from *Darris's Cabinet*, hand-coloured engraving, 1813.

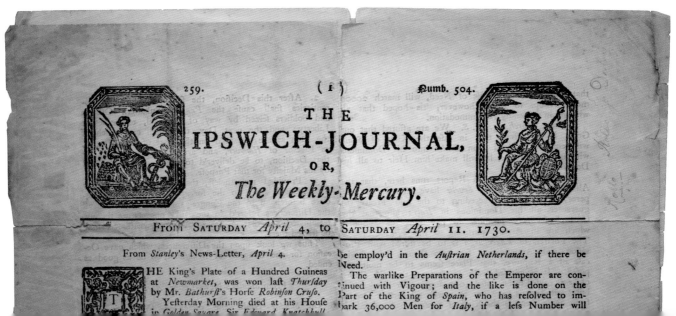

The reinvention of wood engraving

Wood engraving was the most widely used medium for printing images from the late eighteenth and throughout the nineteenth centuries. This technique had the advantage of being relief printed, allowing images to be printed on a letterpress press alongside, and at the same time as, the textual matter. This was a huge saving in labour and time compared to copperplate engraving.

Thomas Bewick (1753–1828) transformed the perception of wood engraving within the printing industry and his influence quickly spread. The book below (*left*) established him as a major figure. However, it was not so

much his large illustrations of animals that caused such a sensation, but rather the small vignettes depicting minor and often amusing aspects of country life. In the example below (*top right*) a youth, presumably attempting to take eggs from a nest, falls into the river still clinging to the broken branch.

Orlando Jewitt (1799–1869), a wood engraver who specialized in the depiction of Gothic architecture (*opposite, left*), was initially influenced by Bewick but developed a style that enabled him to depict his subjects objectively in rich detail. He achieved great success through his work for publishers such as Oxford University Press.

Left Thomas Bewick, title page of *A General History of Quadrupeds*, with wood-engraved illustrations letterpress printed, Newcastle upon Tyne, UK, 1821 (first published in 1790).

Top right Thomas Bewick, wood-engraved illustration from *A General History of Quadrupeds*, letterpress printed, Newcastle upon Tyne, 1821.

Bottom right Engraver unknown, printed and published by the Catnach Press, *c.* 1820–30s. No doubt cut and printed at speed, this example is typical of the standard of wood engraving for popular reading matter.

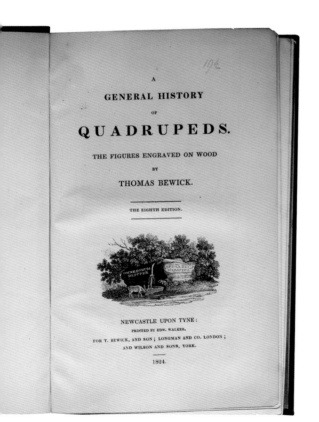

Calling cards as a symbol of style
Convention required that a lady's card was slightly larger than a gentleman's, but that the latter was heavier. These three examples (*right*) reflect the way calling cards evolved. The first (*top*) is handwritten, a practice superseded by the far more eloquent, though less personal, skills of the engraver's calligraphic hand (*centre*). The last example (*bottom*) is also an engraving. The letterforms, with their distinctive extremes of thick and thin lines, are reminiscent of Bodoni's letterpress types, but here the engraver has incorporated decoration within the thick strokes. The card has a hard, glossy surface.

Left Orlando Jewitt, wood engraving, Oxford, UK, *c.* 1840s.

Right Three calling (or visiting) cards, *c.* late eighteenth/ early nineteenth century.

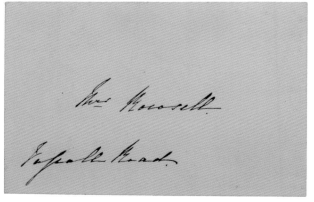

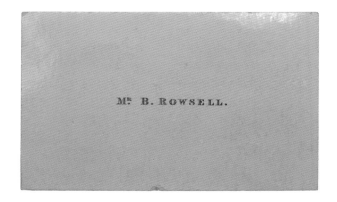

Information design: travel

Alongside travel guides showing the calculated distances from a certain point (*top left*), which were particularly popular in the UK, US and Canada, various ways of describing a journey – miles covered, time taken or, more simply, places passed through on the way to a destination – were conceived. An example below (*bottom left*) shows a particularly interesting development, with place names presented sequentially rather than geographically.

In the documents top left and bottom right, the nature of engraving – the hand tools, the resistance of the copper, the smallness of scale – all appear to contribute to the resulting fine, elongated serifs and the exaggerated distinction between thick and thin lines of the letters. This distinctive appearance was a major influence on Fournier and Bodoni in the design of typefaces for the letterpress printer during the last half of the eighteenth century.

The earliest known timetables relate to the high- and low-water crossing times of ferries. The design of the tabular work in the example below (*top right*) is concise, eloquent and of a standard not uncommon during the early nineteenth century.

Top left *A Table of the Roads and Distances from London to any Part of England and Wales*, engraving, *c.* 1760.

Bottom left *The North-West Road from London to Holyhead*, letterpress, UK, date unknown.

Top right Combined sun, moon and tide timetable, letterpress, London, 1828.

Bottom right Detail of a map, engraving, *c.* 1780.

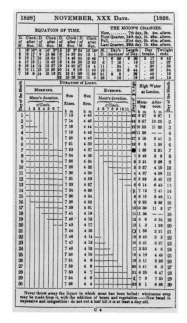

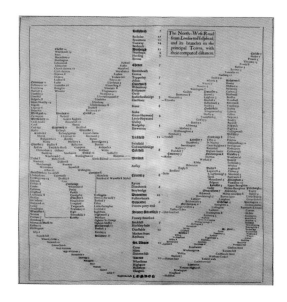

The speed table below (*top left*), which provides a calculation of minutes per mile and miles per hour, is remarkably erudite in its arrangement. There is a very real sense that the engraver was as intrigued by the potential of design in presenting facts as the facts themselves.

Issued by local authorities, early passports evolved into a part-printed document of identity (*top right*) in the nineteenth century, which included a detailed description of age, height and facial features. As international travel became increasingly popular for leisure and culture, or necessary for business, enterprising service providers had the bright idea of dual-language cards (*bottom left and right*).

Top left Speed table, engraving, UK, date unknown.

Bottom left and right Two dual-language cards, France, *c.* 1800.

Top right Passport issued by the town of Calais, letterpress, 1814.

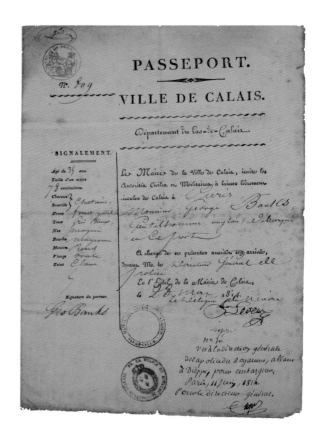

Information design: miscellaneous
In the bill of mortality (*top left*), each year is assigned a column that is subdivided into three: month, total number of deaths, and deaths caused by the plague. However, these lists were untrustworthy, especially regarding plague victims, because relatives sought to avoid stringent quarantine regulations.

Tables specifically geared to a niche market were published in periodicals such as *The Gentleman's Magazine* (*top right*, in this case members of the land-owning gentry). The tabulated material provides information regarding weather forecasts and corn prices. The tabular

work in the *Book of Prayers* (*bottom left*), in contrast, required considerable planning and, no doubt, test pages to be composed before the book was set. While it is presumed that the client would provide a full and detailed manuscript, the task of interpretation (design) fell to the compositor.

The detailed plan for rolling carts and wagons (*bottom right*) advocates a radical, broad-rimmed wheel designed to reduce the damage to paths and roads caused by standard models. There is no information regarding the construction of these wheels or the materials with which to build them.

Top left Bill of mortality, letterpress, UK, 1665.

Bottom left *Book of Prayers*, UK, *c.* 1800.

Top right *The Gentleman's Magazine*, letterpress printed by Nichols & Son, London, January 1805.

Bottom right Plan for rolling carts and wagons, hand-coloured engraving, London, 1772.

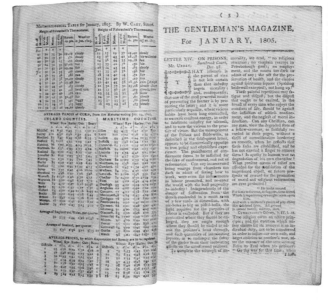

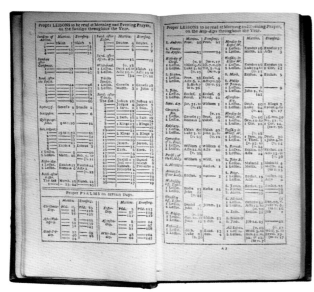

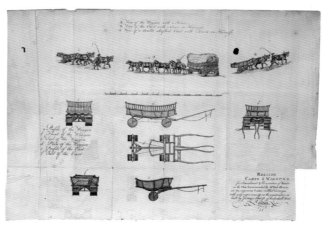

By the beginning of the eighteenth century, transportation in London was regulated, with each 'vehicle' requiring a licence, and charges standardized. A fare plate had to be displayed 'in the most convenient place' in a carriage or on a boat. In the early example below (*top right*), information regarding journeys is described in full (the concept of presenting it in tabulated form came later).

Hieroglyphic puzzles (or rebuses) such as the one below (*top left*) became popular during the eighteenth century, sold as novelty items in printsellers'

shops. The ability of the rebus to attract the curiosity of the viewer made it a popular device for advertisers.

The back cover of the chapbook (*bottom*) carries useful information, displaying a number of conversion tables relating to money, roman numerals, and ale and beer measures.

Top left Hieroglyphic puzzle (or rebus), wood-engraved illustrations and text printed letterpress, Paris, date unknown.

Bottom Chapbook, *Against Revenge*, letterpress printed and published by J. Catnach, *c.* 1800.

Top right Fare plate displaying rates for hackney-chairmen and watermen, engraving, London, 1742.

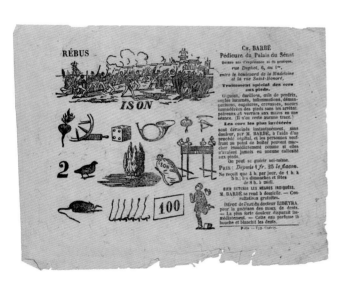

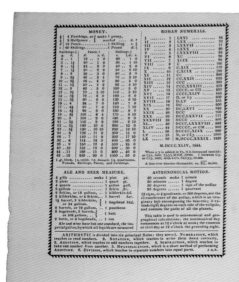

The roots of display type design
The title page (*top left*) of Fournier's
Manuel Typographique displays his
ornamented types, with which he hoped
to give the letterpress printer the means
to compete with the engraver. The spread
(*top right*) shows examples of his shaded
types, characterized by a white line cut
into thick strokes.

In contrast to this innovative work in
Paris, the English typefoundry Joseph
Fry & Sons produced letters modelled
on John Baskerville's and, later, William
Caslon's fonts. The imitation of successful

type designs was standard practice,
leaving the jobbing printer with little
typographic variation. In the specimen
sheet (*bottom right*) italics and small
caps were available in each size but
there were no alternative weights. Fry
resorted to the use of Blackletter in the
heading for emphasis and variation.

When Giambattista Bodoni (1740–1813)
took charge of the Stamperia Reale at
Parma in 1768, he chose types primarily
from the Fournier foundry. However,
Bodoni had also been cutting his own
punches from the outset. Although

Top left and right The title page and
one spread from Fournier's *Manuel
Typographique*, vol. 1, letterpress,
Paris, 1764.

Bottom left Vignettes from Fournier's
Manuel Typographique, vol. 1,
letterpress, Paris, 1764.

Bottom right *A Specimen of Printing
Types* by Joseph Fry & Sons, London,
1785.

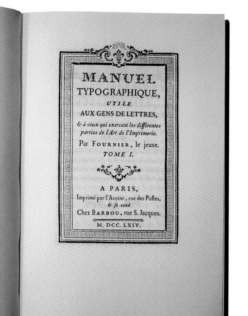

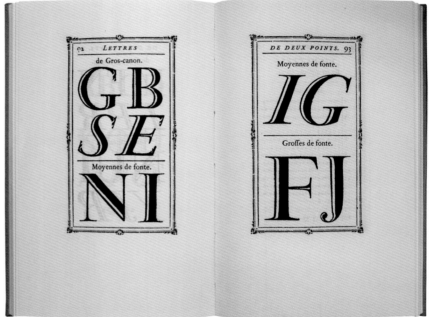

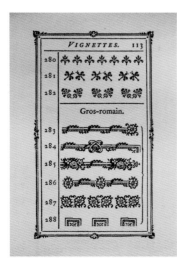

initially influenced by Fournier and Baskerville, he developed a more dramatic version that accentuated the distinctions between thick and thin lines and inspired later display fonts such as fat face, used prominently in the Edinburgh theatre poster, right.

From 1815 the range of display types exploded. Variations or conglomerations of successful display types became commonplace. For example, the first line of the poster detailed below uses an outline, drop shadow fat face.

The Edinburgh poster reveals a less obvious advantage of letterpress over other forms of print. Changes to performances occurred daily, and each required a new poster, often with little time to spare. The necessary changes for Wednesday's performance have been marked up for the printer on the poster for Monday's show.

The lifespan of printed matter was decreasing, and information relating to rapidly changing events required additional emphasis. The wave of new display types met this need admirably.

Top left Poster (detail), letterpress printed by T. Rea, Sunderland, UK, 1817.

Bottom Spread from Giambattista Bodoni's first type specimen *Fregi e Majuscole*, Italy, 1771.

Top right Theatre poster, letterpress, Edinburgh, UK, 1821.

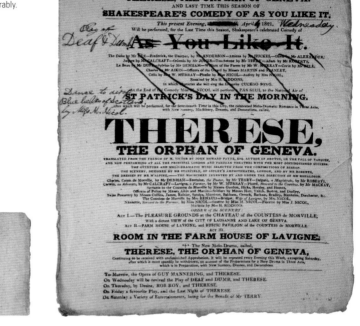

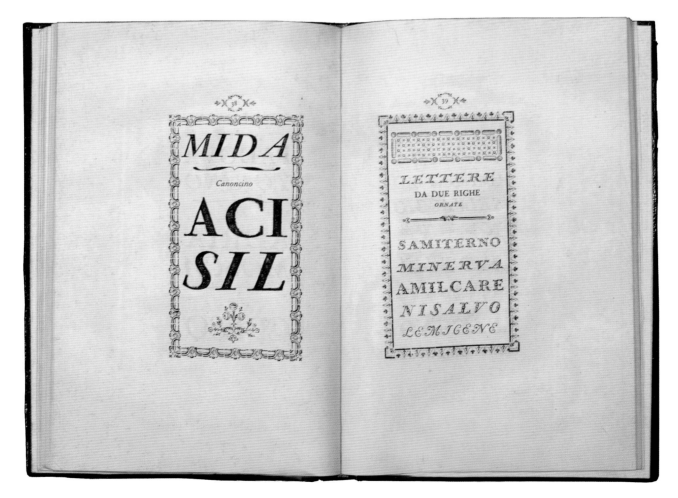

CHAPTER TWO
CELEBRATING THE CHALLENGE OF CHANGE

Previous page Cast-iron handpress, Amos Dell'Orto, Monza, Italy, 1842.

Top left Postage stamp, Whiting & Branston, London, *c.* 1830. The huge growth in business transactions meant that more paper money needed to be printed. A solution to the issue of forged printed currency was sought, resulting in the development of compound plates.

Bottom left Office stamp incorporating compound plates. The reach of the Empire enabled British printing and its technology to be exported all over the world. However, the nineteenth century saw this dominance severely curtailed.

Right The Stanhope, the first press made entirely from iron, manufactured in England *c.* 1800. It was far stronger than any wooden press and, despite its larger size and print area, required less physical effort to work. Handpresses such as this remained the mainstay of the jobbing printer until larger print runs created demand for a power-assisted, one-man press.

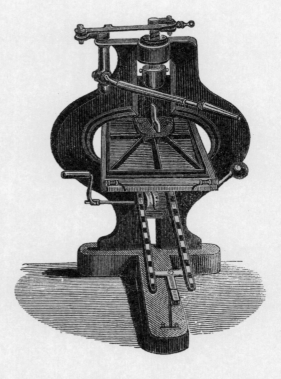

Between 1800 and 1850 the population of Britain and many European countries doubled. During the same period, the cost of living dropped by approximately 50%, while wages remained roughly the same, leaving many people with more money. There was a sense that the individual, through hard work, might take control of his, or even her, destiny. Linked to this was a growing rejection of the florid excesses of the baroque style in favour of something more tangible, measurable and reasoned: neoclassicism.

Horizons broadened as social and cultural mobility became easier, and aspirations more ambitious. Work and leisure were no longer shaped by the aristocracy but by a newly mobile, ambitious middle class whose aspirations helped both to forge and fuel the other transformation of this period: the Industrial Revolution. Initially stimulated by the exploitation of natural resources, especially coal and water, its early accomplishments belong to Britain but then quickly spread throughout the world.

Economic growth increased the demand for printed money, but the means to print it in large quantities to a precise standard was lacking. The outcome of a series of initiatives from the Bank of England was the invention of mechanical engraving using a rose engine, essentially an adaptation of a lathe, and compound plate printing, by which two-colour printing could be achieved in one pass of the press. These innovations did not, ultimately, play a major role in the design of banknotes, but they were highly influential on the appearance of print between 1820 and 1850.

A sign of things to come, especially for the jobbing printer, was a newly invented iron handpress by Charles Stanhope. It was not only stronger than any wooden press, but also required less physical effort to work. For this reason it was also possible to print more copies per hour than on the wooden press. Thirteen years later, George Clymer, in Philadelphia, introduced his lavishly decorated Columbian iron press. These presses, although mechanically sophisticated compared to wooden presses, were not powered machines. They remained, in essence, an extension of the printer's arm but largely satisfied demand – with the exception of newspaper and periodical production.

Handcraft to mechanized industry

During the latter decades of the eighteenth century, it became increasingly common for printers to specialize in particular kinds of job. This rationalization was led by the rapid growth of newspaper printing, driven by the absolute necessity of meeting regular deadlines. With the increased pace, journeymen and apprentices alike were often confined to a narrow set of tasks. Division of work was becoming ever more prevalent.

As a result, many industries experienced a decline of traditional, formal training agreements. Apprenticeships were considered irrelevant to the needs of new trades arising out of the Industrial Revolution. Increasingly difficult to enforce, statutory apprenticeship schemes were being abolished, leaving industrial training to the vagaries of economic forces.[1] The term 'master' no longer meant someone who was a master of his craft, but, instead, someone who was a master of others.

Similarly, the print industry between 1800 and 1850 was experiencing a general transition from handcraft to mechanization. Indentured apprenticeship – intended to provide an in-depth, practical understanding of all aspects of print – began to weaken, replaced by a subdivided system of specialized training. Increasingly restricted work practice was reducing the apprentice's ability to understand the general working of the office. The ethos of the workshop had always been one where 'ignorance is not simply pitiable, but contemptible, that clumsiness is a matter for ridicule, and that humility marks the beginning of receptivity'.[2] Such pressures caused many to be content to specialize.

The jobbing print office remained a place where a practical understanding of all the craft activities pertaining to print and its related commercial outcomes might be pursued.

Here, printing would continue to be done on a handpress or, later, a foot-driven treadle-press, well beyond the nineteenth century. There was every possibility that owners of small jobbing print offices might have little regard for their moral obligation to young apprentices – beyond their ability to earn them a profit – but the nature of the work and scale of production meant that every aspect of print and printing was likely to be experienced first-hand.

Jobbing print offices, where, significantly, formal apprenticeship had only a tenuous hold, were a regular target of print unions and larger-scale employers alike. They were described as 'rat houses' and accused of recruiting child labour. It was also argued that what little training they provided was inadequate because the equipment was old (unmechanized) and poorly maintained, while the kind of work undertaken (jobbing) was inappropriate, providing none of the opportunities for the apprentice to acquire an 'intelligent knowledge of their art'.[3] In short, the jobbing

Far left and left Detail of an engraved copperplate (*far left*) and closer detail of a single character (*top*) with its printed result (*bottom*), date unknown. The letterforms are Tuscan-style with bifurcated serifs and drop shadows. Commercial application of skills such as this was sought throughout the nineteenth century, although, increasingly, much of the engraver's work was transferred to a new technology, lithography, especially from the 1840s.

Opposite, top left A page from Giambattista Bodoni's *Manuale Tipografico* (comprising two volumes), Italy, 1818. While Bodoni's early typefaces and their arrangement show a distinct French influence, his later work, designed from the 1780s onwards, became bolder and sharper as the areas of space around each character increased and the use of ornament decreased.

printer was considered the cowboy of the nineteenth-century print industry.

It can certainly be assumed that many jobbing printers would prefer simply to pay 'assistants' to do as they were told. The owner of a jobbing print office probably resented being told precisely what such a training should entail. The success and prosperity of the jobbing printer's business depended on him forging a reputation of distinction in an increasingly adversarial high street. He would argue that he knew best what he required of his employees. This marks a distinct break with the traditional function of the medieval printers' guilds, which did not recognize individual differences between printers' workshops in a town but, instead, represented printers where work and training was of a guaranteed standard.

The concern for standards by the print unions and the print establishment as a whole was undoubtedly sincere, and it was certainly the case that the nature of the early jobbing print shop meant that equipment was not state of the art. But perhaps more significant for critics was the fact that the jobbing printer was guilty of flaunting the rules. Out of necessity he was finding solutions to new problems, often with very limited means. An unbiased critical evaluation of the jobbing printer's work, to say nothing of approval, would not be voiced from within the printing fraternity until the second half of the nineteenth century.

Early nineteenth-century European typeface design

The Italian Giambattista Bodoni (1740–1813) had a profound influence on the appearance of nineteenth-century printing through his prodigious design of type and the bravado with which he displayed it. At the age of twenty-eight, Bodoni took charge of the Stamperia Reale in the Duchy of Parma where his job was essentially that of a personal printer, producing documents required for the court. However, the international reputation of Bodoni's work grew to such an extent that, in 1790, he was given the freedom to initiate his own projects in the Stamperia Reale. From this remarkable position, he had the freedom to design, compose, print and publish books regardless of time or cost.

His early work reflects the refinement of the engraved writing manuals and an admiration of Fournier and the English printer John Baskerville, both of whose type designs retain some calligraphic qualities while acknowledging the burgeoning neoclassical style. Bodoni's types are self-consciously virtuoso statements: dramatic extremes of vertical thick and thin lines, often large in size, arranged with generous inter-character and inter-line spaces, all set within wide margins and often with little or no decoration.

The intention of such displays of typographic bravado was to elicit a sense of awe in the viewer through typography alone. However, critics of Bodoni's work accused him of printing books to be viewed rather than read, describing them as self-indulgent and self-congratulatory 'vanity projects'. Bodoni's work certainly lacked intimacy and charm, but these are the characteristics he made every effort to avoid. Instead, he sought detachment and controlled, sophisticated elegance. More controversially, Bodoni maintains a formidable presence on the page, refusing to play the conventional role, subservient to that of the author. In this way,

Below Punches cut by Giambattista Bodoni for the Stamperia Reale at Parma, Italy, *c.* 1780s.

Bottom A printer's card, letterpress printed from a standard stereotype, with a space for inserting the buyer's message, *c.* 1840.

he established, for both the type designer and compositor, the freedom to reinvent and experiment.

Although types in their more extravagant decorative form were, by 1800, falling out of favour with the printer of books, the growth in jobbing work, especially posters, meant that there remained a need for distinctive-looking types, particularly in larger sizes. In 1798, the French foundry of Joseph Gaspard Gillé issued a series of *fascicules* of decorative types, borders and *fleurons polytypés*. A form of stereotype, 'polytype' was a generic term describing a copy of an original wood-engraved letterform, produced by making a mould from the face of the original using plaster, or similar material, from which facsimiles were cast in metal. These were then mounted onto a wood block to bring the face of the facsimile up to type height. The advantage in creating letterforms in this way was the ability to produce far larger letters than was possible using the conventional steel punch and matrice (see page 15).[4]

Stereotyping in its various forms was a common activity by 1800, especially among engravers who made copies of decorative 'stock images' to sell to letterpress printers. But as the demand for larger types increased, engravers[5] added ornamented letters to their catalogues of stereotyped images. How many engravers or typefounders produced stereotyped typefaces is impossible to assess, but the process was widely known. For example, in America, the Boston Type and Stereotype Foundry, established in 1817, and the New York typefounder and stereotyper Adornam Chandler, in 1822, issued letterforms 'cast in stereotype plates and the letters separately fixed to wooden bottoms. A great quantity of this kind of job type has been used for three years past.'[6]

In the development of large decorated types, the London typefoundry established in 1818 by Louis John Pouchée

(1782–1845)[7] is most important, due to not only the size and variety of treatment displayed, but also the quality of its engraving. These alphabets, displayed in his catalogue *Specimens of Stereotype Casting*, are rich in detail that spills over the edge of the letters, softening but never obscuring their shape. However, they also have a robustness that reflects the dramatic new wave of (traditionally made) bold display types released by several British foundries.

Right C. A. Carlssons Lithogr., lithograph, Stockholm, *c.* late nineteenth century. Outdoor advertising in the form of shop signage had long been the most important way of informing the public of business activities. Images had initially been important, but with the introduction of formal education during the nineteenth century, businesses began to explore other, more helpful ways of explaining what goods and services they could offer the public. This provided more work not only for the sign-writer and jobbing printer, but also for new roles such as the bill-sticker, sandwich-board man and placard holder.

Display typefaces: British typefoundries

By 1800, the influence of Bodoni's work was dominating European and North American printed matter, and his types proved to be the intermediate step in the creation of a style of typeface appropriately called fat face. Its significance lay in the fact that it was designed specifically for jobbing rather than book printing.[8] With its ever-increasing exaggerated forms taking their lead from the signage of the streets, fat face was quite revolutionary and marked possibly the first time that considerations of historical precedence, or of typographic principle, had so little influence on the design of a typeface.

The innovative Robert Thorne of the Fann Street Typefoundry, London, is acknowledged as the designer of the first fat face in 1803. There had been earlier versions,[9] but Thorne's typeface had the characteristic flat, hairline serifs with minimal, if any, bracketing, and a contrast in line-width so exaggerated that the width of the thick stroke is half the capital character's height. Fat face was designed to function at large sizes, and the new, stronger iron press made printing larger areas relatively easy.

Thorne is also accredited with designing the first Egyptian typeface (initially referred to as Antique), although the first dated example of this design is in the London-based typefounder Vincent Figgins's *Specimen of Printing Types* (1815). (Thorne did not produce a catalogue between 1803 and 1820, so it is impossible to say precisely when his Egyptian was first produced.) Characteristics of the Egyptian typeface are an evenness of line width and the distinctive unbracketed slab serifs: 'serifs like rocks'.[10]

Figgins's *Specimen of Printing Types* was also the first to display shadowed letters. Based on the forms and proportions of the fat face, these types included the illusion of three dimensions. In Figgins's second type specimen catalogue (1817), he added Tuscan types (originally called Ornamented) with curled and bifurcated serifs, which are generally divided at the centre of the stem. The impact of Figgins's first specimen catalogue was immediate, and with the frequent publication of subsequent issues and inserts, each containing new or extended ranges of fonts, enormously influential both in Britain and elsewhere, particularly France and Germany.

However, the most significant category of new type was the sans serif, which first made a modest, single-line appearance in William Caslon's specimen catalogue of 1816.[11] While links between early nineteenth-century display types and sign-writing, though likely, remain speculative, sans serif originated from a conscious attempt to revive the spirit of the earliest stone-cut Roman letterforms. Sir John Soane's architectural drawings depicted incised sans serif letterforms prior to 1800.

The 1816 line of sans serif letters reappeared in the specimen catalogue of Caslon's successor, Blake, Garnett & Company, around 1819, but seems to have been an unsuccessful experiment because neither this nor any other sans serif version was seen again for over a decade. In 1832 both Vincent Figgins and William Thorowgood issued their own versions, described by the former as 'sans serif' and the latter as 'grotesque'. All these early versions of sans serif appear crudely drawn at times, but 'its tremendous blackness'[12] quickly became a major asset to the jobbing printer. Figgins's first sans serif shows an 8-line specimen (96 point; a line being 12 points) and in the following year a 20-line (240 point) specimen, dramatically represented by a single character filling the page.

Nothing demonstrates the change under way in printing better than these catalogues of type specimens by Figgins,

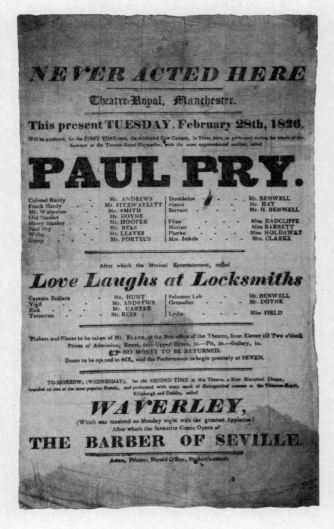

Thorowgood and Caslon. The enormous size of the letter-forms in relation to the page provides a very different experience for the viewer. The characters become images, their normally negative, interior forms (counters) transformed into positive, bold shapes trapped within heavy black contours. One characteristic that connects all these new types, or 'job-letters',[13] is that it seems quite plausible that they were designed: in other words, they were drawn on paper before manufacture, perhaps by a professional sign-writer commissioned by the typefounder for his punch-cutter to follow.[14] Despite their tremendous flourish, there is a rationality about them, a common logic applied to curves, counters and terminals that is reminiscent of the sign-writer's working methods.

All of these new types were available in large sizes for the purpose of display, but the casting of larger type provided the typefounder with a multitude of practical problems. The molten metal would frequently cool unevenly in the larger mould and produce concave surfaces. Weight was another issue. Since a single 10-line (120 point) 'W' might weigh a pound (454 grams), the enormous storage difficulties and delivery costs of a whole font cast in solid metal at this size can be imagined. Later in the century, typefounders would experiment with casting letters onto arched 'feet' in order to reduce the weight and cost of raw material. The high cost of larger-sized fonts resulted in some printers renting out letterforms by the character to other printers. There are also many examples of printers resorting to cutting their own versions of popular typefaces from a wood block.

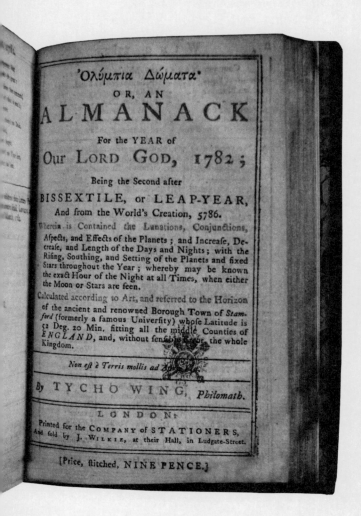

'Ολύμπια Δώματα·
OR, AN
ALMANACK
For the YEAR of
Our Lord God, 1782;

Being the Second after
BISSEXTILE, or LEAP-YEAR,
And from the World's Creation, 5786.

Wherein is Contained the Lunations, Conjunctions,
Aspects, and Effects of the Planets ; and Increase, Decrease, and Length of the Days and Nights ; with the
Rising, Southing, and Setting of the Planets and fixed
Stars throughout the Year ; whereby may be known
the exact Hour of the Night at all Times, when either
the Moon or Stars are seen.

Calculated according to Art, and referred to the Horizon
of the ancient and renowned Borough Town of Stam-
ford (formerly a famous University) whose Latitude is
52 Deg. 20 Min. fitting all the middle Counties of
ENGLAND, and, without sensible Error, the whole
Kingdom.

Non est è Terris mollis ad Astra via.

By TYCHO WING, Philomath.

LONDON:
Printed for the COMPANY of STATIONERS,
And sold by J. WILKIE, at their Hall, in Ludgate-Street.

[Price, stitched, NINE PENCE.]

Left Almanac, printed by J. Wilkie, London, 1782. Almanacs took many forms, including single sheets, booklets and novelty gifts, as well as the pocket-sized book illustrated here.

Almanacs became a familiar item in Europe during the fifteenth and sixteenth centuries. Concerned with forecasting times, such as the rising and setting of the sun and moon, and high and low tides, they also began to discuss moral and social issues and predict political developments. By the mid-nineteenth century, almanacs included medical information, jokes, anecdotes, cookery and gardening information, cures and tonics, and even short stories. The almanac became the only universally received item of printed literature common to most households.

Right Hand-drawn design for an almanac/calendar in preparation for an engraving, probably intended for the inside of a pocket watch or similar, date unknown.

Popular reading: broadsides, chapbooks and almanacs

The rapid expansion in the reading public had been created not only by increasing numbers involved in state-run education, but also Sunday schools run by religious organizations, adult education classes, Mechanics' Institutes, mutual instruction groups and the like. But urbanization itself, in bombarding town-dwellers with print in the form of handbills, posters, broadsides, broadsheets, chapbooks and almanacs, in addition to newspapers and periodicals, played an enormous role in encouraging the general population to learn to read.

This increasing enthusiasm for reading, while generally accepted as a good thing, also brought with it concerns: 'A habit of reading [fiction] breeds a dislike to history, and all the substantial parts of knowledge; withdraws attention from nature, and truth; and fills the mind with extravagant thoughts, and too often with criminal propensities.'[15] Religious organizations were against light reading, recommending, instead, the Bible and hymn book or, perhaps, Bunyan and a few other religious classics. The concern was that fantasy and impurity would lead the reader astray. Material written and designed for the entertainment of the general populace took several forms, and much of it did include stories of moral and physical weakness. Its appearance – hurried, cheaply produced and often slip-shod – did not help.

Broadsides were the traditional non-serious reading matter of the poor. In the mid-eighteenth century there was often no other form of cheap literature, especially in rural areas, other than these sheets pinned up in homes and taverns. (A broadside is printed on one side only, whereas a broadsheet covers both sides.) Broadsides could be any size and their subject matter was diverse, including popular

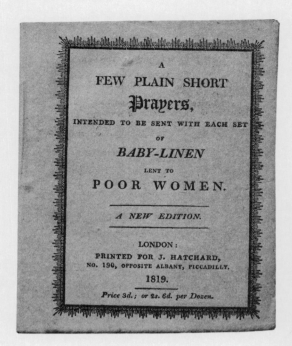

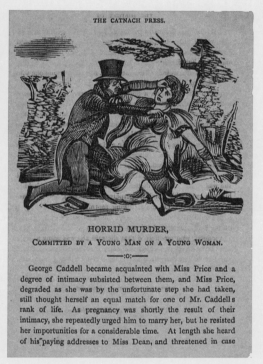

Left Booklet, *A Few Plain Short Prayers*, printed for J. Hatchard, letterpress, London, 1819. This booklet was distributed with bed-linen lent to poor women. The growth of industrial capitalism and its social consequences – poverty, political protest and widespread concern about a failure of moral standards among the poor – caused a number of organizations to make it their mission to put the scriptures in the hands of the lower classes.

Right Chapbook, *Horrid Murder*, printed and published by the Catnach Press, London, *c.* 1820–40. James Catnach was among the best-known printers/publishers of chapbooks. These booklets were generally poorly printed and splattered with typographic and grammatical improvisations. Writers were paid one shilling, and illustrations were reproduced from second-hand wood blocks that often bore little relevance to the subject.

ballads, satire, news, crime and war. They were also used for formal pronouncements of law and order, and as a medium for protest, political controversy and personal dispute.

These sheets were invariably illustrated with what were intended to be sensational images, often printed from crude woodcuts, and sold on the streets. Ballad-sellers adapted their trade to the bustling city streets by dressing up and performing, perhaps in pairs, the music they were selling. Others hung their sheets on railings, sold them on stalls or simply stood on the street corner with their sheets pinned to their clothing. However, crime – 'a stunning good murder'[16] – was the bestseller. The popularity of broadsides waned as the cost of newspapers fell, while the rise of music halls after 1832 caused ballad sheets to give way to song books.

Closely related to the broadside was the chapbook. These were sheets folded into an eight-, sixteen- or, occasionally, thirty-two-page booklet, the finished item often being little more than 10–13 centimetres (4–5 inches) tall. The type was worn and the woodcut illustration could be second-, third- or fourth-hand, in awful condition and even irrelevant in subject matter. Additional colours might be applied by hand. The compositor, using and reusing the often crude materials to hand, calculated his arrangement of type and image to attract the eye. It was important to distinguish the current issue from that of the previous week. Chapbooks were printed onto poor-quality paper, but nevertheless, being made from rag stock, were suitably robust. These little books were cheap (the word 'chap' is thought to derive from 'cheap'[17]) and sold unstitched and untrimmed, the idea being that readers would sew and cut the pages themselves.

For many customers, a chapbook represented a first serious step into the world of literature. Content tended to be popular fiction, often romance containing religious over-

tones, with titles such as *Seven Champions of Christendom*. But they also carried a mixture of anecdotes, verses, riddles, puzzles and jokes. Chapbooks continued to be published well into the nineteenth century, although they evolved into children's booklets, which, in turn, gave way to the popular penny magazines. American booksellers and printers often imported English chapbooks for distribution or reproduction. However, local printers, notably in New York and Philadelphia, later began producing uniquely American versions, frequently based on 'frontier adventure' tales.

Almanacs developed from the medieval calendar, which comprised ecclesiastical and astronomical information. It was during the seventeenth century that almanacs became widely associated with prophecy, with William Lilly's *Merlinus Anglicus Junior* in 1644, and the success of this publication became the model for numerous rivals. However, some almanacs carried no prophecies at all and contained only verse or short stories, or were a focus for ideological debate. There was little physical standardization: some were sold as broadsides, others were books, often small and sometimes designed with the additional function of being a

Left *Thames Tunnel Paper*, printed by J. V. Quick, wood-engraved illustration with letterpress, London, 1843. This free sheet informed the public of the opening to foot passengers of Isambard Kingdom Brunel's Thames Tunnel.

Right Child's pictorial alphabet book (or ABC primer), wood-engraved illustrations, London, *c.* 1840s. These booklets initially had strong links with religious services (Sunday school systems were generally established around the turn of the nineteenth century) and contained moral lessons. This page, however, centres around a playful subject.

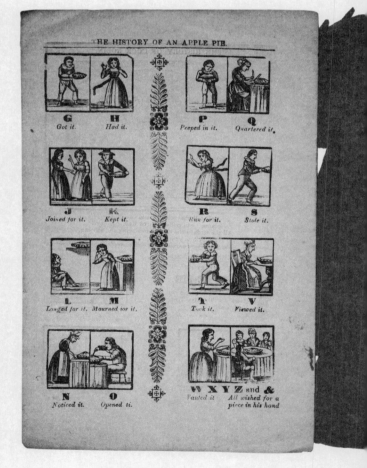

diary. They were commonly syndicated, bound by printers who added regional news of markets, auctions, and other parochial activities and advertisements so that locally modified almanacs could be sold at public events.

Most religious denominations had their own almanacs, as did various politically inspired organizations. It was the ideology of such organizations that gave the almanac its distinctive, alternative aura, that the natural balance of the planet and its constituent forces might, in some way, be irreparably damaged by the Industrial Revolution's newfound 'unnatural' power sources. Connections were made between steam and electric, and warnings of apocalyptic catastrophe.[18] Working conditions in factories and on the huge building projects – especially the digging of tunnels for steam trains – were commonly compared to biblical descriptions of hell.[19] There was a very real sense that humanity might be overreaching itself and heading for indefinable disaster. Perhaps because of this sense of trepidation for the future, there was also a fascination with the past, especially all things medieval and mythical. The political and social ramifications of the burgeoning Industrial Revolution would remain a source of both celebration and revolt throughout the nineteenth century.[20]

The appearance of these almanacs was distinctive. While the imagery was often sensationalist, the small, tightly set text commonly used a mix of biblical and scientific references. A regular feature was the use of tables and other diagrams. From the earliest examples, these featured predictions of celestial activity related to information concerning high and low tides, sun rise and set, weather and seasonal forecasts, etc. Always printed letterpress, following issues were able to reuse the same tables, with required amendments quickly made by the compositor. The originality and

Left Title page, *The Life of Napoleon* by Doctor Syntax, illustrated by George Cruikshank, engraving, London, 1817. Cruikshank (1792–1878) combined illustration with caricature and satire, lampooning styles, manners and, most famously, personalities. This illustrated title page depicts Napoleon's rise and eventual domination, followed by his defeat, fall from grace and enforced isolation. The lettering was engraved by another hand.

Bottom *Banknote – not to be imitated*, engraving by George Cruikshank, London, 1819. One of Cruikshank's most notorious works, it depicts on a mock banknote a gallows and a row of hanging bodies – death being the punishment for handling forged banknotes. The forgers were rarely caught and almost all of those executed were simply illiterate and ignorant of their crime. Following public pressure, the death penalty for handling forged banknotes was later dropped.

effectiveness of their design, to say nothing of the technical achievement, are often remarkable. These tables would later be adapted to convey information for railway transport schedules.

Of equal importance in bringing regular reading matter to the general public was the penny magazine, which originated in the United States in the 1820s. The concept was copied in England and then the rest of Europe. The Society for the Diffusion of Useful Knowledge, founded in 1826, began publication of the *Penny Cyclopaedia* in 1833, selling 75,000 copies in weekly instalments of one penny. The German *Pfennig-Magazin* began in 1833 and reached 100,000 subscribers. Its editor, the Swiss-born J. J. Weber (1803–80), would continue this success with the *Leipziger Illustrirte Zeitung*, modelled on *The Illustrated London News*.

Newspapers and early advertising

When *The Times* was first published in London in 1785, it joined many publications already available on a daily or weekly basis. In fact, the first daily newspaper to be published had appeared in 1702, the single sheet *Daily Courant* in Britain. The first in America, *The Boston News-Letter*, was published by Benjamin Franklin two years later. Due to censorship, France did not have a daily newspaper until the *Journal de Paris* in 1777. Periodicals had been published in various guises since *The Weekly Newes* first appeared in 1622.[21]

Many early regular publications were established, owned and published by enterprising printers. The income they generated was, almost from the start, not only from the sale of the papers but also from the classified notices they carried. Notices were arranged in columns, each brief statement identically presented, rather like the 'small' or 'wanted' ads today. Journals quickly began to specialize in the kind of information carried. One might contain notices concerning government by-laws and proclamations; another might have information regarding auctions of property, servants and slaves, or household goods. However, the nature of notices changed as their purpose became increasingly persuasive in function. Because the visual appearance of competing advertisements remained identical, sellers resorted to writing more and more outlandish claims.

A comment regarding the appearance of early notices published in *Tatler* as early as 1710 is telling: 'Asterisks and Hands were formerly of great use for this Purpose. Of late Years ... Cuts and Figures have been much in Fashion.'[22] The use of asterisks and hands suggests that printers were readily aware of the necessity to attract the reader's attention and were searching their type cases for little-used sorts to catch the eye. A 'hand' was what the print trade called a fist (or

space. As a result, headings tended not to extend further than the width of a single column, and the text, often arranged without leading, was set in a point size that strained the bounds of legibility. However, even after the tax on newspapers was abolished, the appearance of British newspapers remained much the same until the influence of American newspaper design, using banner headlines and illustrations, and readymade advertising displays became standard practice in the late 1880s.

Meanwhile, the jobbing printer, having predominantly small print runs of unpredictable commissions, to say nothing of limited money to invest, found the handpress – albeit the improved iron handpress – the most appropriate means of production.

index) and was, in fact, a hand with a pointing finger. Flowers and astrological symbols might also be used for the same reason. 'Cuts and figures' were illustrations printed from small hand-engraved wood blocks. These initially served as an index to the different groupings of announcements. For example, a column of sailings might be indicated by an illustration of a ship in full sail. In due course, such illustrations came to be requested by individual advertisers, making the pages cluttered, and, once again, restrictions were imposed.

The growth in literacy was fuelling the increasing popularity of broadsheets, chapbooks, almanacs, magazines and newspapers. But it was the newspaper offices, and *The Times* in particular, that responded with a drive for mechanization. For the first twenty-five years of *The Times*, the printing of 500 copies (a single folded sheet, printed both sides) occupied the press room for an entire night. This was achieved using two handpresses with which four men (two per press) could print fifty sheets, one side only, per hour, or 500 sheets in ten hours. By the early 1800s, this was already inadequate. The first steam-powered printing press, invented by the German engineer Friedrich Koenig (1774–1833), was installed at *The Times* offices in 1814. Between 1801 and 1831, when heavy taxation held newspaper production back, the number of copies bearing a pre-printed revenue stamp alone more than trebled from 16,085,000 to 54,769,000 a year.[23]

Taxation also had a big influence on the appearance of newspapers because it forced editors to forbid any 'waste' of

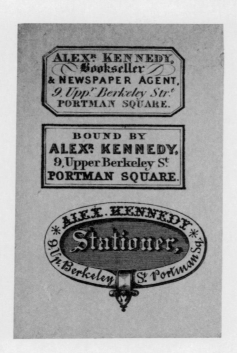

Far left Printer's catalogue of monograms (or crests), lithography with die-sunk specimens, 1860s onwards. Customers could choose the design and have their own company name and details inserted.

Left Sheet of labels reflecting the different functions of a stationery business, engraving, c. early 1800s.

Advertising and the growing influence of the USA

The USA was keen to break its reliance on Old World traditions. Empowerment was fuelled by improved communications facilitated by the local newspaper, which from the start had been a major feature of American life. It is estimated that in 1810 the annual production of newspapers in America had already reached 22 million copies, with 185 paper mills in the country and 51 printing offices in Philadelphia alone.

Philadelphia during the early years of the nineteenth century was the seat of revolutionary government, taking the lead in many matters of general and cultural interest, and business. Among these was the publication of a directory, in 1794, in which every city inhabitant and their trade was listed along with a report on the progress. In 1818 John A. Paxton issued an improved version that included a section containing 67 full-page advertisements. This marked a significant advance for the jobbing printer, given the opportunity to design unregulated arrangements of display type and images.

However, like their counterparts in Britain and Europe, American newspapers struggled to find a satisfactory way of accommodating the needs of their advertisers. In spite of a few individual attempts, the appearance of newspaper announcements remained limited to identical columns. This was exacerbated by severe paper shortages, forcing newspapers to squeeze more text into less space by shrinking type sizes for both news and advertising. But even when there was sufficient paper, requests from advertisers to buy larger spaces were resisted because regular users threatened to withdraw.

Although short-lived, these restrictions came at a time when the powers of advertising were well understood and encouraged advertisers to look for alternative methods. These included various forms of outdoor advertising, which had, since the beginning of the nineteenth century, been on the increase with little

or no control. Hand-painted directly onto walls – sometimes covering an entire building – advertising dominated the main streets of all major American cities. 'Sandwich men' carried portable displays as early as the 1820s, while vehicles bore banners and streamers.

The first American typefoundries were a product of these exciting, expansive times. Prior to this, American printers had been dependent on imports. Imported type, along with ornaments, flowers, pictorial cuts, illustrations, astronomical, mathematical and chemical symbols, had given early American printing a distinctly European appearance. Initially American foundries copied as closely as possible the fonts already in use and of proven commercial success. Unlike his European counterparts, the American printer, from the outset, accepted jobbing as an integral part of his business. However, because the tools and equipment held by early American print shops were imported, they shared the same frustrating limitations of the jobbing printer in Britain and Europe.

What did begin to emerge were engraved patriotic motifs, the most common being the bald eagle, cast in metal by various foundries, perhaps holding a ribbon in which a customer's name could be placed. Stage-coaches, sailing vessels and horses also appeared in great profusion: from the tiniest image for a trade card to large illustrations suitable for poster use. A glance at American typefounders' specimen catalogues of the 1820s and 1830s reveals hundreds of such symbols for sale. The best of these wood-engraved designs achieved remarkable levels of energy and bravado, coupled with finesse, to achieve something quite distinctive. As American (as well as European) specimen books adjusted to the importance of the jobbing printer, typefoundries began to divide their catalogues into three sections: first, text types followed by display types; second, ornaments and borders; and third, pictorial and decorative images.

Left Two billheads for bakers, both letterpress, 1847 and 1848, London. Clearly in competition with each other (both billheads are addressed to the same customer), these bakers have a sheaf of wheat symbolizing their area of business and the days of the week laid out, as well as the most popular items to enable a more speedy recording of deliveries.

Right Detail from a poster, printed from hand-cut wood letters, c. 1830. The perennial problem for the compositor was a shortage of characters of the required size, style and weight. As a last resort, it was not uncommon for him to cut his own wood letters, with varying degrees of success.

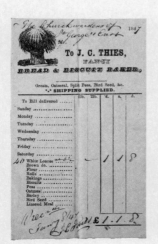

VENUS

Display typefaces: American wood type

In the United States, where unregulated advertising covered whole buildings, the demand for large-scale posters was acute. Darius Wells ran a jobbing office in New York. He had experimented with cutting wood letters by hand before finding a means for mass-producing them in 1827, and published the first known wood type catalogue in March 1828. Wood was cheap, plentiful and, compared to metal, far lighter in weight. In the preface to his catalogue, Wells described the three key advantages of wood type: price – less than half that of metal type; durability – the fine lines of metal type were surprisingly susceptible to breakage; technical perfection – specifically the difficulty in producing large metal type, which occasionally resulted in the face being uneven. William Leavenworth considerably improved the process in 1834 by introducing the pantograph which, when combined with the milling router, formed the basic machinery required for making wood type for the remainder of the nineteenth century.

In these early years, wood type manufacturers made a remarkable claim that they would design and cut a whole font of type based on a drawing of just one character. This is how Wells explained it in his specimen catalogue of 1828: 'Those wishing any particular size or proportion of type, different from any in this Specimen, have only to draw one letter, and forward it on, and they can have a fount made perfectly agreeing with the specimen sent.' He also states that any typeface can be supplied with shade, 'opening the letter on one side' for a small additional cost. These fonts could also be supplied at any size. Such an offer represents a radical cultural as well as technical departure from anything experienced by European, including British, printers. Clearly, if the combination of pantograph and router,

Top right Two-colour wood type, 'elongated' and 'extra-elongated' from Miller & Richard, UK, *c*. 1850. Unlike metal type, wood type could be bought and sold by the character. Here characters are described as being for sale 'by the dozen' or, presumably, half dozen.

Bottom right Wood type, Condensed Egyptian (or Antique). Wood type is remarkably hard-wearing. However, the drying process of the wood itself means that each character, as it contracts, can vary very slightly in height, requiring the printer to add slivers of paper to its base. Fortunately the oil content of the printer's ink is helpful in maintaining a smooth, polished surface on the face of the type.

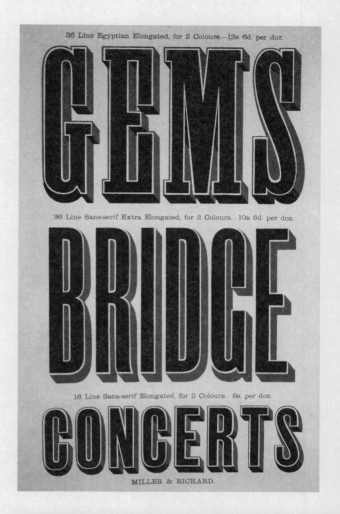

36 Line Egyptian Elongated, for 2 Colours.—12s. 6d. per doz.

GEMS

36 Line Sans-serif Extra Elongated, for 2 Colours.—10s. 6d. per doz.

BRIDGE

16 Line Sans-serif Elongated, for 2 Colours.—8s. per doz.

CONCERTS

MILLER & RICHARD.

coupled with the cheapness of the raw materials, enabled the wood type manufacturer to provide such a service at no additional cost, the potential for unrestrained typographic experimentation was unprecedented.

The high levels of skill, together with the time required to cut individual characters at each size from metal by hand, to say nothing of the understanding of historical precedents and the complex technical constraints, all appear to have dissolved at a stroke with the adoption of wood and the development of the pantograph and router. The lack of physical and technical restraint was matched by a newfound freedom in design, something that was to become increasingly dominant in American printing in the latter half of the century.

From the 1830s onwards, the contribution of the American wood type industry to typefounding and jobbing printing in Europe was highly influential. European wood type manufacturers were not established until the 1850s. In turn, it was American wood type manufacturers who introduced German, French and British versions of fat face, sans serif, Egyptian and Tuscan designs to American printers. The cheapness of the raw material enabled the wood type manufacturer to experiment with the ornamentation of existing styles in a way that would be impractical for the typefounder. A font that would be used only occasionally became a financially viable purchase. The more distinctive the typeface appeared, the more likely it was that a client would wish to claim it exclusively for his promotional material. Such developments encouraged both printers and clients to think of type as a commodity.

The first uniquely American design innovations began to appear in the late 1830s. For example, the practice of reversing a type on a solid or decorated background was explored

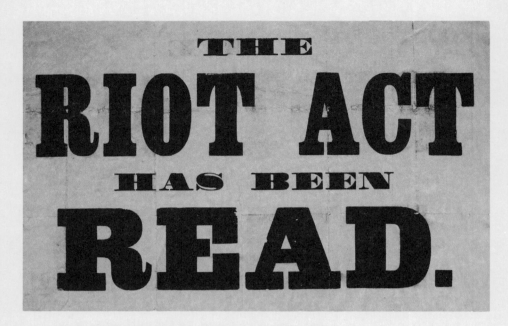

by the wood type manufacturers for use in advertising. The printer used soft wax to hide the joins between characters. A variation of the reverse, and very much an American innovation, was the streamer. Here, letters with 'extensions' at the top and bottom were set into words and caps (the name given to the start and finish of the streamer), turning the word into an image and providing a far larger presence than the word, or words, alone.

The mechanical process of making wood type had been a well-kept secret. However, once established, the principal British typefoundries such as Caslon (from 1857) and other specialist wood type manufacturers, including Bonnewell and Joyce & Co., published catalogues of great verve and scale, encouraged, no doubt, by the commercial success of their American counterparts.

Meanwhile, the design of metal display types continued to be led by European typefoundries until about 1860–70. From this date the American typefoundries joined the wood type manufacturers in being more independent, confident and assured. They also became remarkably successful, exporting not only their fonts but also the whole gamut of tools and materials associated with printing across the Atlantic.

FIFTY-LINE ANTIQUE COMPRESSED.

H. W. CASLON AND CO., LONDON.

Bodoni's legacy

The *Manuale Tipografico* appeared five years after Bodoni's death, completed under the care of his widow and Luigi Orsi, his foreman for twenty years. Print runs of Bodoni's books were often quite small and the *Manuale Tipografico* is no exception, with just 290 copies available. The reputation of Bodoni's work, coupled with its comparative rarity, made it highly collectable.

The two letterpress-printed tickets opposite (*top* and *bottom left*), dating from the first half of the nineteenth century, demonstrate Bodoni's influence. Their design is quite a departure from earlier engraved equivalents (see page 26). The scale is larger and the space around the text is prominent. Both have a grand sense of occasion, conveyed by elegant restraint, but the absence of cherubs, musing figures and distressed

Below Frontispiece and title page of Giambattista Bodoni's *Manuale Tipografico* (two volumes), Italy, 1818.

ille est Magnus, typica quo nullus in arte

Plures depromsit divitias, veneres.

MANUALE

TIPOGRAFICO

DEL CAVALIERE

GIAMBATTISTA BODONI

VOLUME PRIMO.

PARMA

PRESSO LA VEDOVA

MDCCCXVIII.

classical masonry signals a new, far simpler way of communication – one that particularly suited the letterpress printer.

By the 1840s, the compositor had a far greater range of types at his disposal. For the Cappella Sistina ticket he has used a fat face for the name of the chapel, as well as an outlined, drop-shadowed slab serif and a cursive. Despite this diversity, the design radiates unity and dignity.

In contrast, the Bement's Hotel card (*bottom right*) shows just how amenable fat face type can be, here looking suitably congenial despite the less sophisticated setting.

Top Admission ticket, letterpress, designed and printed in the 1840s and still in use in 1851, Italy.

Bottom left Admission ticket, letterpress, France, 1819.

Bottom right Trade card, letterpress, Albany, USA, *c.* 1840s.

Display type variations

Bold departures by Fournier and Bodoni showed the way for what became an unlimited range of variations, extensions and exaggerations in display faces. One of the most influential foundries in this field was that of Vincent Figgins (1766–1844), who released his first catalogue in 1815. All of his early type specimen catalogues are 'pocket-sized'

despite the large size of some of his types. It was not uncommon for a page to show just three characters (*top left*) or fewer.

In the admission ticket below (*bottom left*), small fat face types add flair and momentum to the design but are strong enough to work well even in close proximity to the heavy, slab serif Egyptian face.

Top left Vincent Figgins's *Specimen of Printing Types*, showing a 20-line fat face, London, 1832.

Bottom left Admission ticket, letterpress, London, 1829.

Right Poster for an auction, letterpress printed by Robert Dawson, Norwich, UK, *c.* 1830s.

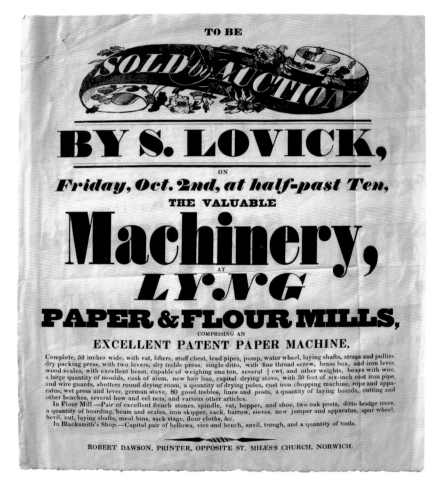

Display faces also changed the way posters worked. The compositor, in an attempt to provide the poster with maximum impact, acted as editor by reducing the size of extraneous copy and increasing the prominence of salient words (*opposite, right*).

The variety available to the nineteenth-century compositor of any given type style is reflected here. The notice below

(*top*) features an ultra-condensed version of an Egyptian typeface that came to be known as Playbill. Its extreme condensed form made it an ideal choice for the tall, narrow posters of the era.

A standard Egyptian wood type (*bottom*) is used for the word 'opera' and character-spaced to good effect, although spacing material has marked the printed surface between the 'o' and the 'p'.

Top Notice, letterpress, Dijon, France, *c*. 1860.

Bottom Poster, letterpress, Shrewsbury, UK, *c*. 1830.

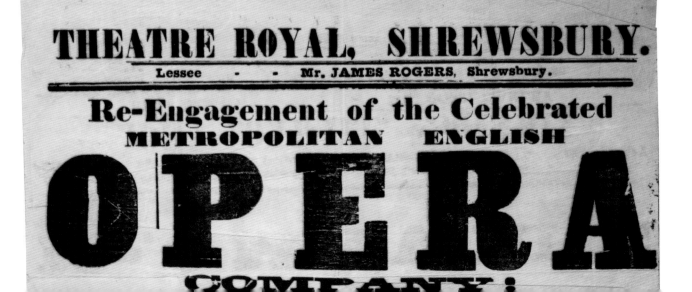

First shown in 1815 by Vincent Figgins, Egyptian was particularly suitable for hurried work and high press pressure (larger areas of black require more pressure to attain a flat colour). The disadvantage of fat face (used above the word 'opera') lay in its fine serifs, which were easily broken.

The two sheriff's notices below (*top left and right*) demonstrate the evolution of the notice from a formal, bookish

appearance to something more poster-like. Both concern the sale of 'goods and chattels' to raise money to pay debtors.

In the UK, 'battledore' was used as a secondary term for a hornbook, a handled wooden panel for children that contained the alphabet. The tablet was later superseded by a folded card such as this (*bottom*). Its outer cover was hand-coloured in grey before printing. The jovial boldness of fat face types

Top left and right Two notices, letterpress, USA: New London, 1720, and New York, *c.* 1840s.

Bottom Battledore, letterpress, UK, *c.* 1830s.

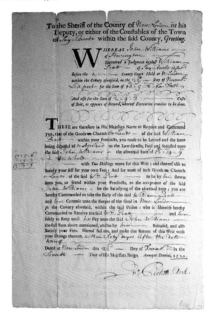

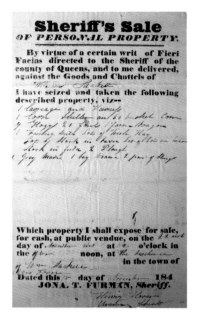

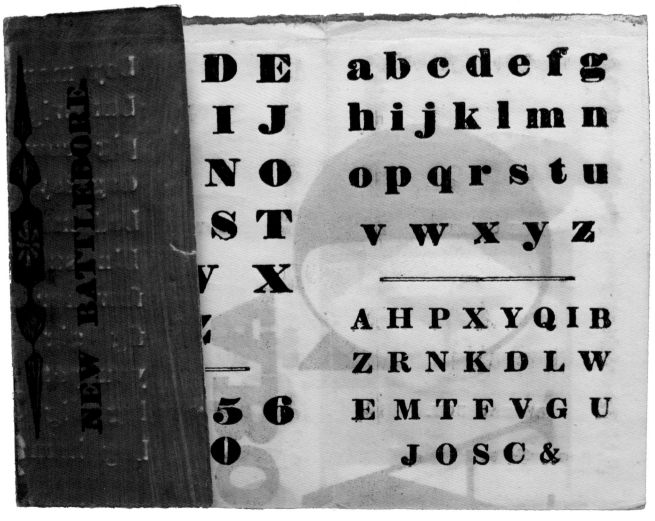

made them a popular choice for the design of children's material.

The text of the poster below can still be read as continuous prose but the essential points have been brought to the fore. Boxing was made illegal in the UK in 1750, and for some 150 years fights were either held clandestinely or, as in this case, described as a 'novelty' event.

This poster and the American sailing notice overleaf use bold display faces, yet remain articulate and attractive. The rich variety of printed material in the following pages shows how manufacturers became ever more ingenious in devising new ways to make types stand out, from the use of streamers and decorated display faces (page 81) to large-scale (pages 82–83) and two-colour wood type (pages 84–85).

Below Poster, letterpress printed by W. Boag, Newcastle upon Tyne, UK, *c.* 1840.

NOVELTY!

The Gentlemen of NEWCASTLE, and its Vicinity, are respectfully informed, there will be a grand Display of
THE ART OF

BOXING

AT THE
NAG's HEAD, Old Flesh Market
On Wednesday & Thursday, Dec. 23 & 24,
BY

SIMON BYRNE

The CHAMPION of ENGLAND.
YORKSHIRE
ROBINSON,
AND TOM
REYNOLDS.

Doors open at 7 o'Clock. —— Admission, Two Shillings.

W. BOAG, PRINTER, DEAN STREET,

Below Poster, notice of sailing,
wood engraving with letterpress,
printed by H. Ludwig, New York,
c. mid-nineteenth century.

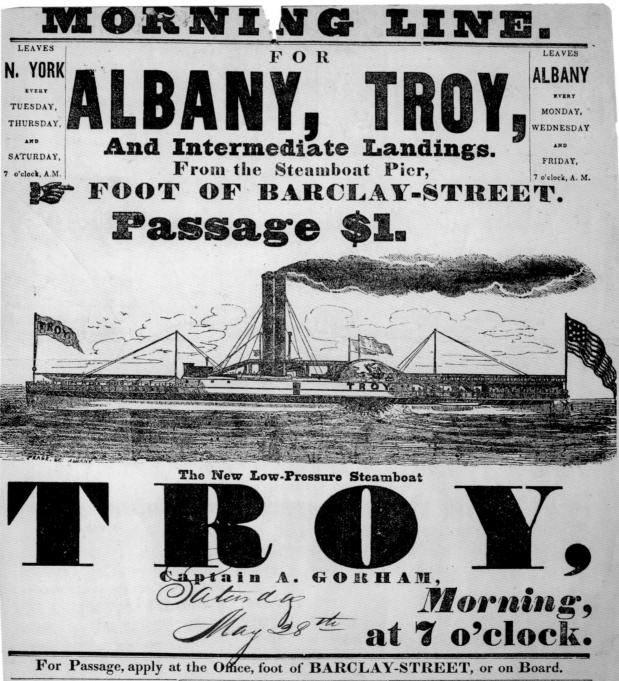

Top left Poster, letterpress using wood and metal types, printed by T. Forge, Barking, UK, 1861.

Bottom Poster (detail), letterpress, using decorated wood letters and metal type, UK, 1837.

Top right Broadside, letterpress printed by Davy & Berry, Norwich, UK, c. mid-nineteenth century.

BARKING TOWN
REGATTA.

The Inhabitants of Barking, Ilford and their vicinities, are respectfully informed that owing to the general satisfaction given on the last occasion, it has induced the promoters to solicit a continuance of their favours

ON THURSDAY, JULY 25, 1861,
WHEN

THREE BOATS
And other Prizes will be Rowed for in Five Heats by
16 FISHERMEN OF THE TOWN
Whose united ages amount to 1055 years,

The first Man in each of the undermentioned Heats will be entitled to Row in the Last and Grand Heat.

Between the 4th and Grand Heat will be an interesting match with the successful winners of former Regattas

FOR A PURSE OF MONEY.

The First Heat to start at 1 o'clock; Grand Heat at 4 o'clock   To start from Bouys in the Barking Mill Pool round a Boat moored off Mr. Hewett's Ice House, returning, round a Boat moored off the Town Quay, back again and round the Boat at the Ice House, returning to and round the Boat in the Mill Pool to the Town Steps.

Age	First Heat	Colours		Age	Second Heat	Colours
79	JOHN WADMAN	Red and Blue		69	JOHN TOPSON	Red and White
71	THOMAS BIRT	Orange		69	JOHN THOMAS	Yellow and White
72	SAMUEL BAKER	Crimson		68	EDWARD JOHNSON	Red
70	GEORGE BYE	White		68	BENJAMIN GOFF	Dark Blue
292				274		

Age	Third Heat	Colours		Age	Fourth Heat	Colours
67	JOHN HARRIS	Black and Yellow		67	HENRY CASWELL	Pink and Blue
66	WILLIAM DORE	Green		58	RICHARD PORTER	Purple
65	WILLIAM WHENNELL	Light Blue		52	JOSEPH TEMPLEMAN	Pink
64	JOHN MILLER	Slate		50	SAMUEL BAXTER	Pink and White
262				227		

THE WHOLE TO CONCLUDE WITH A DUCK HUNT.

The Committee and Managers respectfully solicit the patronage of their Friends, as there are nearly 100 Old Fishermen who will be regaled should the Funds admit.

Subscriptions will be thankfully received by Messrs. BYFORD & SPASHETT, Managers. Mr. HARVEY, Umpire. Mr. J. LINSDELL, Treasurer. Mr. H. W. KNOWLES, Secretary, and by the following Gentlemen, Mr. Turpin, Mr. Hale, Mr. Wagstaff, Mr. Thomas Linsdell, Ship Inn; Mr. Earle, Still; Mr. Porter, Blue Anchor; Mr. J. Holmes, George; Mr. Parsons, Bull; Mr. Jesse Fuller, Peto Arms; Mr. Carter, Dakin Head; and at the various Inns in the neighbourhood.

AN EXCELLENT BAND WILL BE IN ATTENDANCE.

T. FORGE, Printer, Barking.   Local and other Trains on the London, Tilbury and Southend Railway.

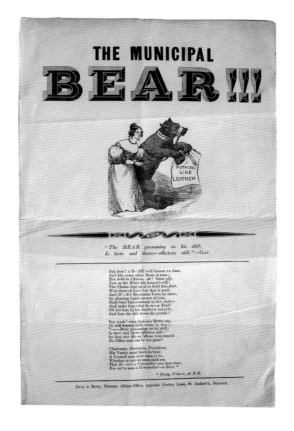

THE MUNICIPAL
BEAR !!!

"The BEAR presuming on his skill, Is here and there—officious still."—GAY.

See here! a B—RE well known to fame,
And like some other Bears is tame;
But held in Chains, ah! bitter pill,
Just as the Blues his keeper's will!
The Chains that used to hold him fast,
Were those of Lace but that is past;
And N—K's Sumptuous Form so nice,
In pleasing bands as erst of yore,
Shall bind him constant to her rule;
And make him what he is—a Tool!
Oh! led him by his leathern muzzle,
And here she did it—in the puzzle!

But mark! what does our Motto say,
(A well known table wrote by Gay;)
"—Bear presuming on his skill,
Is here and there officious still;"
So does our Be-re whose vain conceit
No Office sure can be too great!

Chairman, Deacon, President,
His Vanity must have its bent;
A Council man now aims to be,
Whether or not we soon shall see,
That H—rr's a Councillor you may stare,
But we're seen a Councillor—a Bear.

* Nutty P-loc-r, A.S.S.

Davy & Berry, Printers, Albion Office, opposite Cockey Lane, St. Andrew's, Norwich.

TO BE SOLD BY
AUCTION
BY
J. B. RUSH,

On FRIDAY, the 13th Day of OCTOBER, 1837,
AT THE GRIFFIN INN

Below Bonnewell wood type catalogue, showing an 80-line or 960pt (40 cm / 16 in.) character, UK, 1865.

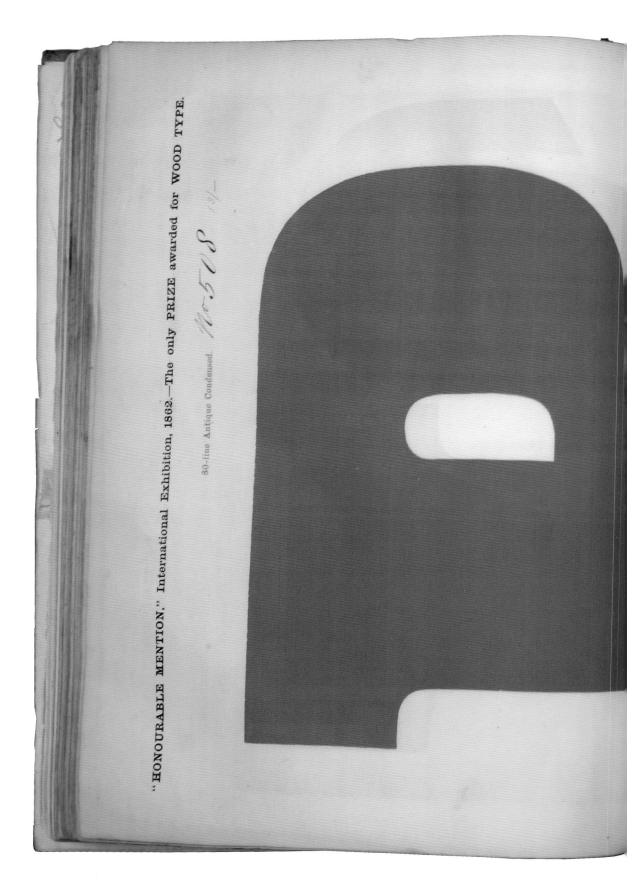

"HONOURABLE MENTION." International Exhibition, 1862.—The only PRIZE awarded for WOOD TYPE.

80-line Antique Condensed.

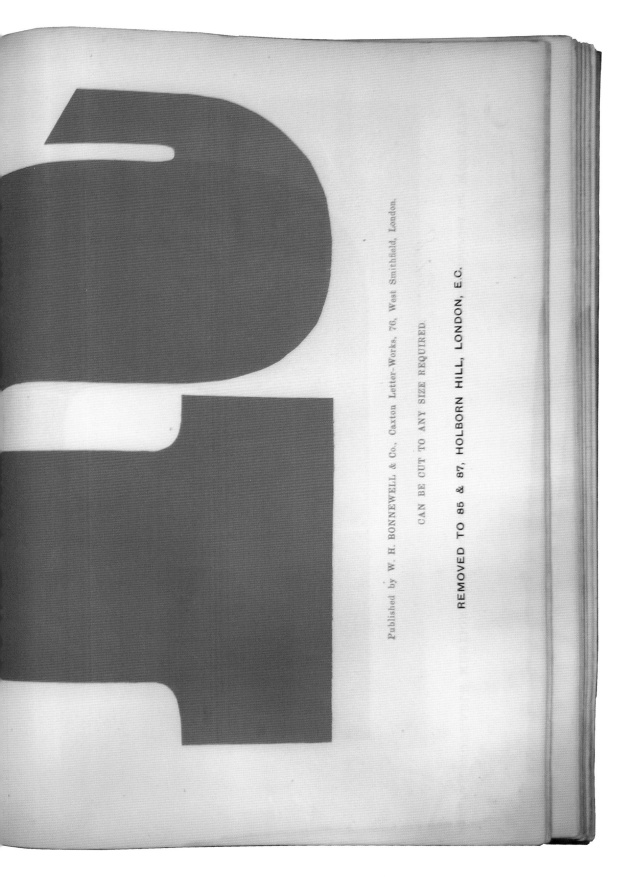

Published by W. H. BONNEWELL, & Co., Caxton Letter-Works, 76, West Smithfield, London.

CAN BE CUT TO ANY SIZE REQUIRED.

REMOVED TO 85 & 87, HOLBORN HILL, LONDON, E.C.

SPECIMENS OF WOOD LETTER.

CONDENSED ANTIQUE, for 1, 2, or 3 COLOURS.

These Founts, for 1, 2, or 3 Colours, are kept in stock in sizes from 6-line to 40-line, with Figures, &c., complete.

Published by W. H. BONNEWELL & CO., Caxton Letter Works, and Printing Material Manufactory, 85 and 87, Holborn Hill, London.

CAN BE CUT TO ANY SIZE REQUIRED.

See JURORS' REPORT, Class 28, No 5213.

Opposite Two-colour wood type specimens, Condensed Antique, Bonnewell & Co., London, *c.* 1870.

Below Two-colour wood type specimens, Antique Shaded, Bonnewell & Co., London, *c.* 1865.

ON," International E82.—The only PRIZE awarded for WOOD TYPE.
e Antique Shaded, in Two Colours, 10s. per doz. Pieces. *No 73*

Gothic Shaded, in Two Colours, 10s. per doz. Pieces. *No 74*

EWELL & CO., ter Works, 85 & 87, Holborn Hill, London, E.C.

Early security printing

Although English lotteries were financed and administered by the government, responsibility for ticket sales and promotion was given to 'lottery office keepers', who competed with each other for sales. Consequently, leading lottery offices such as George Carroll (*top right*) explored every technique to gain attention, exceeding anything that advertising had hitherto conceived. Scale of production as well as haste meant that technical standards were often poor. Here, the pressman did not clean his press properly before printing the red.

Forgery was an issue with lottery tickets, but nothing compared with paper money. In 1818 a public competition was held in London to find a solution. J. H. Ibbetson was one of the contenders and produced a booklet to promote his work (*left*). Somewhat controversially, the winning entry came from Sir William Congreve, Director of the Bank of England, and involved both compound printing and a rose-engine engraving machine. Congreve patented the compound printing system in 1820 but a few years later turned over the patent rights to the Whiting & Branston Printing

Left Booklet by J. H. Ibbetson entitled *A Practical View of an Invention for the Better Protecting of Bank-notes Against Forgery*, London, 1820.

Top right Lottery poster, letterpress printed in two colours, London, *c.* 1825.

Bottom right Trial print from a rose-engine engraving, Whiting & Branston, London, *c.* 1820s.

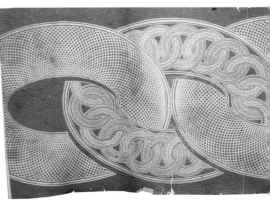

Company, which went on to enjoy great success in establishing the process associated with security-sensitive items such as tickets and bank bills.

Compound printing was achieved with a plate made up of closely interlocking forms that could be inked in different colours and then printed in a single pass through the press. Although the process was never used for the production of banknotes, it did make a considerable impact in the field of security printing. The characteristic worm-like shapes often incorporated into two-colour printing from a compound block (*centre right*) became a common sight.

The distinctive appearance of compound printing, with its panels, lozenges and arbitrary colour changes used in conjunction with decorative rose-engine engraved backgrounds or borders, became firmly established as a graphic idiom. Rose-engine engraved stereotype stock blocks of every shape and form were made available and used, for example, with counterfoils (*bottom right*) or as a purely decorative surround for a panel space in which a company could have its own name inserted (*top right*).

Top left Test rose-engine engraving, Whiting & Branston, London, *c.* 1820.

Top right Ribbons, stock stereotype blocks, source and date unknown.

Centre right Postal permit, probably Whiting & Branston, *c.* 1820–30s.

Bottom right Share certificate of the Grand Imperial Ship Canal, engraving, Brighton, UK, 1827.

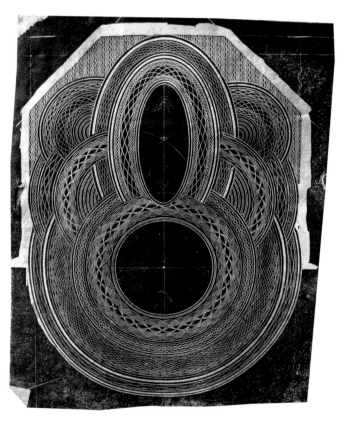

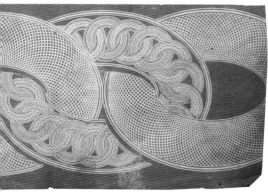

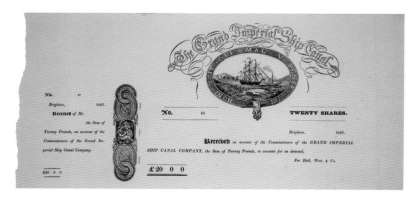

After receiving the patent rights for the Congreve printing system, Whiting & Branston put a great deal of effort into publicizing the process. While hoping for major commissions from banks, they produced items such as security bands (*bottom right*), labels and even handbills (*top right*). Preliminary sketches have survived, giving an insight into the planning required. A sketch (*centre left*) bears little resemblance to the far more elaborate finished handbill (*top right*).

Pirating of successful products was widespread and a number of companies adopted the compound printing process for their labels as additional protection. Others asked their printer to provide something that had the characteristics of security printing, without the expense.

The two banknotes (*opposite, top and bottom left*) are both interim proofs and incorporate a compound plate for their borders and rose-engine engraving. Although compound plates were never used for the printing of money, Whiting & Branston made a number of speculative proposals.

Top left Label incorporating rose-engine engraving and embossing, date unknown.

Centre left Preliminary sketch for a handbill (the final version, much changed, is shown top right), Whiting & Branston, London, *c.* 1820s.

Bottom left Preliminary sketch for a handbill, Whiting & Branston, London, *c.* 1820s.

Top right Handbill, lottery company, Whiting & Branston, London, *c.* 1820s.

Centre right Medicine stamp duty band, printed from compound plates, *c.* 1830s.

Bottom right Tax duty band, printed from compound plates, *c.* 1830s.

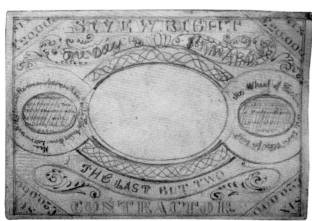

The untrimmed engraving below (*right*), showing the indent of the plate pressed into the paper, was produced in conjunction with a pantograph. A pantograph was a mechanical device used to enlarge or reduce drawings. At this time (from *c.* 1827 onwards) it was also being used in the USA to copy, enlarge and reduce wood typefaces.

To achieve an engraved image such as this, a shallow relief, usually in the form of a medal cast in metal, was required. Controlled to run in a series of lines, one end of the pantograph ran over the surface of the medal. However,

as the stylus undulated over the surface, the line being drawn on the copper sheet shifted slightly. The technique was used occasionally in the design of security-related material, but remained relatively rare.

Whiting & Branston also explored embossing, a technique that derives from processes used in the preparation of seals (applying wax to secure documents) and the minting of coins. Firstly, a metal die bearing a hand-carved, hollowed-out image in low relief is required. Then, a second, 'female' die is made from the original ('male') die.

Top left Banknote (interim proof) for Whitby Bank, probably Whiting & Branston, London, *c.* 1830–40s.

Bottom left Banknote (interim proof) for Deal Bank, probably Whiting & Branston, London, *c.* 1830–40s.

Right Handbill (and detail, below) for a clockmaker, engraving, London, *c.* 1830.

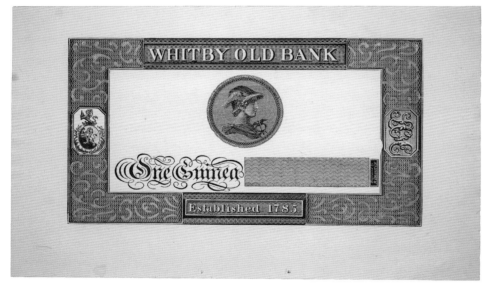

When the two dies are brought together under pressure, the sheet of paper in between is moulded to the image in relief on the original die. Paper structure, thickness and moisture content are all important factors, not only for the success of the embossing, but also the item's ability to maintain its intended form.

Whiting & Branston often incorporated embossing, generally employing Henry Dodds & Co. of London, widely considered the best in this field. The image of Queen Victoria (*top left*) is one of a set of portraits of prominent British figures. There is no record of these ever being for

sale; it is assumed that Charles Whiting used them as a showcase for his work.

Assignats (*opposite, top*), representing confiscated lands assigned to the bearer by the revolutionary French government, were devised as a substitute for metal currency during the financial emergency between 1789 and 1796. Although they appeared in a variety of styles and sizes, all were watermarked and carried a blind embossed stamp depicting symbols and slogans of the revolution. Later issues such as this carried the words: 'The law punishes the forger with death; the nation rewards the informer.'

Top left Portrait of Queen Victoria, blind embossed on coloured grounds, Henry Dodds & Co. and Charles Whiting, London, *c.* 1830s.

Bottom left Admission ticket, blind embossed on a coloured ground with letterpress. Embossing probably the work of Henry Dodds & Co., London, 1834.

Top right Trade card, Comet Engraving Co., Chicago, *c.* mid-nineteenth century.

Bottom right Admission ticket to the coronation of George IV, involving rose-engine engraving, compound plates and blind embossing, 1821.

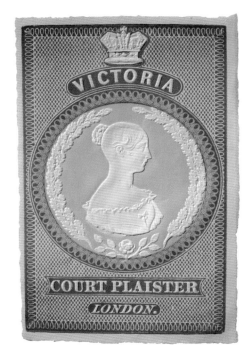

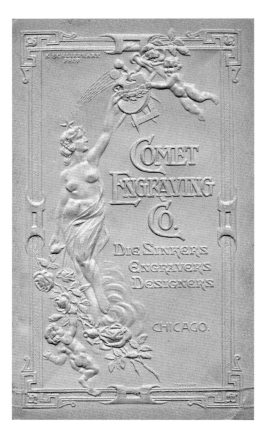

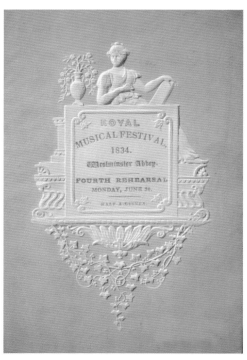

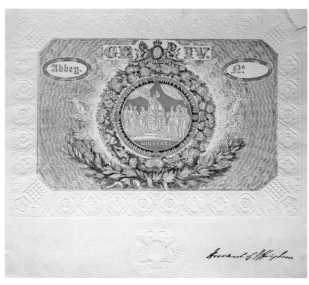

Formal printed cheques with spaces for customers to fill in (*bottom left*) were introduced during the early nineteenth century. The decorative flourish at the point of detachment from the counterfoil was a standard security feature almost from the start. The blind embossed element on the right is a tax stamp.

The engraved admission permit (*bottom right*) has a quiet orderliness that was losing favour to complexity. Concepts of formal sophistication were changing, in no small part due to the influence of Whiting & Branston.

Top Assignat, engraving, France, *c.* 1790s.

Bottom left Cheque, engraving, London, 1875.

Bottom right Admission permit, engraving, London, *c.* 1800.

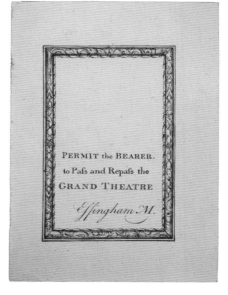

Information design

The earliest directories were merely lists of names. In England, directories began to appear annually in 1734, but a major practical improvement occurred with the publication of the *Universal Director* in 1763, which listed names under trades. The introduction of house numbers was also a key factor in the useful function of directories. The first two American directories were published in 1785.

The first *Post Office London Directory* appeared in 1817. Frederic Kelly took it over in 1837 and improved its design considerably, adding a 'trades' and a 'streets' section. By the time this Edinburgh directory (*below*) was published, a number of design elements had been standardized. A long dash avoids the necessity of repeating surnames, and the deep indent on all second address lines aids access to names down the left side of the column.

The calendars and timetables illustrated opposite all date from the

Below *The Post Office Annual Directory, Edinburgh, UK, 1831–32.*

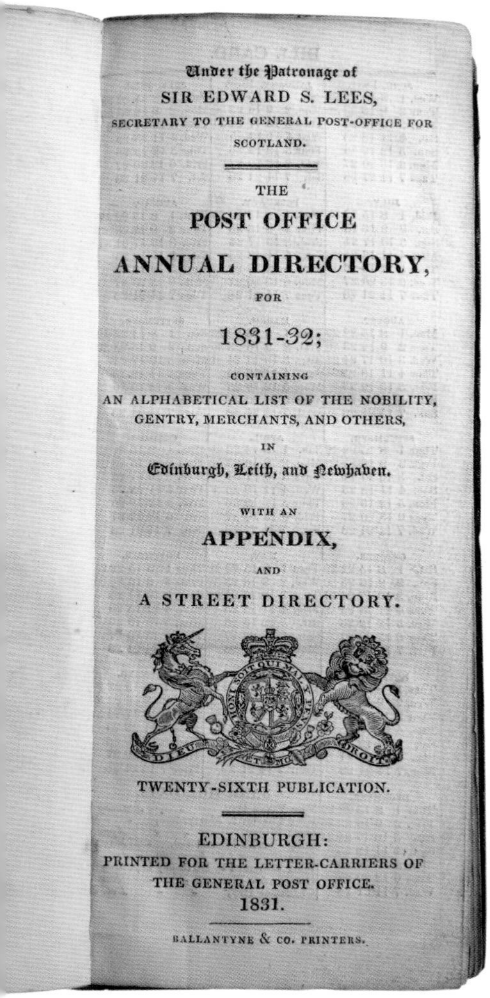

Under the Patronage of
SIR EDWARD S. LEES,
SECRETARY TO THE GENERAL POST-OFFICE FOR SCOTLAND.

THE
POST OFFICE
ANNUAL DIRECTORY,
FOR
1831-32;

CONTAINING

AN ALPHABETICAL LIST OF THE NOBILITY, GENTRY, MERCHANTS, AND OTHERS,

IN

Edinburgh, Leith, and Newhaven.

WITH AN

APPENDIX,

AND

A STREET DIRECTORY.

TWENTY-SIXTH PUBLICATION.

EDINBURGH:
PRINTED FOR THE LETTER-CARRIERS OF THE GENERAL POST OFFICE.
1831.

BALLANTYNE & CO. PRINTERS.

MEI   EDINBURGH   126

Mathews, P. spirit dealer, 6 Greenside street
—— Robert, esq. writer, 17 London street
—— William, pocket-book maker, 306 Lawnmarket
—— Mrs, 10 St Patrick square
Matthew, James, esq. Dean bank
Mathewson, Hugh, J. P. officer, 149 Westport
—— John, late letterfounder, 22 Duke street
Mathie, Mrs, lodgings, 15 Catherine street
Maughan & Company's laboratory, 32 Howe street
—— E. J. surveyor of taxes, Canonmills cottage
—— Captain Philip, 37 Melville street
—— R. deputy compt. of Excise, & inspector of taxes, 18 Howard place
—— Mrs R. lodgings, 12 Hill square
Maule, George, builder, 58 Broughton street
—— John, architect, 69 Broughton street
—— Misses, 5 Cassels place
Maury, Anthony, confectioner, 138 George street
Maver, J. M. builder, 9 Charlotte place
Maxton, Anth. esq. of Cultoquhey, 12 Saxe Coburg pl.
—— Boog, and Co. saddlers and accoutrement makers, 20 North bridge
—— John (merchant, Leith), 29 Albany street
—— Robert, land-surveyor, 65 York place
—— Mrs Josiah, 29 Albany street
Maxwell, Henry, esq. 125 George street
—— James, auctioneer & appraiser, 32 Frederick st.
—— J. L. of Edin. and Leith brewing Co., 19 New st.
—— John Clerk, esq. of Middlebie, adv. 14 India st.
—— John, victual dealer, 49 Fountainbridge
—— John E. teacher, 107 Nicolson street
—— Robert, builder, 47 Cumberland street
—— Robert, tin-plate worker, 39 Bristo street
—— General Sir William, 125 George street
—— Lady, school, 25 Horse wynd, Cowgate
—— Mrs Colonel, 13 Gloucester place
—— Mrs James, 2 Salisbury place, Newington
—— Miss, 11 Darnaway street
MAYNE—see p. 122
Meadowbank, Lord, 13 Royal circus
Medical Theatre and Dispensary, 9 Society
—— Hall, Thos. Butler and Co, 73 Princes street
Mealling, J teacher, 41 Lady Lawson's wynd
Mearns, Henry, painter, Stead's place
Medwyn, Lord, 17 Ainslie place
Meek, John, grocer and victual dealer, 88 High st.
—— John, esq. W.S. 12 Terrace
—— John, slater, 68 Grassmarket
—— Robert, hosier, 21 Salisbury street
—— Thomas, baker, 133 Rose street
—— William, builder, 16 Allan street
Meik, Mrs, P. 35 Ann street
Megget & Roy, esqrs. W.S. 279 High street
—— & Symington, hide and leather factors, and bark agents, 28 Blair street, and Citadel, Leith
—— Aiken (of *Megget & Symington*), 3 Salisbury road
—— Thomas, esq. W.S. 18 Drummond place
Meheux, Mrs Lieut. 6 Annfield
Meikle, G. merchant, 70 Grassmarket—ho. 4 Park street
—— James, esq. solicitor-at-law, 2 Queen street
—— Mrs, dressmaker, 9 Charlotte place

127   DIRECTORY.   MER

Meikle, Mrs, lodgings, 1 George street
Meiklejohn, Rev. Dr, professor of church history, 12 Nicolson square
—— John, esq. W.S. 22 Duke st.—ho. Viewfield cottage
—— John, classical academy, 23 Downie place
—— J. grocer, 70 Canongate
Mein, James, spirit dealer, 56 St Leonard street
—— William, victual dealer, 40 Potterrow
—— Mrs, 17 St Patrick square
Meiklum, Mrs, 18 Atholl crescent
Meldrum, James, shoemaker, 25 Jamaica street
—— John, transparent blind painter, 4 Calton street
—— Mrs W. board and lodgings, 3 Roxburgh street
Melrose, And. & Co. tea dealers and grocers, 83 South bridge, 122 High street, and 301 Canongate
—— And. (of *A. Melrose & Co.*) 19 west Nicolson st.
—— James, watchmaker, 175 Canongate
—— John, tailor and clothier, 21 Nelson street
—— Mrs James, lodgings, 94 Pleasance
Melville, A. heckle & awl-blade maker, 47 Leith wynd
—— George, esq. 11 Minto street
—— George, writer, 1 Raeburn place
—— Hugh, shawl manufacturer, Fountainbridge
—— J. M. esq. W.S. 110 George st.—ho. 22 Heriot row
—— John, esq. W.S. 11 Minto street
—— Robert, esq. Drumdryan house
—— Mrs John, 2 Crichton street
—— Miss Whyte, 27 Moray place
Melliss, P. linen warehouse, 108 So. br.—ho. 13 Blair st.
Melvin, David, teacher, 37 Candlemaker row
—— James, grocer, and spirit dealer, 19 Dublin street
Menelaws, Wm. grocer & wine merchant, 143 & 145 George street—house 40 Charlotte square
—— William, baker, 133 Canongate
Mennon, John, teacher, 138 Nicolson street
Menteith. See page 132
Menzies, Alexander, lodgings, 49 Thistle street
—— Allan, esq. W.S. 12 Thistle street
—— Archibald, musician, 55 Cumberland street
—— Douglas, & Son, bootmakers, 1 Alison square
—— George, (of *J. & G. Menzies*), 8 Adam street
—— J. and G. engravers and printers, 199 High st.
—— James, Regent coffeehouse, 14 Waterloo place
—— John, boot and shoemaker, 80 Potterrow
—— John, bootmaker, 11 Hanover street
—— John, esq. 24 York place
—— John, Commercial inn and coffeehouse, 14 Waterloo place
—— Robert, esq. W.S. 17 Hart street
—— Robert, printer and publisher, 304 Lawnmarket
—— Major, late of the 42d Regiment, 17 Dean terrace
—— Robert, esq. shipbuilder, Leith—house Trinity
—— Thomas, spirit dealer, 87 Rose street
—— William, bookseller, 9 middle Arthur place
—— William, shoemaker, 16 south Richmond street
—— Captain William, 114 George street
—— William, sheriff-officer, 8 Milne court
—— Mrs Robert, 27 Castle street
Menzies, Mrs Catharine, 61 Clerk street
—— Mrs, 4 Graham street
—— Misses, milliners and dressmakers, 27 Castle st.
Mercer, George, esq. of Gorthy, 20 York place
—— Geo. Commercial bank—house 4 Montgomery st.

first half of the nineteenth century. Almanacs were published by printers, stationers and local newspapers. The circular example (*bottom left*) was designed to be placed in the crown of a top hat. Primarily functioning as a calendar, it also carried information about the moon and the rising and setting of the sun – an important consideration before the introduction of regular street lighting.

The Italian '50 year almanac' (*top left*) has leap years highlighted in red and includes a printed cut-out strip marked with the days of the week, which is fed through the sheet. Compact, effective and accessible in design, the table (*top right*) provides tidal information along with the rising and setting times of the sun and the moon. The railway timetable card (*bottom right*), on the other hand, is believed to have been an early experiment and was perhaps printed for railway staff rather than passengers. ('C' stands for Croydon, 'B' Brighton and 'D' Dover.)

Top left Almanac, Italy, *c.* 1800.

Bottom left *Tilt's Almanack for the Hat*, letterpress, 1845.

Top right Timetable of natural light conditions and tides, London, 1828.

Bottom right Railway timetable card, letterpress, London, 1844.

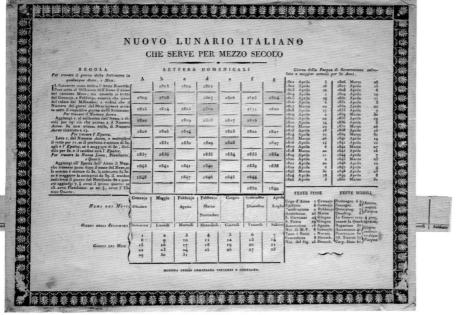

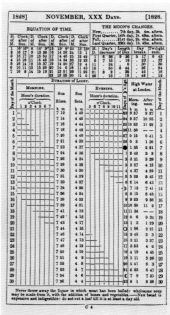

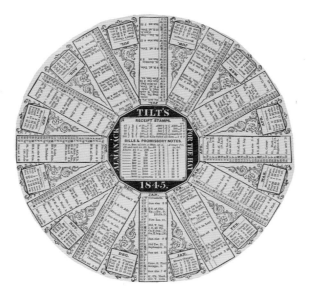

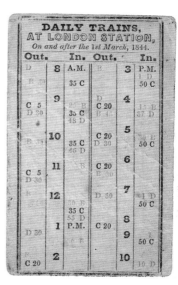

By the early nineteenth century, delivery systems for goods and parcels had developed in the wake of the passenger coach network, often setting off from the same inns and booking offices. Independent carriers operated in major cities with covered vans or wagons, and between cities using coaches, boats and, later, railways.

Engraved illustrations were often stock blocks, images chosen from a printer's catalogue. For the bill of lading illustrated below (*top left*), the printer of the Philadelphia-based shipping company used two copies of the same image. However, the printing of bills of lading and postal tickets was often more perfunctory (*bottom left*).

The Fly Vans handbill (*top right*), which doubles as an invoice, displays pick-up points and destinations. The Austrian passport and French hotel bill opposite use the same ornamented font as this.

Single-sheet passports (*opposite, top left*) were the norm until the early twentieth century when protective

Top left Bill of lading, letterpress with stereotyped wood engravings, Philadelphia, USA, 1849.

Bottom left Postal ticket, letterpress, USA, *c.* 1882.

Top right Fly Vans handbill, letterpress, Worthing, UK, 1839.

Bottom right Two-colour receipt, Liverpool, UK, 1846.

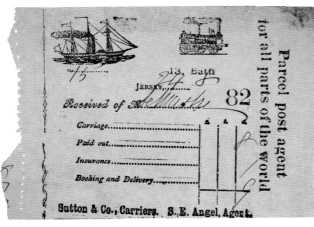

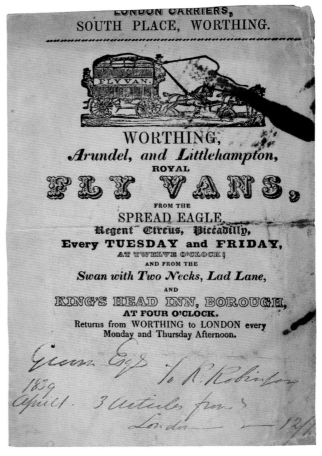

covers were introduced. The blue ground tint used on the passport – an unusual feature in the early nineteenth century – was created from multiples of a decorative unit (*top right*). The use of ornamented and fat face types in the design of formal documents such as this and the papal document (*bottom left*) demonstrates the rapid acceptance of these types, which had been considered unconventional just a short time before.

Passenger control on horse-drawn coaches relied largely on the use of a waybill (*bottom right*), which listed passengers, pick-up and drop-off points and the amount paid.

Top left Passport, letterpress, Austria, 1825.

Bottom left Papal document, letterpress, Naples, Italy, 1850.

Top right Decorative units from Bodoni's *Manuale Tipografico*, 1818.

Centre right Hotel bill, engraving, France, 1823.

Bottom right Waybill, letterpress, Boston, USA, 1842.

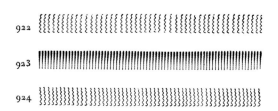

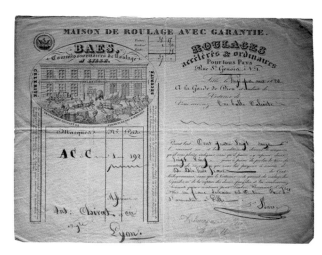

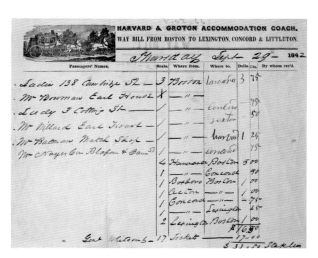

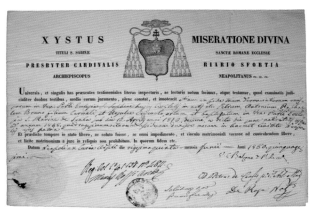

Popular reading material: England

Initially magazines differed very little from books in terms of size and layout – with the exception of the contents page, which was always crammed with detail (*left*). Magazines quickly realized that they had to address a specific market. *The Gentleman's Magazine*, aimed at the landed gentry, had at its height a circulation in the hundreds of thousands.

Chapbooks continued to be published well into the nineteenth century. These cheap, primitively printed booklets were sold by street vendors, and it was essential that they caught the eye of the passing public. Lurid or alarming titles such as those below (*top and bottom right*) and opposite (*bottom left*) were found to work best.

Chapbooks often carried salacious stories presented as fact. The obvious popularity of such material was both feared and criticized by church and social leaders alike. However, chapbooks remained very profitable – and the more sensational the headline, the more

Left *The Gentleman's Magazine*, (January issue), letterpress printed by Nichols & Son, London, 1805.

Top right Chapbook entitled *The Burning Shame or Morality Alarmed in this Neighbourhood*, printed and published by the Catnach Press, London, *c.* 1840.

Bottom right Chapbook entitled *Terrible Disaster at a Welsh Colliery*, London, *c.* 1830.

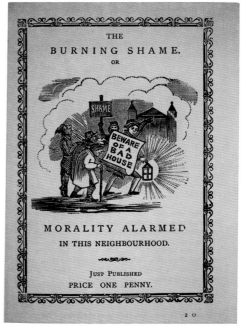

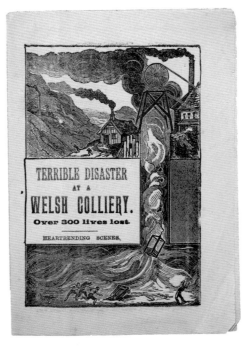

96

profitable the outcome. It was not until much later in the century that newspapers began to compete on cover price and subject matter. The copy of *The Times* below (*top left*) is a special issue mourning the death of Nelson – one of the few occasions that this newspaper had an image on its cover.

The Saturday Magazine (*top right*), published by the Committee of General Literature and Education, and sponsored by the Society for the Promotion of Christian Knowledge, ran between 1832

and 1844. Its aim was to provide the general population with subject matter more wholesome than murder and cannibalism. During this period, song books and sheets (*bottom right*) also became popular, buoyed by the success of music halls.

Execution broadsides were illustrated with a stock block, the central portion of which was pierced to accommodate the required number of figures (*overleaf, top left*). Hanging days were recognized as public holidays and attracted crowds.

Top left Cover of *The Times* newspaper, London, 10 January 1806.

Bottom left Chapbook entitled *A Dialogue between Farmer Trueman and his Son George about the Cannibals in India* (cover and spread), printed by J. Evans & Son, London, date unknown.

Top right *The Saturday Magazine* (March issue), London, 1838.

Bottom right Song sheet entitled *A Garland of New Songs*, letterpress printed by John Marshall, Newcastle upon Tyne, UK, *c.* 1840.

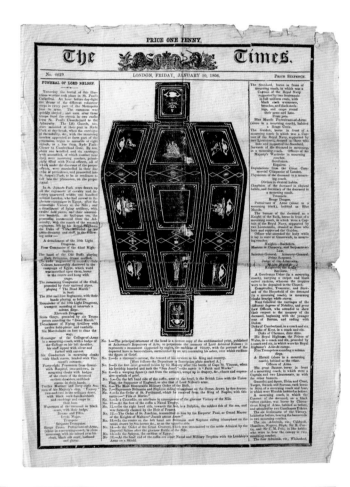

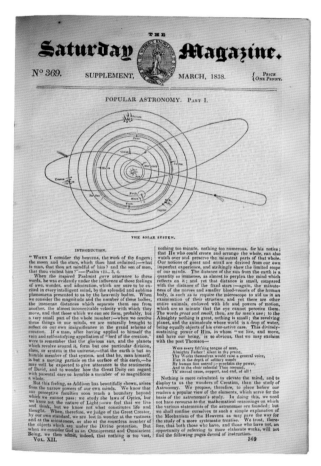

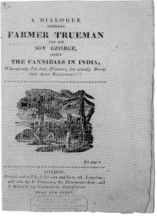

Printers used the opportunity to sell broadsides that purported to carry up-to-date accounts of final court proceedings, confessions and even – in the example below (*right*) – a copy of a final letter to the condemned man's wife. However, such broadsides were generally produced well in advance of the occasion.

Court proceedings, even where the death penalty was the inevitable result, were commonplace and so the copy was often written beforehand and then embellished with details at the last minute. Printed with some care, the four-page chapbook below (*bottom left*) is a particularly fine example. The engravings were, apparently, cut for this publication.

Top left Broadside, letterpress with a wood engraving by G. Smeeton, London, 1834.

Bottom left Cover of a chapbook entitled *The Life of Daniel Good*, letterpress printed with wood engravings by J. Paul, London, *c.* 1840.

Right Broadside, letterpress printed with a wood engraving by Martin & Hillatt, London, 1837.

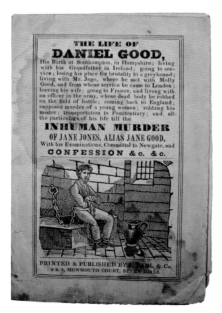

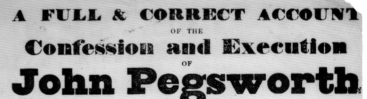

Children's learning material

The Death and Burial of Cock Robin (*top left*) is a children's pictorial alphabet book (or ABC primer). This booklet, sold trimmed and bound, and with a separate cover, is a step up from the average chapbook, although printing quality is much the same and the hand-colouring is cursory. *Cries of London* (*bottom left*), printed and published by J. Fairburn, is also coloured by hand, but more care has been taken. It is likely that *Picture*

Lessons (*bottom right*) was also printed by Fairburn.

Unimpeded by historical precedent, the use of colour in letterpress printing was far more prevalent in the United States than Europe. The Reward of Merit (*top right*) was designed to be hung around the neck of its recipient (a ribbon was threaded through it). These cards – many carrying a moral text – played a key role in primary education in the United States during the nineteenth century.

Top left Booklet, *The Death and Burial of Cock Robin*, letterpress printed with hand-coloured wood engravings, *c.* 1840s.

Bottom left Booklet, *Cries of London*, letterpress printed with hand-coloured wood engravings and published by J. Fairburn, London, *c.* 1830s.

Top right Reward of Merit, letterpress printed in three colours with wood engravings, USA, *c.* 1850.

Bottom right Pictorial alphabet, *Picture Lessons*, letterpress printed with hand-coloured wood engravings as a composite sheet (probably by J. Fairburn), London, *c.* 1830s.

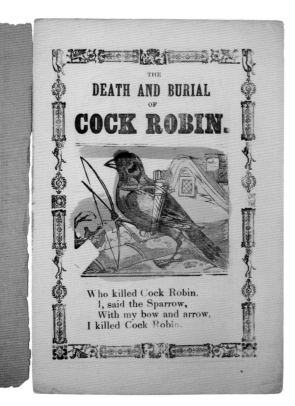

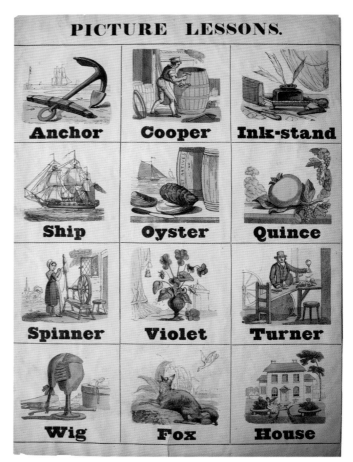

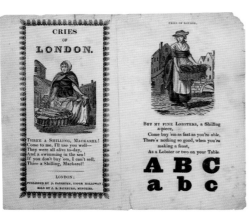

Children's aids

At the turn of the nineteenth century, spelling and reading aids varied considerably in quality. Some were virtually useless. In *The Busy Bee: or Literary Hive* (*bottom left*) little thought has gone into the choice of words (or even the number of letters each contains), and the images appear to be entirely random. In contrast, the children's French/English language aid (*top left*) has been carefully considered, with an intriguing, imaginative result.

Views on childhood were changing. Towards the mid-century, the idea that games designed to stimulate the imagination might be beneficial to children was being taken seriously. If they could include basic skills, such as cutting, folding and gluing, so much the better. Cut-out toys were particularly popular in northern Europe, with sheets of toy-soldier prints (*bottom right*) being among the earliest forms.

Games that enabled parents to help their children with school work were also

Top left Language aid with hand-coloured engraving by G. de Montaut, *c.* early 1800.

Bottom left Spelling and reading aid entitled *The Busy Bee: or Literary Hive*, letterpress printed with engravings and published by the Catnach Press, London, *c.* 1800.

Top right and opposite, top left Alphabet cards with hand-coloured engravings, France, *c.* 1800.

Bottom right Cut-out toy-soldier sheet, letterpress printed from wood engravings and hand-coloured, France, *c.* 1830.

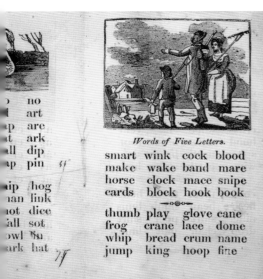

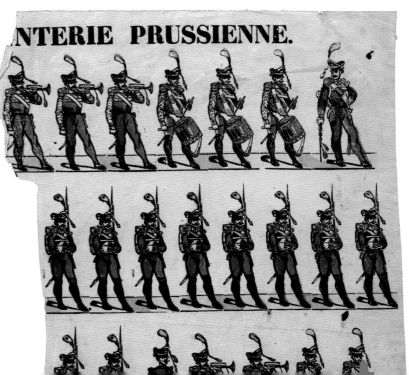

becoming popular. Alphabet books and card sets were among the most common aids, often using images to reinforce the phonic impact of initial letters. These two examples (*below, top left* and *opposite, top right*) are from a pack of cards illustrated with professions.

During this period there were efforts to make books more robust. For some time, maps had been fortified for outdoor use by pasting the printed paper onto calico, a process that was successfully transferred to children's books (*top right*).

Rag books, in which the content was printed directly onto calico, eventually replaced these.

Some of the earliest children's colouring books originated in Germany during the first half of the century (*bottom*) and were often printed using the new commercial printing method: lithography. Early colouring books often had twin images, the first pre-coloured by hand, the second left for the child.

Top right Reading aid, hand-coloured engraving pasted onto calico, France, date unknown.

Bottom Colouring book, lithography, Germany, *c.* 1820s.

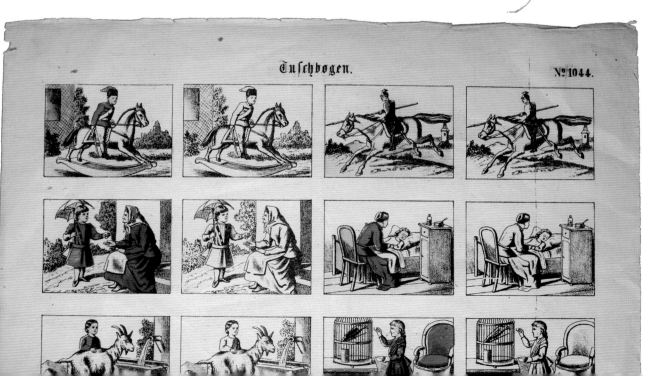

Changing typographic style

Letterpress provided an economical medium for billheads, but until the nineteenth century it is probable that an engraved billhead was considered the superior, more refined print process. By the turn of the century there was a renewed interest in letterpress, especially in France, largely due to the new fonts being issued by the Fournier foundry in Paris.

The two billheads (*top and centre left*) are evidence of the letterpress jobbing printer using precursors of fat face types, seen in the two later examples (*top and centre right*). With the confidence of the letterpress printer growing, the only concession to the legacy of the engraver is the decorative 'bought of', which has been printed using a stereotype block.

The changing appearance of personal bookplates (engraving) and book labels (letterpress) provides an intimate record of middle-class tastes in typographic style. In the book labels and plate (*bottom*), the Lawrence Strangman and Gerald Fitzgerald items have the stateliness of neoclassical style, while the untrimmed Henry Cheever example hints at a less restrained style to come.

Top and centre left Two billheads, letterpress, Paris, both 1813.

Bottom, from left to right Book label, letterpress, nineteenth century; book label, letterpress, nineteenth century; bookplate, engraving, nineteenth century.

Top right Billhead, letterpress, Paris, 1837.

Centre right Billhead, letterpress, London, 1843.

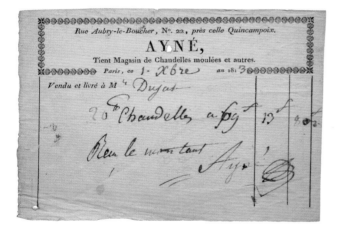

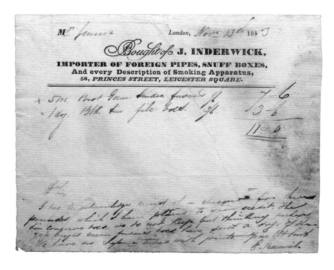

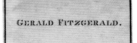

Monumental design
John Johnson's book *Typographia* (*left*)
is a cross between a printer's manual
and a historic survey of printing. The
final chapter includes a review of new
print-related technologies, including
stereotype printing, larger steam-driven
presses and one-man hand machines –
innovations about which Johnson was
less than enthusiastic. The appearance
of this volume is particularly striking and
certainly nothing like the conservative
design that was typical of such books.

All the elements used to represent
the wall and arch are taken from
decorative border material. After the
publication of this book, for a period
it became a popular exercise for
compositors to construct 'monuments',
at the centre of which might be placed
a suitably solemn statement. Unusually,
in one of the promotional pieces for
Beyerhaus, Berlin, a butterfly takes
centre stage (*bottom right*).

Left Title page of John Johnson's
Typographia, or The Printers' Instructor
(two volumes), London, 1824.

Top and bottom right Two decorative
pieces, reproduced in the *Journal für
Buchdruckerkunst, Schriftgießerei
und Verwandte Fächer* to promote
Beyerhaus, Berlin, 1835.

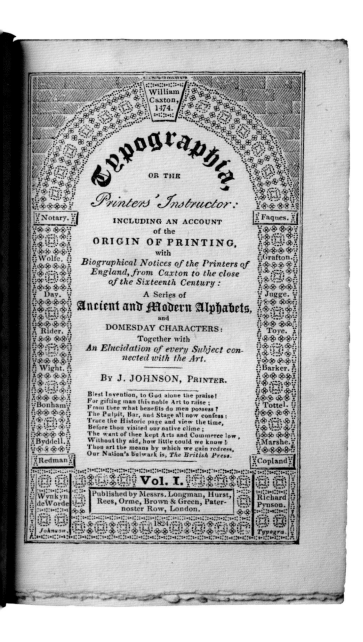

Kaleidoskop - Einfassungen von *A. Beyerhaus* in Berlin.

CHAPTER THREE
MECHANIZATION AND INTERNATIONAL AMBITION

Right Events such as London's Great Exhibition of 1851 were hugely important and provided the opportunity to celebrate creativity, inventiveness and engineering prowess. The revolution in manufacturing, driven by mechanization, meant that there was great competition between companies selling comparable goods. Factories grew to enormous sizes, and the increased use of power-assisted machines kept productivity on the increase. Mass production required mass markets.

Whereas in Britain enthusiasm for the machine was constantly tempered by concerns for its broader aesthetic, cultural and social implications, the United States was quick to embrace it, encouraged by a lack of cheap, available labour (in contrast to Europe and Britain) as well as the presence of an increasingly affluent, highly homogeneous mass market. Major cities on the eastern seaboard were developing into important metropolitan centres, while within the vast, open continent, cities such as New Orleans and Detroit were growing rapidly. As sections of the west were settled, newspapers were established in each new town and compositors and pressmen who had joined the migrations found that they could obtain work with ease.

Although the United States was not responsible for the invention of many of the machines, pioneering American manufacturers were invariably quicker to introduce their use than their European counterparts. They were also very good at adapting existing machines to fulfil new tasks, promoting the concept of interchangeability and standardization within mass production. This meant that from early in the nineteenth century, both industrial manufacturing and consumer products incorporated numerous identical parts designed by anonymous engineers. Machines were being built to make parts for the manufacture of other machines.

Despite, or perhaps because of, advances in mechanization, the appearance of the traditional fine engraved line had a lasting impact on some areas of print, particularly business stationery and security printing such as banknotes, passports and postage stamps. The introduction of affordable postal rates in England in 1840, and in America in 1847, meant that business stationery took on a more significant role and ensured that engraving remained a popular medium throughout the century.

The elaborate decoration that had been applied to the copperplate-engraved letterforms of eighteenth-century Europe was now being added to letterforms whose origins were nineteenth-century display faces designed for letterpress. These bold, heavy types were redrawn on engraving plates, decorated and elaborately wrapped in and around illustrations. The smaller company might still prefer to illustrate its activities via symbolic images (for example, bees for industriousness or sheep for woollen goods), but finished products were increasingly being depicted in a simpler, more direct way.

By the 1860s, the term 'print shop' – although considered derogatory by some in the trade – was in common usage in the United States and signalled a more relaxed attitude to commercial imperatives.[1] For an increasing number of people, shopping was becoming a pleasant, more leisurely activity. Browsing shop windows was a common pastime, and businesses aimed to utilize the commercial potential of the shop frontage. Where previously the shop sign might have been depicted on a letterhead, it was now more often the whole shop front. Rivalries encouraged increasingly sophisticated advertising methods.

The growing demand for graphic illustration, and the potential for individuals to make a living from it, is reflected in the popularity of books such as Thomas Houghton's *The Printers' Practical Every-day-book*, published in 1841, which was the first to dedicate a substantial part of its content to jobbing work. The opportunities afforded the printing office in the mid-nineteenth century had improved inestimably in the previous thirty years. With a wide variety of types now available and founders willing to sell display fonts in smaller lots, the compositor had a considerable choice of styles, weights and sizes at his disposal. Creative invention was becoming part of the printer's domain.

In his chapter on job work, Houghton emphasized the need for design that was 'appropriate for its purpose'. In the context of jobbing work, 'appropriateness' took on an altogether different and certainly broader meaning than that of previous manuals. The jobbing printer was being presented with unique problems that required novel solutions. Houghton recognized that the responsibility for creative outcomes was being placed directly on the compositor, and thereby increasing his status within the print office to the detriment of the pressman.[2]

Top left Three-man Rutt rotary press, c. 1825. One man feeds paper, another turns the cylinder by hand, and the third removes the finished print (at the rear).

Bottom left Applegath & Cowper's perfecting machine (c. 1828) enabled the printer to print both sides of the paper simultaneously. Speed was also increased by the feeding of paper to the press from huge continuous rolls.

Right Publisher John Walter's web-fed rotary presses at The Times newspaper offices, 1869. This press was more compact, required fewer men to operate it and could produce about 10,000 perfected sheets of an eight-page newspaper per hour.

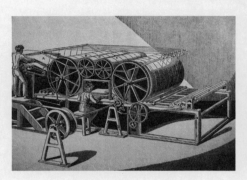

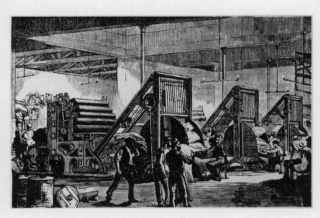

The influence of mechanization on the status of design

The speed of printing was not limited by the efficiency of the machine itself but by the feeding of paper sheets, which still had to be done by hand, one at a time. The initial solution to this problem was to increase the number of feeder stations. By the early 1860s, *The Times* newspaper had two ten-feeder Hoe rotary machines. Each employee, or 'feeder', was estimated to feed 1,500 sheets an hour (see page 59).

The limitations of feeding by hand were overcome by the development of a reel-fed machine – a 'perfector' – that could print both sides of the paper simultaneously. In Philadelphia, William Bullock manufactured such a press in 1865, while in England the first prototype was built a year later by John Walter III. In 1869, four Walter presses were installed at the offices of *The Times*. The scale and speed of these machines had completely changed the job of the printer in the newspaper sector of the industry. In a single generation, the pressman's job had been transformed from that of a craftsman using a wooden handpress to something more akin to an engineer.

For other sectors of the printing industry, including the majority of book printers, the printing process changed little. But with demand for print growing exponentially, the only way to enable the hand composition of type to keep up with increased printing speed was to buy more foundry type and employ more compositors. Attempts to mechanize the composition of type were being made as early as 1850, but compositors had little to fear from these crude inventions.

Likewise, in the United States, changes in the duties of compositor and pressman were emphasizing the growing division between these two roles. While the pressman's job remained essentially the same, the compositor was being given more autonomy, more time and space in which to arrange or design the matter that the pressman then printed. These changes of status within printing offices reflected the evolving nature of printed material in general as demand became increasingly diverse and more individual.

Traditionally, the typographic arrangement (or lay) of the page had been a house style from which the compositor rarely strayed. In such circumstances, where everyone knew what the outcome would be from the outset, compositor and printer could share equal status within the printing office. But once the compositor became an originator, the creator of a unique outcome, the printer as pressman was perceived as doing little more than carrying out the instructions of the compositor.[3]

The sudden abundance of every material commodity – some essential, many entirely frivolous – was something that preyed on Victorian minds. There was a genuine concern that the uniform perfection of the mass-produced object might dull the senses. English writer, critic and artist John Ruskin (1819–1900) despaired of the sheer quantity as well as the quality of manufactured material goods and feared for the moral values of a society that could have all it needed, and even more of what it merely coveted, stating: 'I want to explode printing and gunpowder – the two great curses of the age; I begin to think that abominable art of printing is the root of all mischief.' The new purposes to which print was now applied demonstrated for Ruskin a worrying disregard for traditional standards in terms of taste, design and manufacture. For Ruskin, it was mechanization that was the cause of falling standards, and, more specifically, a lack of pride or responsibility taken by any one person within the printing office.

Concern for 'taste' – taste being a measure of good judgment – was a subject much discussed during the mechaniza-

Left Hotel advertising register printed by Maynard, Gough & Co., New York, c. 1860. This sheet displays a number of businesses in the immediate vicinity of the hotel, each of which was persuaded to pay a fee to the printer. In return, the printer negotiated with the hotel, and then designed and printed the sheet. Such an activity was, essentially, the business model for the emerging advertising industry.

Right Detail from the bottom of a receipt of payment from the advertising department of the newspaper Kentish Gazette, UK, 1825. It shows the pricing policy and substantial additional cost of duty on all advertising at that time.

tion of industry. The success of manufacturing, by providing regular incomes and cheaper goods, was also providing the working classes with increasing buying power and, critically, manufacturing was offering choice. Among the population at large, for whom domestic objects such as furniture had previously been bought just once in a lifetime, and clothes only replaced when, literally, worn out, many more now had the opportunity to buy for reasons purely of fashion.

Taste would also become a much discussed issue for the jobbing printing fraternity, many of whom wished to maintain the authority of their activity's historic associations of craftsmanship, integrity and sound judgment, while accepting that the nature of their work meant association with contemporary and temporary social events, services and fashion. This dichotomy would be the root subject of thousands of columns of anguished comment in the print trade journals as well as arts and cultural magazines.

Advertising and the advertising agency

By 1850 canals, roads and railways in Britain and much of Europe had opened up new markets and reduced transportation costs dramatically. In 1869 the American Congress authorized the construction of a system of transcontinental rail lines, and by 1875 trains carried mail from coast to coast. Transport itself, and railways in particular, became big business and major clients for the printing industry. Manufacturing was being scaled up as mechanization and assembly-line working methods enabled factories to produce goods in large numbers at low cost and uniform quality. For the first time, it was cheaper for people to buy a product than make or grow it themselves.

With improved methods of transportation, factories and workshops could distribute their products over an ever-increasing area and, thus, required printed material that promoted goods far beyond their place of manufacture. The most effective way to achieve this was to advertise in the local newspaper of every town and city within the target area. The planning and arrangements required in booking advertising space in, perhaps, fifty papers, using different sized pages, was time-consuming. Recognizing this problem, an agent might offer to take over these essentially administrative tasks for an agreed fee. At the same time, newspapers began paying such agents to sell space on their behalf to advertisers. In this way, an entirely new business – the advertising agency – came into existence.

During 1851, *The Times* often had forty-four columns of classified advertising daily.[4] Alongside volume, advertising was also becoming a more sophisticated activity, as evidenced by the publication in the United States of *The Newspaper Press Directory*. This contained not only a list of all the principal newspapers and numbers of copies sold, but also an

Left A stereotype is a duplicate printing plate made by pouring molten metal into a mould. The casting was usually taken from engraved wood blocks of an image or letterform, or – as in this case – from set type. The stereotype would be fixed to a wooden base, bringing it to standard type height. The advantage of printing text from a stereotype was that it was easy and cheap to store, enabling the type to be put back to use on other jobs.

Right Engraved wood block and a print taken from an engraved wood block. The wood used for wood engraving had to be hard, carefully dried, accurately finished to type height and cut to the size required. Larger wood engravings could be made by bolting several blocks together.

appraisal of the editorial stance regarding social and political issues. Charles Mitchell, an advertising agent and publisher of this directory, recognized that the advertiser must be able to choose the papers that offered the appropriate audiences for his goods or services.

Nevertheless, despite their falling cover price, many people could not afford to buy newspapers, and many more could still not read. This, along with the various restrictions regarding the appearance and size of advertisements, to say nothing of the cost for the space, meant that many businesses chose to use alternative means of advertising, and bill-posting in particular. However, street advertising was universally criticized for being criminally irresponsible for the unverified claims made (called 'puffing' or 'puffery') as well as its defilement of public places.[5] This was made far worse by the unregulated way notices and posters were displayed. It was common practice for posters to be pasted over the top of the competition under cover of darkness by 'gentlemen of the paste and brush',[6] who fought running battles to ensure that their clients' posters remained visible.

Street advertising featured a wide range of typefaces, styles and sizes on the same poster, often with striking wood-engraved illustrations. This was in direct contrast with advertising in newspapers, which was still strictly regulated in terms of size and typefaces. By the late 1860s, American newspaper publishers began to relent as pressure grew. Rival manufacturers of sewing machines and typewriters were among the earliest to carry large images of their products in newspaper advertisements. Nevertheless, full-page newspaper advertisements did not become commonplace until the final decade of the century.

Unlike newspapers, magazines initially made most of their money from subscriptions and did not generally accept

notices, let alone advertising, until the 1870s. The view remained that publicity was vulgar and advertising was a sham and would, therefore, be detrimental to the integrity of the journal. Resistance finally faltered during the 1870s when the American magazine *Century* broke with tradition and actively sought advertisers by offering moderate rates.

Far left Theatre playbill, letterpress printed by the Theatre Royal Press, Bradford, UK, 1856. As theatre productions became more extravagant, playbills became longer. Featuring useful information such as synopses, playbills were also sold as theatre programmes.

Left Theatre handbill and programme, letterpress printed by G. Stuart, London, 1846. This single sheet, combining the typical appearance of a Victorian theatre playbill on the left with editorial notices on the right, was probably distributed in and around the vicinity of the theatre to encourage ticket-buyers. The folded two-page arrangement paved the way for the booklet format of modern times.

Packaging and the retail business

One of the most significant areas of commercial growth between 1850 and 1875 was in trading. Across the developed world there was an increase of over 50% in the number of wholesale and retail traders, among whom the proliferation of small shopkeepers was particularly noticeable.[7] In these shops, foodstuffs were typically stored behind the counter, requiring the sales person to collect the produce from the shelves or portion out loose goods such as flour and biscuits (sold by weight) from open containers.

The demand for the packaging of goods had been small until the nineteenth century. Business tended to serve its immediate locality, but as roads were improved and railways built, the possibility of establishing a national or even international foodstuffs business became a reality. This transferred the initiative for packaging from the shopkeeper to the manufacturer, while transportation generated packages using materials such as glass, metal, wood and card as well as paper.

The concept of choice as part of the shopping experience encouraged the design of packaging that not only held and protected the goods, but also attracted the attention of the customer. Paradoxically, pre-sealed packaged goods had a certain exclusivity that local produce lacked, while the printed price, based on net weight, was popular because of its intrinsic honesty.

The expansion of American activity in every form of packaging grew enormously during the latter half of the nineteenth century, as did the transatlantic trade in packaging material, for example, tinplate from Wales to America and box-board from the United States to Europe. All containers needed labels so that customers could see at a glance what, and how much, they held. Colour printing was more prevalent as lithography became increasingly mechanized

and the essential role of the illustrated image displayed on labels was recognized.

Entering a shop had required, to some extent, a commitment to buy, and so the idea of shopping being an altogether more relaxed experience, where the shopper might browse at leisure, led to the establishment of the department store, first in Europe and then in America. The department store appears to have grown, in the main, out of drapery stores, which gradually extended their range of goods to include lighting and furnishing. A little later, the same developments took place by combining foods, or confectionery, newspapers, magazines and tobacco, or pharmaceutical goods. The freedom offered to customers to inspect and choose from a variety of similar goods was, in itself, still a privileged experience, and stores were built to accentuate this sense of luxury. It also gave manufacturers the incentive to study customer behaviour and review the effectiveness of their packaging, labelling and any point-of-sale support.

Top left Hand-coloured lithograph, presumably a watch paper, depicting the construction of Brunel's Thames Tunnel in London, date unknown.

Bottom left Map showing the Metropolitan Railway, printed over a copy of an earlier engraved map of London, c. 1870s.

Right Travel ticket, letterpress, New York, c. 1870.

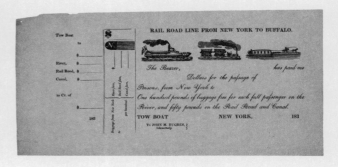

Posters and the entertainment business

Growth in the use of posters is probably the most visible example of the changing functions of the printer. The general design of posters developed from the traditional, symmetrical layout of the title page of the book. With the introduction of display sizes and designs of types, the jobbing compositor had the means to break away from the traditional appearance of the book.

Such opportunities are particularly apparent in the design of theatre posters in which it was now possible for each act listed to be represented by a different typeface, tightly packed one above the other, to provide the perfect evocation of the theatrical variety show. The availability of display types also influenced the nature of the written copy. Commas and full stops, for instance, became superfluous when statements or various theatrical acts could be distinguished by a different typeface. If the name of the act was long, it would be set with a condensed face; if short, an extended face would be used. The technical advantage of letterpress, meanwhile, was demonstrated by the frequency with which a playbill would be edited, reset and reprinted for each day's performance.

Posters for other purposes – auctions, horticultural sales, public notices, etc – were given a more dignified appearance through the judicious use of white space and hierarchical signals. Great strides had been made in the expressive sophistication of the compositor's work. Design for purpose no longer meant only that a text should be readable – it also had to be designed so that its purpose could be identified before the viewer committed to reading.

Information design for transport systems

With the arrival of the railway came the need to present a considerable amount of information in a concise format, including times, fares, the names of stations where trains might or might not stop, interconnecting services between increasing numbers of rail companies, and the various facilities available on board. Inventive solutions had to be devised to enable such a wide range of facts to be displayed in tabular form, and the compositor had to plan this complicated task with the utmost care.

Not surprisingly, passengers occasionally complained about the complexity of these early timetables. Indeed, one example, published in Britain in the 1850s, was called *The Unintelligible Railway Guide*. From 1840, guides and timetables began to appear in pocket-sized book form. Timetables were published by railway companies but also by enterprising local and national printers who included advertising – revenue that enabled them to sell the booklet cheaply. Pre-eminent among the publishers of railway timetables was the Englishman George Bradshaw, whose guides first appeared in 1839 (and continued until 1961).

Related to travel is the development of touring maps. Both timetables and maps require that decisions regarding editorial and design are made in unison, principally to establish how much information can be included before function is impaired. The appearance of railway timetables was (and remains) strongly influenced by the nature of letterpress – most significantly, in the characteristic horizontal and vertical axes, with distances between stations described by the arrival/ departure times alone. Alternatively, maps depicting the journey, initially engraved and, later, printed with lithography, provided the traveller with the information required to fill in the 'spaces' between stations.

Right A lithographic stone is flat and porous, and once its surface has been prepared it must not be touched. Any contact with oily material (even a human hair) will leave a trace and print as a black speck.

This stone features several drawing techniques. The fact that lithographic printing was the result of hand-drawn letters and images gave the artist the same creative freedom as copperplate engraving. It was also quicker and therefore cheaper.

Britain, because of its relatively small size and accessibility, developed touring maps in advance of the United States, where huge distances limited the concept of travel for pleasure, by and large, until the era of the car. The earliest of Britain's touring maps were published in the 1840s. Glued (tipped-in) to stiff covers and small enough to fit into a coat pocket, these maps were designed specifically for the railway explorer, showing the latest line completions and stations.

Lithography and the advent of colour printing

While letterpress remained the only significant and practicable means for the printing of text, gradually the full creative and commercial potential of lithography – invented around 1798 by the Bavarian Alois Senefelder – was being realized. In essence, the lithographic process exploits the fact that water and grease repel each other. Marks were drawn onto a flat, porous stone using a pen or brush with greasy ink or crayon. When the stone was dampened and a grease-based printing ink rolled across its surface, the ink would only adhere to the drawn image. This image could then be transferred to paper via a simple press. Once prepared, the stone was extremely sensitive, which meant that virtually any kind of mark could be made. As a result, the very versatility of lithography – its ability to mimic other print processes – caused its identity to remain elusive during the first part of the nineteenth century.[8]

Shortly after 1850, some forty years after letterpress printing had begun to be mechanized, powered lithographic presses started to narrow the commercial gap between the two processes significantly. The fact that all lithographic-printed letterforms and images were hand-rendered offered considerable creative advantages over letterpress. The emphasis on drawing meant that lithographic artists brought with them an unfettered approach to graphic communication and, especially, the creation of unconstrained, occasionally eccentric letterforms. The process lent itself particularly well to jobbing and, in particular, printing work in which words and images were inextricably combined, such as maps, plans and other diagrammatic material.

Lithography also competed successfully with engraving because every aspect of its production was simpler, quicker and, importantly, additional colours were a ready option. Before

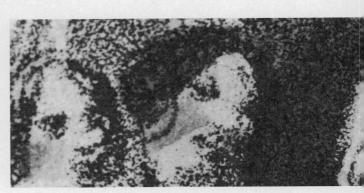

1840, the use of colours other than black had been rare, an exception being the printing of lottery tickets. It was with the introduction of two-colour wood type that the communicative potential of colour printing inks began to be exploited. During the 1840s, posters promoting circus, theatre and festive events first began to appear. By the 1860s, pictorial woodcuts and other decorative motifs in three or even four colours were being used in the design of posters, aided substantially by the early wood-letters of Wells & Webb, Bonnewell and others.

As the factors that had commercially restricted the process were overcome, lithography, and in particular its use of colour, began to have an effect on the interiors of shops in which packaging and point-of-sale items started to appear. Products and commodities could now be illustrated on the lid or label of a container. The draughtsmanship of the lithographic artist and his mastery of the process were impressive from the outset.

Owen Jones (1809–74) was one of the earliest British pioneers in lithographic colour printing and brought it to prominence with his book *Plans, Elevations, Sections, and Details of the Alhambra*, begun in 1836 and completed in 1842, which included numerous colour plates of Moorish designs. From the 1840s onwards, Jones produced a number of books focusing on decorative design, his most celebrated being *The Grammar of Ornament* in 1856.

Colour printing from wood blocks continued to compete with colour lithography in Britain longer than anywhere else – made possible, perhaps, by the tendency for British lithographic printers to mix their inks with white to acquire a more opaque consistency. This gave the printed image an appearance similar to that achieved using wood blocks, encouraging the term 'side-by-side' lithographic printing.

The best early lithographic work was produced in France from 1834, beginning with the design and production of a series of imaginative coloured alphabet and design books created by J. Midolle. During the next three decades, innovations and increasingly sophisticated techniques in colour lithographic printing (namely chromolithography) continued to be developed in France at a pace admired throughout the world. The French illustrated chromolithographic poster industry was on the brink of a major expansion, beginning with Jules Chéret, in 1866, establishing his own printing company in Paris, which would revolutionize the appearance of lithography as well as the function and effectiveness of the poster in the final decades of the century.

The superior quality of the inks manufactured in France enabled the French lithographic printer to develop the technical and creative potential of 'building up' images and letters by overprinting numerous translucent colours. Using pens, crayons and brushes directly on stones, the surface of which could be smooth or textured to various degrees, lithography offered infinitely more subtle possibilities than those that could be achieved by printing from wood blocks or even copperplates.

Various print-finishing techniques commonly associated with lithographic printing were also being developed to provide additional tactile as well as visual stimulus. Labels and greeting or business cards were often spot-varnished and given an embossed or debossed texture. The stippled effect – tiny dots of various sizes, densities and colours (often blue, red and yellow, but sometimes with pink for flesh tones as well as grey and black) – would be the basis on which standard full-colour lithography would develop in the twentieth century.

Lithographic printing technology began to arrive in the United States during the 1830s and 1840s, and a succession of

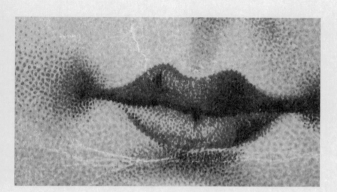

immigrant printers brought further improvements. Early American lithographic work followed the British method of using almost opaque inks, but by the 1850s this was gradually being replaced by the use of translucent inks, overprinted to provide a more subtle, more sophisticated and realistic colour rendition. By the end of the decade chromolithography was being very effectively used for advertising and the design of sheet music covers.

The technical sophistication of American chromolithography is demonstrated by the Julius Bien edition of John James Audubon's *Birds of America*, produced between 1858 and 1862. Bien went on to apply lithography to the production of large-scale maps and charts, an important use of print during the American Civil War (1861–65). Many lithographic printers built up their businesses and technical expertise during this period, designing and printing posters and broadsheets of military camps, battles, and portraits of military and political leaders.

Political unrest in the late 1840s led to a rise in the number of German immigrants – among them, future leaders in nineteenth-century American printing. None was more successful than Louis Prang (1824–1909). In 1860, he founded his own company producing prodigious numbers of colour plates for book illustrations, labels and posters (see page 167). He is also credited with the introduction of brilliantly coloured advertising trade cards in 1873 and, two years later, with the creation of the greetings card.

By the 1870s, steam-powered lithographic presses were in widespread use throughout the United States. With this enterprising, high-volume commercial work came the innovations, both technical and creative, that would result in the distinctive use of multiple overlaid colours, creating rich, exuberant images that often drew on the romance and adventure of the New World. Importantly, lithography also encouraged the use of bold, elaborate, free-flowing lettering, including drop shadows, and unrestrained variations and extensions of every kind. While these letterforms were influenced by the display wood types available for letterpress, they related more directly in style to the work of the engraver because many lithographic companies had their roots in engraving and maintained engraving departments.

From the outset, many American printers were, first and foremost, jobbing printers. Immigrant printers adapted to the new freedom on offer, and in particular, the lack of any preordained hierarchy based on the purpose of the printed material. Also missing was the stigma associated with the design and printing of jobbing work, still so prevalent in the Old World.

Below A Sigl lithographic machine, Austria. In 1851 Georg Sigl took out patents for a powered machine incorporating rollers that dampened and inked the lithographic stone automatically. The production rate suddenly rose to around 1,000 prints an hour.

Lithographische Schnellpresse
erfunden und gebaut von G. Sigl in Wien.

Mechanization and the failures of training

The general introduction of machinery and the growing incidence of large-scale production of every kind encouraged employers to replace skilled craftsmen with semi-skilled or even unskilled workers as skilled jobs were divided up and converted into fewer operations. Severe weakening of apprenticeship schemes was a common consequence.

In the print trade, as elsewhere, it was argued that if the apprentice could no longer learn the full breadth of the print trade from within the industry, it must be made possible to supplement this experience with a mixture of practical and theoretic study in evening classes at regional technical colleges. To admit to the necessity of such a scheme was to publicly accept that the printer's apprenticeship, for so long recognized as embodying the highest moral virtues, was now dysfunctional. The perceived loss of control, especially for an industry that had jealously protected its craft secrets, came with a sense of failure.

Some master artisans opposed any ideology that encouraged modernization, including further education.[9] This anti-liberalism was not a dogma but simply an expression of unspecific hostility, a rejection of all facets of the prevailing social reform (including not only mechanization but also internationalism and individualism), which were despised on the grounds that they were anti-traditionalist.[10] However, the introduction of automated machines, and the application of scientific knowledge to printing processes, was also a rallying call to those campaigning for technical education. Public information took many forms and, with printed matter now playing an increasingly important role in everyday life, there was a growing desire to gain an education – a prospect supported by a growing number of social, religious and political organizations.

The link between creativity and economic performance had long been recognized in France, where 'a French capitalist employs three or four artists, [whereas] in England one artist would supply eight or ten manufacturers … it appears that in England the designer and the person who applies it to the manufacturer are different people. In France the workman is himself the artist.'[11]

The British government, in recognition of the growing inadequacies of apprenticeship schemes, had already provided funds for the establishment of a School of Design in London in 1837, and in 1853 this was considerably enlarged and renamed the National Art Training School, later becoming the Royal College of Art. Unfortunately for the School of Design, there was little consensus about what 'design' was, and no one appeared to know how to teach it. The acquisition of 'good taste' seems to have been the principal aim, with much emphasis placed on the students copying motifs from classical architectural detail.

Although some employers (manufacturers of ceramics, textiles, jewelry, etc) began to use design school attendance as a prerequisite to employment or formal apprenticeship, the printing fraternity remained convinced that only they could teach the necessary skills and maintain the guarantee of a practical outcome. The general criticism that design education isolated the youth from the realities of the workshop was just another way of stating that education instilled an elitist attitude detrimental to the equilibrium of the workplace. These concerns were supported by periodicals such as *The Journal of Design*, a resolutely critical voice of the School of Design.

Art education, therefore, for the printing trade, was of no value. Entry to their industry was to remain by one route only: apprenticeship. Despite its problems, the persistence of apprenticeship in printing, unlike many other trades during the nineteenth century, might be attributed to the poor reputation of early design education, but more important were the growth and influence of trade societies and, in particular, the legal status afforded to trade unions. These developments gave trade unions the power to uphold policy on apprenticeship in order to control entry to the industry to protect the status and pay of its members.

However, it was becoming increasingly clear that the industrial employer, unlike the craft master of the past, was unable, or unwilling, to meet the moral and practical obligations historically associated with apprenticeship.[12] There was mounting comment that such intransigent methods of shop-

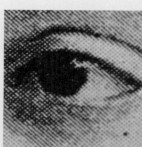

Top left An engraver's interpretation of tonal gradations of a photographic image, achieved by varying the thickness of lines by hand and, for lighter areas, cutting the lines again at right angles to form dots of various sizes.

Bottom left A photomechanical halftone. This image was letterpress printed from a halftone block. Two sheets of glass, each with engraved parallel lines, were glued together so that the engraved lines lay at right angles to each other. When an image is projected through the glass screen onto a light-sensitive surface, the gradated tones of the photograph are changed into dots. Where the tones are dark, the dots on the light-sensitive surface are larger and, therefore, closer together, creating a darker tone.

Right Lithographic print (detail and in full), printed sepia to make the print look like a genuine photograph, *c.* late nineteenth century. Chromolithographers adapted to the black-and-white photograph by making hand-drawn translations of it on lithographic stones, a practice that continued even after photomechanical systems had been developed.

floor-based training were inadequate and, indeed, no longer feasible. Overseers were under constant pressure in administering the day-to-day control of work and maintenance of discipline, while journeymen, a large proportion of whom were working under a system of piecework, could not afford the time and attention required by the young apprentice. Perhaps most important was the recognition that design, and the inquisitive, questioning attitude that comes with it, was near impossible to accommodate where compliance and standardized outcomes were insisted upon.

It must also be mentioned that the working environment of the printer was not, generally, conducive to clear, thoughtful work. Throughout the nineteenth century, compositors worked by gaslight, which was both hot and very bright, or perhaps with the vapours of whale oil or kerosene. The 'newfangled electricity', which had a tendency to pulsate, was detested, and yet a gaslamp could consume up to five times more oxygen than a man. By the end of a midwinter day, with all the windows tightly closed, composing rooms were positively miasmic.[13]

Early photography and its influence on illustration

The invention of photography was announced in 1839. Three famous and influential illustrated journals were founded almost at the same time: *The Illustrated London News* (1842), *L'Illustration* (Paris, 1843) and *Illustrirte Zeitung* (Leipzig, 1843). The growth in journalistic illustration and the development of photography are closely connected, despite the fact that photographs themselves could not be commercially printed alongside text until the final decade of the century. Harnessing the potential of photography was something that printers recognized had huge commercial promise. Many attempts – often producing excellent results – were made, but none proved practical for use with commercial print technology of the time. Nevertheless, photography did have an enormous influence on the way illustrators worked.

The commercial function of a striking image on the cover of a magazine had been acknowledged for some time. Publications such as *The Mirror of Literature, Amusement, and Instruction* (1822) and *The Cheap Magazine* (founded 1831) were printed with a single wood-engraved cover illustration. But the turning point for illustrated journals came with the founding of successful weekly publications such as *The Penny Magazine* and *The Saturday Magazine* (both 1832). It had been common practice for a magazine to send an 'artist-reporter' to make drawings in the midst of, for example, military activities, who then sent these back to the publishing house, where an engraver would interpret the drawings on copper or steel plates – a process that involved condensing, or editing, incidents recorded in a number of drawings into one illustration.[14]

Once photography became a practical proposition, photographers were also employed to record a developing story. One of the earliest examples of illustrations openly based on

Left Double-page spread from *Harpel's Typograph, or Book of Specimens* by Oscar Harpel, Cincinnati, USA, 1870. Harpel's book was the first to celebrate exclusively the work of the jobbing printer. He displayed the everyday printed material of business, 'taken from the current transactions of a regular printing office, and not designed for the pages of the book'.

Opposite Detail of a chromolithographic poster, USA, date unknown. The colours and tones are achieved almost entirely by the use of Ben Day mechanical tints (sheets of pre-printed dots or lines, etc, which could be rubbed down onto the lithographic stone). The density of the smoke, for example, has been achieved by the illustrator applying multiple coloured screens and greater pressure to the tint to increase the size of the dot.

from other, less ambitious jobbing printers, began calling themselves art jobbing offices, art printers or, most commonly, artistic printers.

By mid-century, Cincinnati had become the fourth largest publishing centre in the United States after New York, Philadelphia and Boston. Situated on the Ohio River, it was the gateway to the south through shipping and the west through the railroads, both industries requiring large quantities of printed matter. Huge amounts of passing trade, generally in a hurry and looking for local information, provided opportunities for the enterprising jobbing printer. Tabular clarity and bold display had to cater to the sophisticated expectations of travellers coming from the East Coast cities. As a result, Cincinnati developed a printing reputation for confident, precise presswork, ornamented typefaces and, above all, use of colour.

Oscar Harpel led the way in this regard. Demonstrating remarkable confidence, he published *Harpel's Typograph, or Book of Specimens* in 1870. Uniquely, more a design than a technical manual, the book was devoted almost entirely to jobbing work and was resplendent with numerous specimen settings, all described as genuine jobs, tipped- or sewn-in, many credited to their compositors, and all solutions to routine design problems faced daily by the jobbing printer. In reference to the compositor, Harpel explained: 'Such a [creative] spirit, if properly maintained, can only promote the interests of all concerned, and serve to elevate Printing still higher as a substantial and creative Art.'

In Harpel's view, the purpose of printed matter should have no influence on the quality of its design or printing. The aim of his book was to demonstrate that the everyday label, invitation or business card provided both compositor and printer with opportunities to achieve something unique

by its design and beautiful in its printing. The assumption that the art of printing was restricted to worthy subjects, such as the book, was emphatically denied. Instead, Harpel insisted it was in the communication of ordinary events, goods and services that the printer should excel, and, in so doing, contribute to the enrichment of urban life and, naturally, the success of his clients' businesses.

As the printer's work for his customers became more sophisticated, so his attention turned to the marketing of his own business. Horizons were being broadened, new opportunities recognized and sought. Although very few copies of *Harpel's Typograph* were available in England and the rest of Europe, it was very positively reviewed, becoming a much-discussed point of reference for those calling for a more professional approach by the printing industry to the needs of the business community.

For Harpel, the art of the printing office was to serve commerce: 'tasteful utility'. Its 'artists' were tradesmen compositors whose tools were both 'extremely unadaptable as well as troublesome', and yet if the compositor was 'artistic' in intent then 'beauty could prevail'.[16] This link between art and commerce, and artist and tradesman, demonstrated a pre-eminently democratic attitude. Printers, through their tools and processes, and through their trade journals, would wrestle with the implications of this for the remainder of the nineteenth century.

Despite enthusiastic reviews and huge influence, *Harpel's Typograph* was not a financial success. It appears that Harpel allowed his enthusiasm to overtake any business plan: 'The expense of *Typograph* has been greater than was at first anticipated, in consequence of considerable additions to the original plan.'[17] It had required a year of 'unremitting labor and superintendence'. Subsequent publishing projects did not fare particularly well either.[18] His printing company, Harpel's Mercantile Job Rooms, went out of business in 1875. Six years later, Harpel died at the age of fifty-three.

OPENING OF THE INTERNATIONAL EXHIBITION: THE ORCHESTRA.—SEE PAGE 473.

The changing role of the engraver

The weekly *Illustrated London News* (*opposite*), launched in 1842 and followed a year later by *L'Illustration* in Paris and *Illustrirte Zeitung* in Leipzig, made a big impact on the nature and function of images and popular media. The engraved illustrations in these magazines were influenced by photography, which gave the journals an authenticity previously unknown. Although photographic technology ensured the engraver continued work, it was thought by many to reduce the status of his craft. Instead of interpreting an artist's sketches and embellishing the narrative of an event, it was argued that engravers were now merely copying, or at best translating, a photographic image into a printable form.

The objectivity provided by the camera via the engraver was an important influence on *Scientific American* (*top right*) when it first appeared in 1845.

The masthead of Andrew White Tuer's London-based *Paper & Printing Trades Journal* (*top left*) reflects his predilection for medieval references. The remainder of the cover is given over to engravings of printing machines. Advertisements and catalogues depicting manufactured goods would keep the engraver in business until the end of the century.

In contrast, the masthead of the Philadelphia-based trade journal *Typographic Advertiser* (*bottom*) is a mould-breaking design. Published by the American Type Founders Company, its appearance predicts design to come.

Opposite *The Illustrated London News*, letterpress, 1860.

Top left *The Paper & Printing Trades Journal*, letterpress, London, 1884.

Top right *Scientific American*, letterpress, New York, 1848.

Bottom *Typographic Advertiser*, letterpress, Philadelphia, USA, 1864.

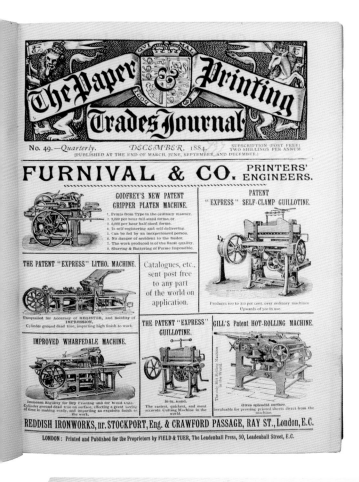

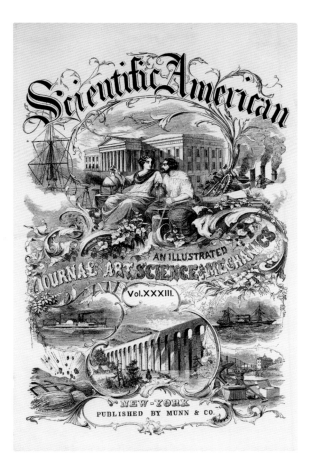

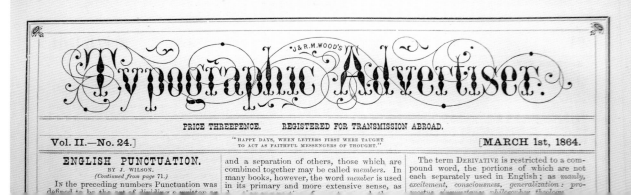

Expressive typography

The masthead of *The News of the World* (*bottom*) was something of a departure for the British newspaper industry. It avoids the traditional and self-consciously serious appearance of other national papers, preferring a style that reflects the spirit of the theatre bill – in keeping with this paper's characteristic mix of caustic comment and frivolity. In contrast, the spacious arrangement of the masthead for *The Police Gazette* (*top*) is more restrained but certainly imposing and suitably authoritative.

Meanwhile, the music hall poster provided the opportunity to utilize the full range of styles, weights and sizes of display type, shown to great effect in the advert for the Theatre Royal (*opposite, right*), Plymouth. The poster incorporates three folds designed to enable the poster to be used also as a programme.

The Vauxhall poster (*opposite, top left*), although smaller and far simpler, appears hurried, and the bottom two lines are carelessly set and printed. The poster for Astley's (*opposite, bottom left*) features a wood-engraved illustration, unusual for the time, and it is possible that it was originally cut for another purpose.

Top Masthead of *The Police Gazette*, popularly known as *Hue-and-Cry*, Dublin, Ireland, 1866.

Bottom Masthead of *The News of the World*, London, 1875.

Top left Poster for Vauxhall Gardens, letterpress and wood engraving, London, 1839.

Right Poster for the Theatre Royal, Plymouth, UK, 1889.

Bottom left Poster (detail) for Astley's Amphitheatre, letterpress, London, c. 1843.

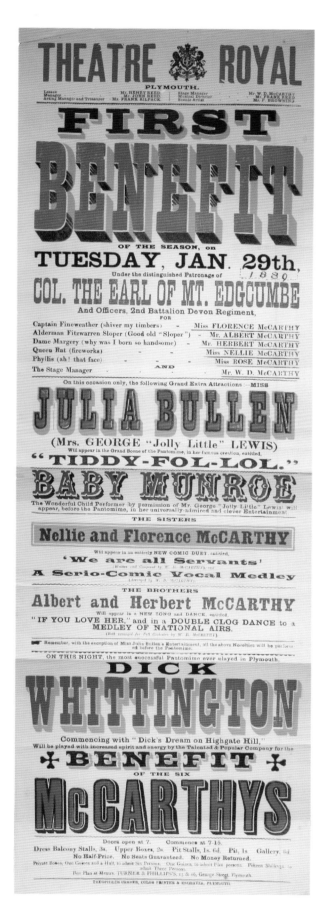

The evolution of labels

To ensure numerical integrity, playing cards were among the earliest products to be packaged. The wrapper was initially held in place with a loop of thread, which was later replaced by a sealing or 'security' label (*top left*). The more robust card slipcase construction was introduced around 1800.

The development of packaging such as the tin can transformed food production, transportation and retailing. The need for labelling resulted in a huge lithographic printing presence in California during the late nineteenth century, serving the fruit-growing industry. The printing enterprise set up by Max Schmidt (*bottom left*) was among the largest of these companies.

By the latter part of the century, all manner of products were available in air-tight metal or glass containers. Catalogues (*right*) displayed such items without comment, leaving the labels to explain the function and merit of the product.

Top left Wrapper for a pack of cards, letterpress with wood engraving, France, eighteenth century.

Bottom left Trade card, chromolithography by M. Schmidt, San Francisco, USA, 1878.

Right Catalogue of packaging and labelling options, London, date unknown.

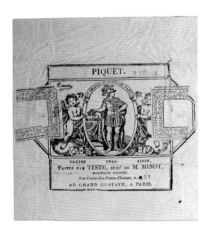

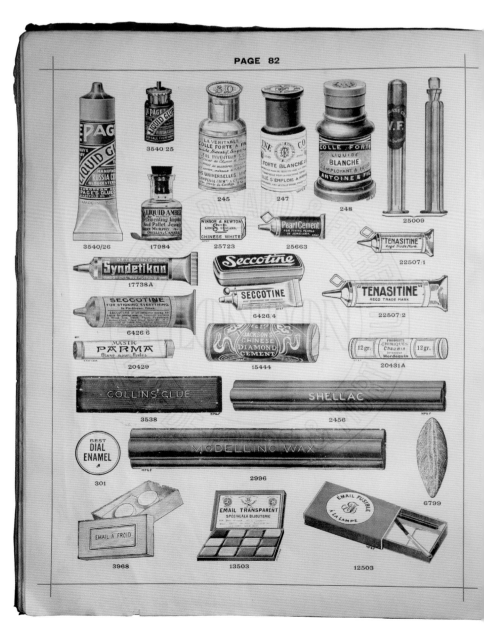

126

The retail business

The photograph (*bottom right*) shows an early twentieth-century shop interior. The customer has to request to see items for sale, which the shopkeeper then brings to the counter for him to view. For the smaller retailer, this way of shopping changed little between 1860 and 1960.

Items for sale were displayed on shelves behind the shopkeeper, so their design played an essential role in attracting the eye. The surface design of the box (*left*), containing a bottle of medicine, bears a close resemblance to the theatre bills of the time.

The counter was often cluttered with advertising material of various kinds, mostly showcards. The retailer would have initially made these himself, but as products became branded and packaged, they were provided by manufacturers (*top right*).

Retailers themselves also had to think of ways of maintaining an advantage over rivals. The fly paper (*centre right*), despite being impregnated with poison, would be placed in the buyer's home for several days and so the retailer took the opportunity to remind the customer of other items he had for sale.

Left Box, two-colour lithography, New York, date unknown.

Top right Showcard for various fastenings, lithography, UK, mid-nineteenth century.

Centre right Fly paper, letterpress on brown paper, *c.* mid-nineteenth century.

Bottom right Chemist's shop interior, early twentieth-century photograph.

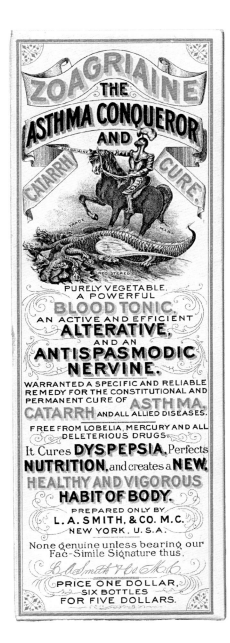

From bill to poster
Progress in the design and expertise of the compositor, together with the influence of the new display types, can be gauged by these four race items. The 1815 bill (*top left*) serves the dual purpose of handbill and programme, including detailed information regarding runners, owners, riders, weights and colours. The following year, the same printer introduced a bolder headline above a stock block of runners approaching the winning post (*top right*).

By 1825, the bill had evolved from being purely a conveyor of information to one also of promotion (*bottom*). The integration of the earlier stock block with the headline type, supported by a heavy double rule, is an effective solution and a bold move away from conventions established in bookwork.

The 1870 poster (*opposite*) is a fine example of the mature nineteenth-century poster, with confident use of heavy wood and metal display types. The engraving is based on the earlier version.

Below Three race bills (two details) for Bridgnorth Races, letterpress pinted by G. Gitton Jr, UK, 1815, 1816 and 1825.

BRIDGNORTH RACES, 1815.

THURSDAY, JULY 6th.

Purse of 50l. given by T. Whitmore Esq. Three-2-miles.

Sir John Dashwood's b. f. Bella 4 yrs old, 8ft. 7lb. S. Darling, pink & black, (to be fold) — 2 — dr
Matthew Fletcher's Efq c. h. by Meteor, 4yrs old, 8ft. 9lb. R. Spencer blue - - 1 — 1

FRIDAY, JULY 7th.

Sweepftakes 10gs. each, with 20 added.....Two miles.

Sir G. Pigot's br. c. Belgium, 4yrs old - — dr
Mr. Whitmore's b. s. by Staveley, dam by Moorcock, 3 yrs old - - - - — ds
Mr. Jenkinfon's b. m. by Windle, out of Cowflip's dam 6 yrs old - - — 3
Sir T. Jones's Tinker Barnes, 6yrs old - — 2
Mr. Charlton's b. g. Don Rodrigo, 6 yrs old — 1
Mr. Plowden's a Subfcriber, but did not name. The other two Stakes did not fill.

Purfe of 50l. given by the Hon. C. Jenkinson. Three-4-miles.

Sir W. Wynn's b. f. Arcadia, 4yrs old, 6ft. 9lb. Rider unknown, green and red - - — 1
Sir John Dashwood's b. f. Bella, 4yrs old 6ft. 9lb. S. Darling, pink & yellow, (to be fold) — dr
Mr. Spencer's Tinker Barnes, 6yrs old 9ft. 7lb. R. Spencer, blue and red - - — dr
Mr. Charlton's b. g. Don Rodrigo 6yrs old, 9ft. 4lb. Barnett, pink and broad ftripe - — bo

Printed by G. Gitton, Junior.

Bridgnorth Races, 1816.

THURSDAY, JULY 11th.
Sweepstakes of 85gs.—Two mile heat.

Sir G. Pigot's br. f. Sabrina by Sorcerer, dam by Penny-royal, 3 yrs old - - - - -
Mr. Whitmore's br. c. Pompey by Windle, 4yrs old
Mr. W. Moseley's b. c. Snowball by Snowball, out of Snowdrop, 3 yrs old - - - - — 3
Mr. Jenkinson's ch. h. Partner by Maltonian, 4 yrs old — 1
Mr. Benson's b. c. by Newcastle, dam by Sir Peter, 3 yrs old - - - - - - - - — 2
Mr. Pelham's b. f. by Castrel, 4 yrs old - -
Sir T. Jones's b. f. by Sir David, out of Pentronella.

BRIDGNORTH RACES, 1825.

In the Afternoon of Thursday the 30th of JUNE,

THE MEMBERS' PURSE OF FIFTY POUNDS, given by *Thomas Whitmore, Esq.* for three and and four yrs old; three yrs old to carry 7st. 7lb. four, 8st. 9lb. Fillies to be allowed 2lb. A Winner of one Plate this year to carry 3lb. of two or more, 5lb. and of a King's Plate, 7lb. extra, (matches and sweepstakes excepted).——The best of Three-2-mile heats.

In the Morning of Friday the 1st JULY,

A SWEEPSTAKES of 10gs each, with 10gs added, for all ages; three yrs old, 6st. 10lb. four, 8st. five, 8st. 10lb. six and aged, 9st. 2lb. Mares and Geldings to be allowed 3lb. Five Subscribers or no race. One 2-mile heat. In the event of being walked over for, the 10gs will be withheld.

Lord Forester's Ynysymaengwyn. 6 yrs old
Robert Pigot, Esq.'s b. m. Miss Robson, 4 yrs old

Below Poster, letterpress with wood engraving, 1870.

Children's games

Juvenile drama was introduced during the second decade of the nineteenth century as a way of presenting children's versions of successful plays of the day. It was common for the proscenium, backcloth and characters to be printed on paper for the child to cut out. The example below (*bottom right*) is a simpler version, with the narrative presented as a series of strips to be pulled across the stage.

The idea of play as an appropriate activity for children was made more tolerable if it involved a semblance of learning or hand-skill. The character 'parts' (*left*) were designed to be cut out and pinned together, requiring dexterity and patience. In one of the board games opposite (*top left*), to complete the picture the child had to cut out the figures and place them in the correct spaces. In another (*opposite, top right*), the pieces are pre-cut

Left Theatre characters, letterpress with hand-coloured wood engravings, France, *c.* mid-nineteenth century.

Right Toy theatre (*bottom*) and cover (*top*), letterpress with wood engravings, London, *c.* mid-nineteenth century.

but include multiplication and rhyming moral lessons.

The oval race track, with a starting and finishing line, is the most enduring of board game designs (*centre*). Other means of 'racing', notably trams (*bottom left*), railways and, later, cars, kept this simple concept topical. Transformation or 'metamorphic' toys such as the lattice interlay (*bottom right*) were also popular during the first half of the century.

Top left Children's board game, chromolithography, *c.* 1860.

Centre Children's game, chromolithograph mounted onto board, *c.* 1860.

Bottom left Children's board game, chromolithography, date unknown.

Top right Cut-out sheet, chromolithography, France, *c.* 1860.

Bottom right Children's novelty, transformation or 'metamorphic' game, chromolithography, *c.* 1860.

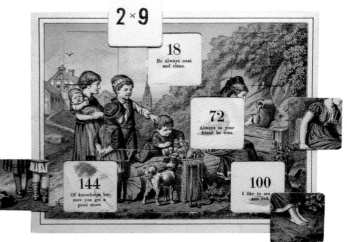

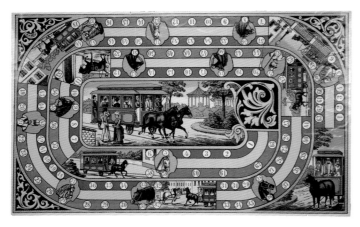

The influence of the camera

The impact of the camera on printing and printed matter was apparent long before photographs themselves could be printed commercially. Stock blocks such as the railroad vignettes (*top left*) and the panoramic postcard (*bottom*) provide images that have likely been made with the aid of a photograph. The group shot on the label (*top right*), meanwhile, leaves no doubt as to the original source.

Even when the halftone process was established as a commercial means of printing a photographic image, the definition was decidedly poor. It was for this reason that the engraver was employed to add clarity, particularly in catalogues and advertising. Two images on the far right (*opposite, top and centre*) are from an advert for an engraving company demonstrating the clarity their engravers could achieve

Top left Railroad vignettes, stock blocks from a type founder's catalogue, *c.* 1870s.

Bottom Panoramic postcard, lithography, *c.* late nineteenth century.

Top right Label, chromolithography, *c.* 1870s.

compared with a standard halftone photograph. The original halftone image is shown complete with instructions and, beneath it, the pristine engraved result.

The methods used by the engraver to describe complex forms can be seen in the image below these (*bottom right*). The illustration (*bottom left*) is printed black only, with tones achieved by varying widths of line.

When photographs were reproduced as halftone images, they were often heavily retouched (*top left*). In this example, barely any of the original photograph is still visible.

Top left Woodwork department of J. G. Schelter & Giesecke Type Foundry, Leipzig, Germany, 1894.

Bottom left Engraving from a photograph, USA, *c.* 1913.

Top and centre right Halftone photograph and engraving (before and after) by Gatchel & Manning Inc., Philadelphia, USA, *c.* 1914.

Bottom right Photo-engraving by Gatchel & Manning Inc., Philadelphia, USA, *c.* 1914.

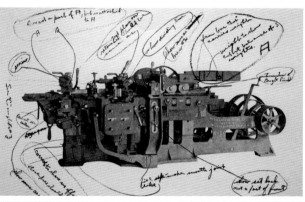

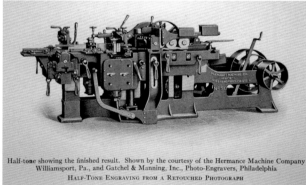

Half-tone showing the finished result. Shown by the courtesy of the Hermance Machine Company Williamsport, Pa., and Gatchel & Manning, Inc., Photo-Engravers, Philadelphia
HALF-TONE ENGRAVING FROM A RETOUCHED PHOTOGRAPH

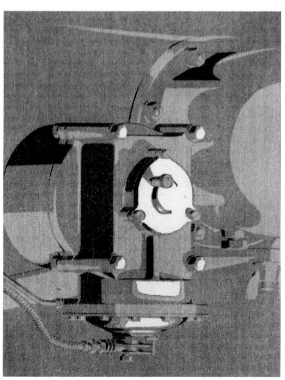

Advances in label design

Early label designs generally used a scroll, ribbon, badge (*top left*) or even a 'label' (*opposite*) to carry words. However, during the nineteenth century, words began to gain a certain independence from the pictorial elements. For example, the words 'Bird & Handle' (*bottom left*) are depicted on a ribbon that does not belong, in any physical sense, to the image. Eventually, the need to rationalize the presence of words would no longer be necessary. The word 'Birds' (*top right*) stands alone as an image in its own right.

From the beginning, competition ensured that cigar packaging (*bottom right*) featured the fullest range of techniques and finishes that the printing industry could provide. The heyday of the cigar industry was from 1870 to 1920, and by the turn of the twentieth century

Top left Label, chromolithography, with letterpress added, Todmorden, UK, c. 1870s.

Bottom left Label, lithography, USA.

Top right Label, chromolithography, c. 1890.

Bottom right Packaging for cigars: wooden boxes with stencils, die-cut labels, edgings and security seals.

there were some 20,000 brand names registered. Printing companies specialized in designing and printing cigar labels, bands, security bands and a plethora of special items to promote the brands. Printing was extravagant, with a multitude of different finishes, and the results were avidly collected.

By the late nineteenth century, the value of corporate branding and the building of brand loyalties was already understood and established. The food labels below (*top left and right*) are two of a series for Thurber & Co., all featuring an 'affixed' paper label, a border and a similar style of illustration. Lithography was enormously successful in the area of food-label printing because of the rich colours that could be achieved as well as the skill of lithographic artists in depicting products to advantage.

Top left and right Branded labels, chromolithography, printed by Forbes & Co., Boston and New York, *c.* late nineteenth century.

Bottom Label for 'dress box' of cigars, chromolithography with metallic inks and embossing, UK, *c.* late nineteenth century.

The Druggists' Printer specialized in label printing and updated the designs of their stock regularly, issuing a catalogue quarterly (*bottom right*). Printers supplied labels untrimmed. The lozenge-shaped example below (*top left*) has been hand-cut, a difficult and time-consuming process. For this reason, labels were often cut with straight edges (*top right*). This latter example and another chemist's label (*bottom left*) offer points of comparison between the technical limitations of letterpress and the variable skills of the lithographic lettering artist.

Meanwhile, H. Silverlock, a distinctive jobbing printer, delivered work to his client held with a bellyband carrying his name and a description of areas of expertise (*opposite*). Presentation of work in this way reflects a change of attitude within the print trade about the status of jobbing printing. At the very least, it indicates that this jobbing printer is proud of his work.

Opposite Labels held with a bellyband, lithography by H. Silverlock, London, *c.* 1860.

Top left Label, lithography by H. Silverlock, London, *c.* 1860.

Bottom left Label, two-colour lithography, London, *c.* 1860s.

Top right Label, letterpress, *c.* 1870.

Bottom right Labels, *The Druggists' Printer* catalogue, Philadelphia, USA, 1874.

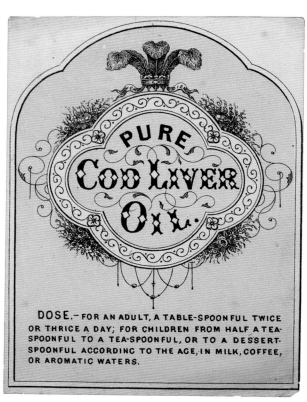

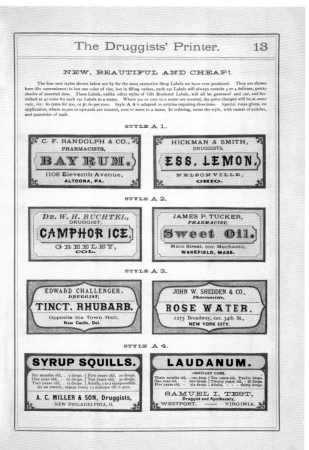

Monograms and crests

In the midst of huge industrial growth there was a fascination with everything medieval, and heraldic design came back into fashion. Cigar makers and their printers drew on this trend, exploiting every possible technique and material to create a sense of pomp and stature for their brands – not only laurels, medallions, insignia and monograms, but also sexual imagery and explicit or implied celebrity endorsement. The

interlocking monogram was among the most popular recurring motifs (*bottom*). The engravers Ortner & Houle, describing themselves as 'Heraldic Seal Die & Medal Engravers', have used a similarly inspired device on their trade card (*top right*).

Collecting monograms became a popular activity, and albums were designed specifically for the purpose (*opposite left, top and bottom*). Rather like stamps, collectors could buy packets of mixed and random monograms. This

Top left and right Trade card and detail for engravers Ortner & Houle, London, 1860s.

Bottom Cigar band (detail), chromolithography with gold embossing and die-cut, date unknown.

page (*right*) offers a selection of 'M' monograms specifically designed to be used for print matter relating to marriages and deaths. Readymade art in the form of stereotypes meant that all the printer had to do was show a customer the foundry catalogue and order their chosen design. While the advantages for the letterpress printer are obvious, this practice effectively ended such work being commissioned from engravers.

Top and bottom left Cover and page of *Album for Crests, Monograms, Coats of Arms*, lithography, with examples attached, mid- to late nineteenth century.

Right Page of monograms (detail) from Fonderie S. Berthier & Durey, Paris, 1890.

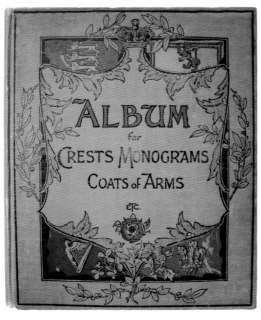

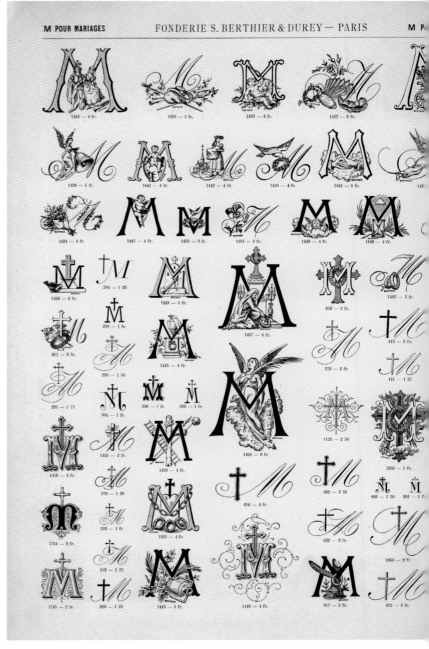

The changing retail business
The two trade cards below (*top left*) demonstrate how attitudes to business enterprise were changing. In the earlier card (*left*), status is reflected through the richness and complexity of the decoration; the premises are almost an afterthought. In contrast, decoration is entirely dispensed with in the later card (*right*), which celebrates the success of the business through the detailed presentation of its premises.

The concept of shopping as a leisure activity was cemented with the emergence of the department store. In the poster (*top right*) the departments within the store are described using a variety of types reminiscent of the theatre poster.

Top left Two trade cards for Richard Johnson Stationer, lithography, Manchester, UK, *c.* 1830 and 1860.

Top right Poster for a department store, printed by Phair & Co., New York, 1859.

Bottom left and right Pencil and wash drawing, and resulting engraving, late nineteenth century.

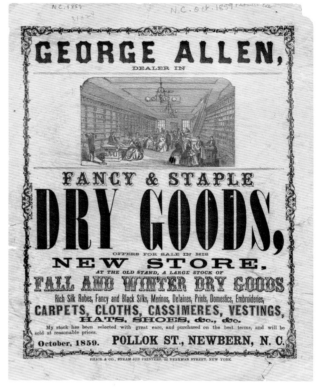

Envelopes

The purpose of the stationer's envelope (also known as a 'paper packet') was similar to that of the shopkeeper's paper bag. However, while the standard shopkeeper's paper bag might carry little more than a name or illustration (*top left*), the stationer's envelope was used as a means of conveying a detailed list of stock-in-trade and services (*top right*).

Shopkeepers could buy stock illustrated envelopes from a printer who would then overprint the shop name. The alternative, though far more expensive, was to have envelopes exclusively designed and printed (*bottom*). These envelopes could be secured with glue, but it is clear (*top right*) that the use of wax remained popular for some time.

Top left Paper bag, lithography, Bournemouth, UK, *c.* mid-nineteenth century.

Bottom Two advertising envelopes, both lithography, USA and UK, *c.* mid-nineteenth century.

Top right Stationer's envelope with letterpress-printed product list, 1857.

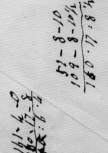

The typewriter
Typewriters began to be used in a commercial setting during the 1870s, and the authority of the typewritten document (*centre left*) quickly became an indispensable business tool. Surprisingly, the crude, mechanistic appearance of the characters was in no way detrimental to its commercial viability; nor were the severe limitations of only eighty-eight key-options. In fact, the resulting idiosyncratic characteristics of the typewritten document came to represent a modern, viable business enterprise.

Top left Billhead for the World Type Writer Agency, Hartford, USA, 1887.

Centre left Billhead for Charles Jenner & Co., Edinburgh, UK, 1891.

Bottom left Advertisement for rotogravure printing technology, using a typewriter as an example.

Right Billhead for Jarrold & Sons, Norwich, UK, 1878.

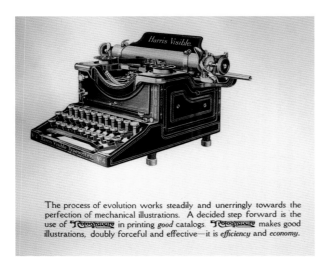

The process of evolution works steadily and unerringly towards the perfection of mechanical illustrations. A decided step forward is the use of Rotogravure in printing *good* catalogs. Rotogravure makes good illustrations, doubly forceful and effective—it is *efficiency* and *economy*.

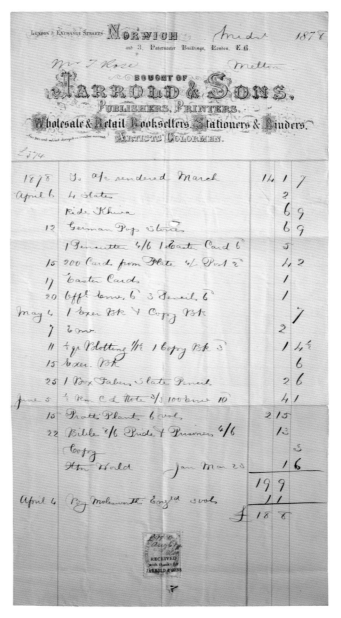

Mayer, Merkel & Ottmann advertising
Based in New York, Mayer, Merkel & Ottmann was one of the largest lithographic printing companies in the United States in the late nineteenth century, specializing in illustrative colour advertising. Their work, characterized by lavish detail documenting everyday life in America, was highly regarded for its lack of showmanship. In contrast to most large-scale printers, they made practically no stock trade cards, preferring instead to tailor cards to individual requirements. The company eventually became part of the Russell, Morgan & Co. mergers (see page 199).

Below Advertisements designed and printed by Mayer, Merkel & Ottmann, chromolithography, *c.* 1874.

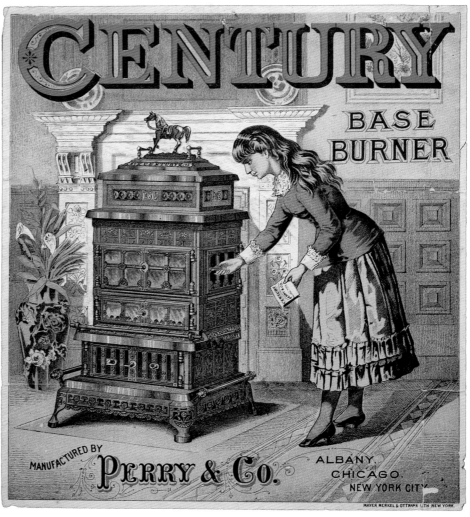

Travel-related print
The concept of travel is encapsulated in the luggage label or tag (*top right*). One of the best examples of form following function, it appears to have arrived perfectly formed and has remained almost unchanged to the present day.

The panel in the stock poster (*bottom left*) was probably left blank for sailing times. The poster promoting the Iron

Mountain Railway Route from St Louis to Texas (*top left*) was issued to encourage immigration into Texas and presents extensive information in a clear manner. The map (*centre right*) depicting the District underground line in London is less refined but includes a great deal more detail. The passport (*bottom right*) was made out by the British Consulate in Tianjin, China, for a British subject travelling to Beijing.

Top left Poster promoting the Iron Mountain Route from St Louis to Texas, printed by the St Louis Globe-Democrat Company, lithography, *c.* 1856.

Bottom left Stock poster depicting the Hudson River, chromolithography, date unknown. (See the detail on page 121.)

Top right Tag label, letterpress with reinforced eyelet, San Francisco, *c.* late nineteenth century.

Centre right Map of the District underground line, London, 1878.

Bottom right Passport, issued in Tianjin, China, 1866.

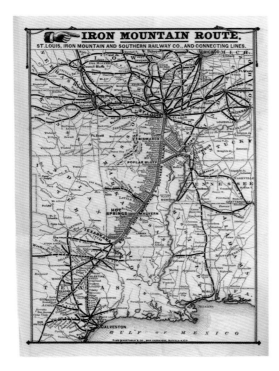

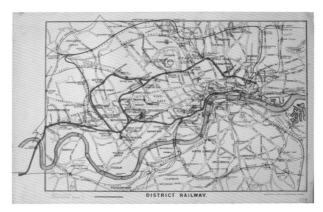

144

Passenger contracts for a land and sea voyage were long and complicated. In the example below (*bottom*), in which the conditions are set out in both German and English, the drama and gravitas of the undertaking are conveyed in the complex design. Legal and practical details are accompanied by images of ships, harbours and trains, providing the prospective journey with a true sense of adventure.

The two freight receipts (*top left and right*) possibly belong to the same shipping company, albeit with a change of name. Although some of the elements remain in the later version, the addition of blue rules and listing of required information suggest that its design is the result of a considered analysis of the use and purpose of this form.

Top left and right Two receipts for the shipping of freight, letterpress, New Haven, USA, 1857 and 1865.

Bottom Passenger contract, lithography, Hamburg, Germany, 1851.

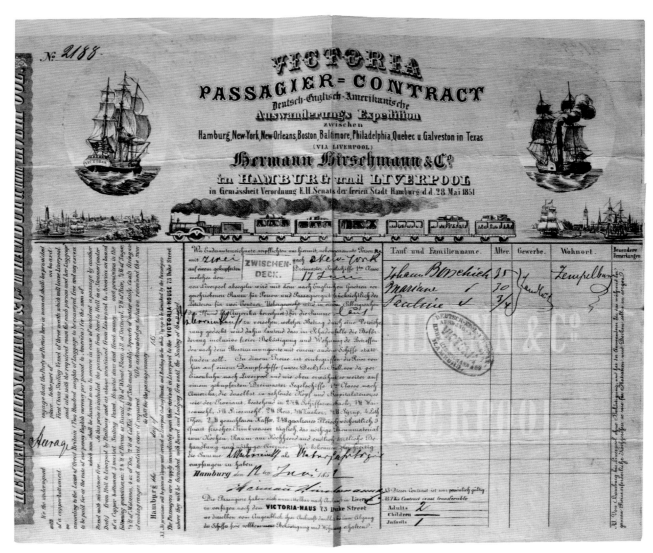

Tariffs and rates

Dating from the turn of the nineteenth century, the sheet below (*top left*) contains thirty-five tickets for a turnpike or toll road. The toll-keeper would cut these out and distribute them on payment. Charges varied depending on the purpose of the coach or wagon, the number of horses or oxen used to pull it, and the width of the wheels. Fewer horses and wider-rimmed wheels caused less damage to the road surface and were, therefore, charged less. To help the toll-keeper, a well-organized table of toll rates (*bottom left*) was essential.

The railway document (*right*) dates from the mid-century. Railway freight was divided into first and second class and charged by weight and distance, necessitating two tables. What constituted first- and second-class goods required long lists and explanation. This example follows the convention, established before 1846, of representing the route along the vertical axis and the increasing freight costs along the horizontal axis. In passenger timetables, the horizontal axis generally provided times of departure.

Top left Turnpike tickets, letterpress, UK, *c.* 1800.

Bottom left Table of toll rates, letterpress, Darlington, UK, 1808.

Right Freight tariff, Norwich & Worcester Railroad, letterpress, USA, *c.* mid-nineteenth century.

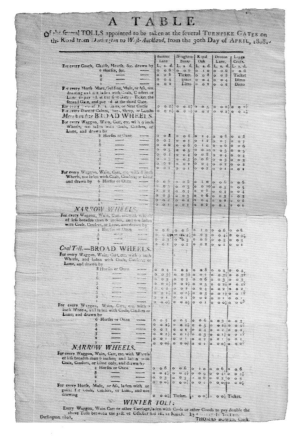

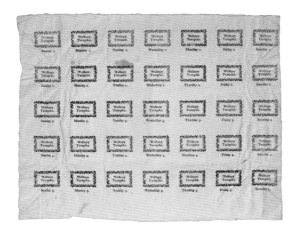

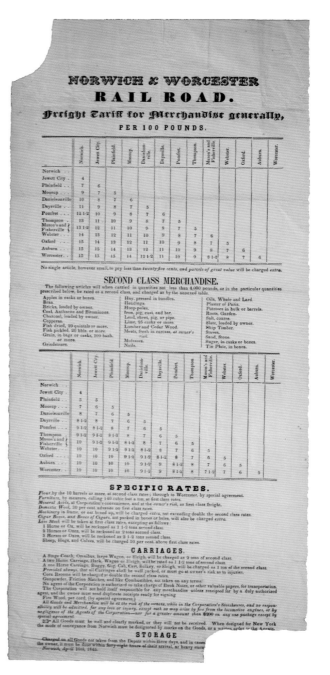

Lists

The list is the most basic organizational aid and a shopping list is the most common. In the past, shopkeepers liked to provide lists of what their customers could buy. The example below (*top left*), dating from the turn of the nineteenth century, was hand-written by a chemist for a printer.

The earlier printed example (*bottom left*) demonstrates the drawback of the vertically aligned list: it requires a great deal more space. Around 1800, paper costs made up over half of the printer's bill. As a result, the shopkeeper has chosen to list his most popular goods and present the remainder as continuous prose.

Mr H. Howell allowed the printer a larger budget and his shop list has been carefully edited and arranged (*right*). The vertical rules, which aid the reader, have been made from short lengths cut for a previous job.

Top left Hand-written list prepared by a retailer for a printer, *c.* 1800.

Bottom left Items for sale (ironmonger), letterpress, late eighteenth century.

Right Items for sale (grocer, tea dealer and ironmonger), letterpress printed by Wilson of Knaresborough, UK, *c.* 1850s.

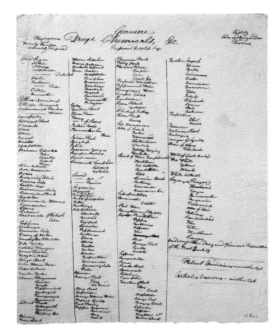

Religious themes

The term 'calendar' was closely associated with 'almanac', and this continued well into the nineteenth century. Information relating to the passing time was often given a religious or moral theme.

The familiar small, rectangular twelve-page calendar came into general use during the 1870s and was produced in the millions. These simple booklets were bought by printers who could add a cover and attach them to 'calendar backs', wall charts, cut-outs and other novelties (*left*).

Religiously themed broadsheets were bought as a protective or reassuring presence in the house. The example below (*right*) includes the Lord's Prayer and the Ten Commandments.

Left Almanac and calendar, chromolithography, embossed and die-cut, 1873.

Right Broadsheet, chromolithography, *c.* mid- to late nineteenth century.

Widespread production of cards with religious and moral lessons began with the introduction of Sunday school systems. By the 1850s, millions of small motto cards (*centre right*) were being produced. There were also attempts to make scriptural texts more interesting. In the example below (*top right*), the word 'Bible' is made up of facts relating to the book itself.

Engravers knew that the general public was impressed above all by their ability to work in minute detail. The Lord's Prayer written in the space of the smallest coin of the time was a standard 'party trick'. In this far more elaborate sheet (*left and bottom right*), rose-engine engraving has been cleverly used to provide a suitably ethereal image.

Left and bottom right Broadsheet and detail (The Lord's Prayer), engraved on steel by W. Palmer and published by De La Rue James & Rudd, London, *c.* 1850.

Right, from top to bottom Broadsheet (detail), engraving, UK, *c.* 1855; moral lesson, single sheet, lithography, mid-nineteenth century; moral lesson card entitled 'My Motto', with elaborate decorative border embossed, die-cut and printed gold, and letterpress-printed text, *c.* mid-nineteenth century; detail of the broadsheet, left.

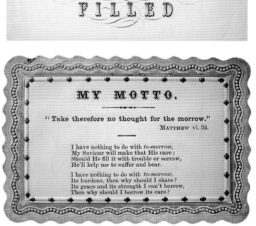

Oscar Harpel and *Harpel's Typograph*

T. C. Hansard's (*left*) and William Savage's (*top right*) books, like every printers' manual since Joseph Moxon's *Mechanick Exercises* (1683–84), concentrated on the design and printing of books. The design element, however, was highly prescriptive and based on time-honoured commercial practice. In both cases, their title pages are models of decorum.

The design of Harpel's title page (*bottom right*), on the other hand, is striking in a number of ways, particularly in the use of colour. Printed letterpress, five colours were used in its production.

This, together with the mix of display typefaces and decorative borders, caused consternation among the book-printing fraternity.

The first 48 pages of the book are taken up with advice concerning composition, imposition, paper, inks and presses – subjects common to all printers' manuals of the time. But the next 176 pages contain job printing specimens. The number and complexity of the examples, many requiring multiple colours, make the book important, but it was Harpel's choice of everyday jobbing work that is most significant.

Left Title page of *Typographia: An Historical Sketch of the Origin and Progress of the Art of Printing* by T. C. Hansard, published by Baldwin, Cradock & Joy, London, 1825.

Top right Title page of *A Dictionary of the Art of Printing* by William Savage, published by Longman, Brown, Green & Longmans, London, 1841.

Bottom right Title page of *Harpel's Typograph, or Book of Specimens*, written, designed, printed and published by Oscar Harpel, Cincinnati, USA, 1870.

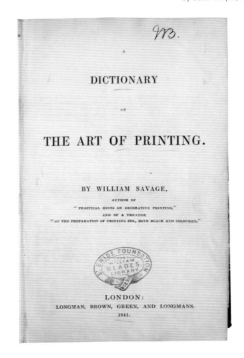

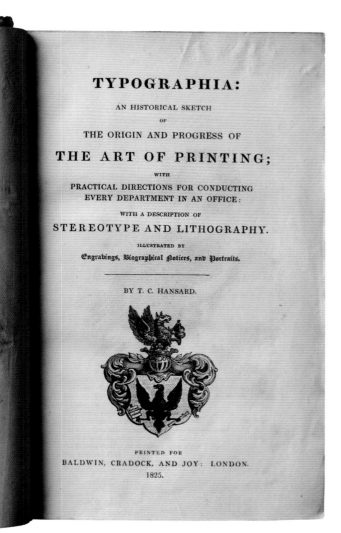

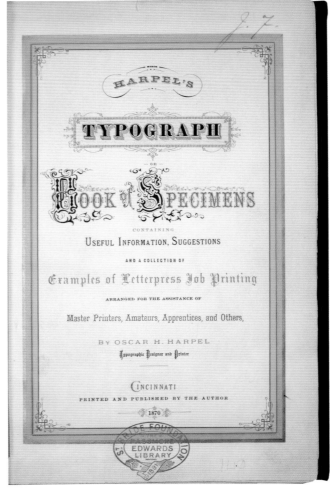

Below Cover and spread from *Harpel's Typograph, or Book of Specimens,* written, designed, printed and published by Oscar Harpel, Cincinnati, USA, 1870.

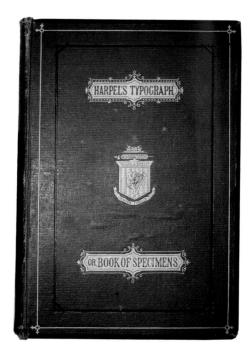

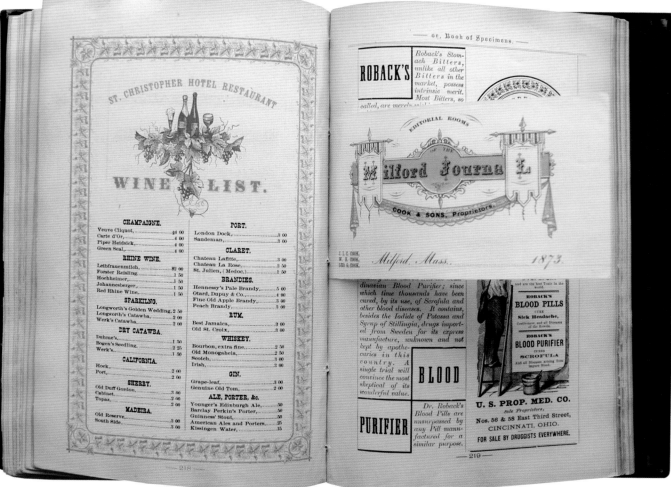

CHAPTER FOUR
ARTISTIC ASPIRATIONS FOR MASS COMMUNICATION

THE HOE MANUFACTURING ESTABLISHMENT, GRAND STREET, NEW YORK.

At the beginning of the nineteenth century, Britain had occupied an unrivalled position in the manufacturing and commercial trade of the world's markets and, for the first fifty years or so, faced few competitive pressures. By mid-century, however, the United States and the industrial nations of Europe were beginning to test that supremacy, and by 1875 Britain's virtual trading monopoly had ended.

Nevertheless, the English experience of rapid industrialization, and the cultural reaction to it – particularly as defined by John Ruskin – that resulted in the Arts and Crafts movement, gave British printing, and British design in general, huge influence and prestige abroad. Printing was now a global trade, and competition encouraged mechanical innovation. Ruskin, who considered art and design to be indivisible, rejected the mercantile economy, arguing that industrialization and mechanization had caused art, artist and artisan to become separated from society. In his view, art, together with labour, should be in the service of society: by reinstating art into the work of the architect or engineer, for example, society would have a more cultured, beautiful and humanistic environment in which to live – one where social justice (improved housing for industrial workers, a national education system, etc) would surely follow.

Ruskin's ideas, together with international competition, caused many traditional practices and attitudes prevalent in the printing trade to be questioned, but none more so than the appropriateness of training. The general opinion was that European – and particularly German – printing was better designed, better printed and cheaper than in Britain (Germany was in the midst of an economic depression that would not abate until the 1890s). The reason for the superior quality of this work was attributed to the excellence of technical training facilities in Germany, and to the absence of such opportunities in Britain, where any reform of training was resisted.

German printing of every kind was admired for its richness and accuracy, but it was chromolithographic printing for which Germany became renowned. However, by the 1880s, after a succession of technical developments, the United States had become a highly successful international competitor, helped by an influx of German printers. In addition, America's competitive machinery industry was providing printers with a stream of technical innovations, enabling higher quality and more efficient output in both letterpress and lithographic production.

Whereas the letterpress printing office was self-contained and self-regulated, and staunchly defended its independence, the alternative print processes – lithography and engraving – were always more relaxed and open to outside developments. From the outset, those who worked on lithographic stone or cut copperplates were referred to as 'artists', and their training placed emphasis not only on their ability to draw but also their commitment to continued personal development. Lithographic artists were encouraged to collect interesting examples of printed material, keep a notebook to record ideas, practise drawing and visit art galleries. Specialist trade journals such as *The American Lithographer & Printer* and *The British Lithographer* provided supplementary sheets illustrating drawing techniques and decorated letterforms for inspiration.

Letterpress, and specifically jobbing printing, received a much-needed boost in 1870 with the publication of *Harpel's Typograph, or Book of Specimens* in the United States (see page 120), in which Harpel insisted that commercial success was aligned with creative endeavour and self-awareness, not just technical precision.[1] This support for the letterpress jobbing printer was continued by the journal *American Model*

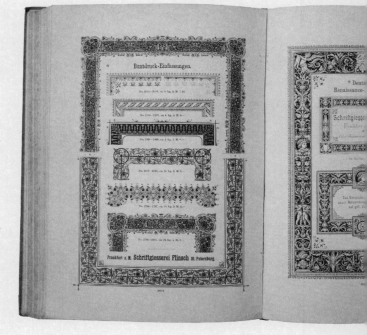

Left Cover of the Cincinnati Type Foundry *Specimen Book*, USA, 1874. In the United States printing companies were rapidly being established along frontier settlements. To provide them with type, White's Type Foundry of New York set up a new plant in the small town of Cincinnati in 1817, producing its first catalogue six years later. By the 1870s Cincinnati was a major American centre for printing.

Right Detail from the type specimen catalogue of Schriftgießerei Flinsch, Frankfurt, Germany, 1876. German printers became renowned for their use of combination borders: decorative frames made from individual units. Two- or even three-colour borders were possible due to improvements in print technology.

Printer (1879–82), the official organ of the International Typographical Union of North America. From the very first of the twelve issues printed during its brief life, it displayed exemplary work with full, often florid descriptions and technical explanations, including the names of individual compositors or foremen.

Equally important was the establishment of *The Printers' International Specimen Exchange* in England in 1880. Edited by Andrew White Tuer, a partner in the Leadenhall Press and proprietor of *The Paper & Printing Trades Journal*, the aim of this annual publication was to nurture a more ambitious, 'artistic' (meaning creative) approach in the composing room. The *Exchange* contained real examples of primarily jobbing work, sent to the publisher from across Europe and the United States. The publisher then bound these into sets and redistributed them to all contributors.

This was a period when, quite suddenly, names of individual compositors as well as companies became significant appendages to printed matter. Who was doing what, where, how and for whom became a subject for discussion not only in the boardrooms of printing offices, but also in composing rooms. Success for the compositor now required that his work be recognized – its merits or defects, originality and technical finesse analysed in a very public manner on an international stage. In the United States, ambitious job-printing companies began to produce their own self-promotional publications carrying examples of their work. Perhaps it was in part the need to impress, to draw attention to itself, that caused the appearance of this work – collectively called artistic printing – to involve increasing amounts of decorative material and display fonts.

What had previously been different aspects of the same trade became progressively specialized activities. For example,

the compositor trained and long practised in book work would have great difficulty attempting what, by now, were regular tasks required of the jobbing printer. Tabular work (timetables, charts and the like) and posters demanding various sizes, weights and styles of type had each become sophisticated tasks requiring considerable planning and an ability to conjure up solutions from what could be found in the composing workshop.[2]

Beginning around 1885, the text-setting work of the compositor was finally, and inevitably, mechanized and keyboard-operated. The introduction of the typewriter in a business context in the 1870s made this transition less traumatic. The demand for such machines was primarily from the newspaper industry (monopolized by Linotype) and the magazine and book publishing houses (Monotype). Few jobbing printers could justify such financial investment and would continue to hand-set type and buy fonts as required.

Right A page from Rand & Avery's *Specimens*, Cornhill, Boston USA, 1867. Jobbing work was in the ascendancy, and those printers with the ability to promote themselves did so with refreshing directness. Rand & Avery's specimen catalogue provides engravings and detailed descriptions of each department of their printing business, including the jobbing department illustrated here.

Job Composition Room.

The Job Department. The specimens of type presented in the following pages of this book, numerous and diverse as they are, convey but an inadequate conception of the vast quantity and assortment daily in use in this department, and we are constantly increasing the variety and amount as new designs make their appearance from the founderies. The field is not limited by "diamond" and "pica," but only by the ingenuity of man. The internal arrangement of the room we are inspecting is similar to that of the Book Composition Room; but the labor performed in it requires quite a different order of talent, and to be a first-class Job Compositor is a high attainment in the art. Whether we have any in our employ who have gained that eminence is for others to decide; and to assist in that decision we present our plea, — this volume, with its specimens of type and of printing, and respectfully solicit for it an impartial examination.

The apprentice and technical college

If, during the 1870s, the concern in Britain regarding foreign competition was limited to a loss of status as a major trading nation, it was during the 1880s that the full and devastating consequences of falling standards hit the print industry as French and German craftsmen began to be employed in London. Even more worrying was the growing number of major print commissions from British companies transferring to European and even, apparently, North American companies. The journal *Printers' Registrar*, in 1879, reported: 'We know of contracts for printing, engraving, and especially for lithography, made by English commercial firms with American, French and German houses, simply because they cannot get the work done so well in their own country.'[3]

A Royal Commission on Technical Instruction was set up in 1889 to compare English and European provision, and its findings concluded that French and German technical colleges not only had higher qualified teachers of typesetting and presswork than those in England, but also that their equipment was superior and their instruction more efficient. It praised the combined work- and education-based training for encouraging an interest in the arts and culture in general, together with the dignity of authority and hard work – all genuine Victorian concerns.

Critically, the commission also reported that a closely integrated, well-organized working relationship between educational institutions and the printing profession considerably shortened the traditional seven years required for apprenticeship. Recognition of the failures of a seven-year apprenticeship under instruction from journeymen directed by the master printer was, finally, being openly stated. The necessity of the print industry generally, and the jobbing printer in particular, to respond creatively to the new needs of the client, rather than focusing on protecting traditional working methodologies and outcomes, was debated in trade journals.

The period 1875 to 1900 was a time of rising union membership and greater statutory protection for trade union activities. Their concern regarding technical education was that if anyone, not just indentured apprentices, was allowed to acquire a knowledge of printing, this would lead to the trade being swamped with young men or, worse still, women, and thus drive down pay.[4] However, by the mid-1890s, a significant number of union members had established themselves within the technical education system as teachers and as members of managing committees and school boards, and so began urging employers to let apprentices leave work early to encourage their attendance at evening classes (day-time courses came later). From this position, unionists could ensure that classes were not only limited to apprentices and young journeymen, but also that their content and delivery remained closely aligned with standard working methods and outcomes.

In 1896 the National Art Training School was granted permission to change its name to the Royal College of Art. Just how very different the approach to design was at art college compared to that experienced by the apprentice-printer at a technical college can be gauged by the six-day entrance exam set by the Royal College of Art at that time.

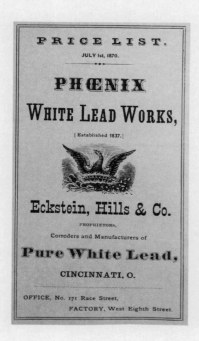

Left Cover of a price list from *Harpel's Typograph, or Book of Specimens* by Oscar Harpel, letterpress, Cincinnati, USA, 1870. This restrained design has been thoroughly edited down to essentials, with curlicues and decorative borders conspicuous by their absence.

Centre and right Two trade cards for printers: the first (*centre*) is from *Harpel's Typograph, or Book of Specimens*, letterpress, Cincinnati, USA, 1870; the second (*right*) is from the Eagle Job Printing House, Poughkeepsie, New York, 1879. This was a period of dramatic change in attitudes to the appearance and purpose of design. There was, in the United States at least, a sense that the values of the past must be left behind. New times required new solutions, and print was no exception. Suddenly, design was conspicuous.

In all, four areas of study were included: Architecture: 'a drawing of a small architectural object' (with a time allowance of 12 hours); Sculpture: 'a clay model of the mouth of Michelangelo's *David*' (6 hours); Painting: 'a drawing in charcoal from life of a head, hand, and foot' (9 hours); Ornament and Design: 'a drawing from memory of a piece of foliage, such as oak, ash, or lime, and lettering by hand of a given sentence' (9 hours). In stark contrast, admittance to printing classes at technical college was granted with possession of a valid union card and evidence of support from an employer.

The Head of the School of Ornament and Design at the RCA was William R. Lethaby, who also held the post of Principal at the Central School of Arts and Crafts, London, inaugurated in 1896. The name of the latter reflects the support it received from the Art Workers' Guild, William Morris (who was a member of the Board of Governors) and the Arts and Crafts movement. Lethaby was a practising architect, and his involvement with these organizations and close friendship with Morris make it clear that while his appointment to the Central School provided their apprenticed students with a more pragmatic approach than they would encounter at art school, it also offered a far more liberal learning experience than the usual technical college.[5] Classes in typography and printing were introduced in 1905.

The lack of practical problem-solving in the curricula of schools of art and design prompted Lethaby to describe them as 'teaching how to swim without water', a comment that perhaps explains his more limited achievements at the RCA, in contrast with the international reputation he earned at the Central School of Arts and Crafts. Here, he instigated an interdisciplinary approach to study, encouraging students to 'see how stained-glass windows were made, and books are bound and gilding done'.[6] All teachers were expected to undertake 'live' projects, which might be self-generated or offered to the School by outside companies or organizations.

These bold policies would be taken up and thoroughly absorbed into art and design education in the twentieth century. The success of Lethaby, and the influence of practising artists and designers employed to teach on a part-time basis, including Edward Johnston, would give the Central School in particular and British typography as a whole an international reputation. Lethaby's ideas were employed by Henry van de Velde, among others, and, after the First World War, Walter Gropius during his initial years as Director of the Bauhaus.

Left Thousands were lured to the Black Hills of South Dakota, USA, by the discovery of gold in 1874, and the booming region attracted many printers. The *Black Hills Times* newspaper, whose offices can be seen left, was started in 1877.

Right Detail of a page from James Callingham's book *Sign Writing and Glass Embossing*, London, 1871.

The United States and artistic printing

During the 1870s, there was a groundswell of cultural optimism throughout the developed world, particularly in the United States. It found expression in successful events such as the Philadelphia Centennial Exposition of 1876 and Oscar Wilde's American lecture tour of 1882, as well as the founding of craft societies, book clubs, libraries and museums across the whole country. Americans travelled to Europe and read the works of Charles Baudelaire, Algernon Charles Swinburne and, most importantly, John Ruskin.

The ideas of these writers coalesced in the 1870s into the Aesthetic movement, and a number of artists including Dante Gabriel Rossetti, Edward Burne-Jones and James Abbott McNeill Whistler, as well as Wilde and other writers, were actively sympathetic. Printers also found tremendous empathy for their craft in this movement, with particular focus on Ruskin's call for an Arts and Crafts revolution. Enthusiasm for this cultural renewal was active on both sides of the Atlantic, but, for the first time, it was American printers who would exert influence on the international course of design for print (that is, the intellectual process required before the physical composition of text and images) and on printing itself. This new wave was called art printing or, more commonly, artistic printing.

By the 1870s, the word 'art' was becoming a popular adjunct of many established businesses. William Morris and his partners, Marshall and Faulkner, had set up their decorative arts firm in 1861 (together with Rossetti and others), primarily designing furniture, wallpaper and embroideries. After restructuring and renaming the company Morris & Company in 1875, Morris opened a London showroom two years later, followed, in 1881, by a showroom in New York. Many, wishing to emulate Morris's

ideals (to say nothing of his critical success), included the word 'art' in the description of their own business. Trade directories list dozens of art furniture, metal and leather workers, and jobbing printers began calling themselves art printers, and their work art or artistic printing.

For the key figures that emerged towards the end of the decade, artistic printing was considered to be nothing short of a revolution. Essential to this was the transformation of the culture within the printing establishment, with the promise of re-evaluating and overhauling long-established practices. Taking a lead from Oscar Harpel, one of the radical, early outcomes was the focus and additional prestige given to the compositor.

The idea that printed media (together with every other craft-based activity) might be an art was widely discussed by artists, artisans and writers on both sides of the Atlantic, but it was in the United States that these concepts were most energetically promoted by a burgeoning, profoundly confident job-printing industry. The American printing fraternity was, through its leading practitioners and journals, calling for a new, distinctly American spirit of unbridled possibilities. This inevitably meant reconciling the idea of unlimited potential with the basic nature of the tools and materials to be found in the composing rooms of the time – an approach that was at the heart of the best artistic printers' work. The compositor who demonstrated the ability to reinvent or adapt standard materials to serve a new purpose was, for the first time, applauded in a very public manner for his creative initiative. In contrast, the work of the book compositor, previously considered the elite within the trade, was now referred to as 'straight matter' because it involved no typographic embellishments, headline fitting or tabular work and, therefore, required fewer skills.

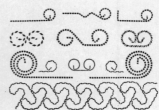

Left Two trade cards for ink manufacturers, Camden, New Jersey, and Cincinnati, USA, c. 1880s. The impulse to design a trade card that would not only impress but astonish the printing industry itself drove American ink manufacturers to give free rein to their own printers. Numerous colours and the latest tools (such as the Wrinkler, illustrated below) were used to produce cards of remarkable complexity, in the hope that the printer might keep them or even pass them around his compositors.

Right Detail of an advertisement for the Wrinkler, sold by Earhart & Richardson, USA, 1885. The device enabled compositors to crimp and spiral brass rule into almost any shape.

'Decorative', 'useful', 'industrial', 'applied' and 'ornamental' arts were all terms commonly used to describe the process of designing and making man-made objects, including printed matter, that fell outside the fine arts of painting and sculpture. Interest in the non-essential aspect of decoration – the idea that it was something that an artist or craftsman chose to provide over and above bare functional necessity – increased its status and value. This celebration of decoration was reflected in a growing interest in medievalism and Japanese culture, evident in the use of complex, stylistic elements and rich colour. Demand from the jobbing printing industry encouraged foundries to invest in the design and manufacture of exotic types, ornamental material and combination borders.

The use of colour was a distinctive characteristic separating the artistic letterpress printer from his predecessors. Instead of the customary primary red and black, the artistic printer chose delicate shades offset, perhaps, by the use of gold or silver. Brass rules were used to divide and subdivide information, and often bent into curves to suggest ribbons, scrolls or flags. Used in combination, these elements, each carrying exotic types, were set to follow these twisting contours. One surface would seemingly be wrapped or folded around another, creating an 'illusionist' effect' reminiscent of the medieval fascination for intertwined letterforms. The final result often had an effect similar to that of a miniature theatre set of some unspecified exotic location.

The American printer was being encouraged to consider the product of the printing office, at least potentially, as art, and this was reflected in the language employed in critiques of print specimens received by *American Model Printer*. Here is a typical critique of a business card, taken from the first issue of the influential journal in 1879: 'A.V. Haight,

Poughkeepsie, New York, sends us his latest business card, which we must pronounce as beautiful. The design is Japanesque, with all the beauties of modern adornment. It is elegant in its simplicity and precise in execution. The colours used are gold, emerald green, bright red, medium violet and orange tints, a field of light blue tint, also a field of gloss black. The lettering is Gothic italic capitals, worked in gold and black, producing a fine gold shade.' (By the 1880s Andreas Valette Haight had garnered a reputation for strident design and technical excellence in Britain as well as the United States, and from 1884 regularly issued collections of *Specimens of Printing*, copies of which were sent to trade journals around the world to review.)

In both the United States and Britain, there was a revolutionary zeal about the enthusiastic way the trade journals reported new designs, techniques and materials, and reiterated the necessity of improving every aspect of design for print and printing itself. New inks, papers, typefaces, printing presses: all these essential elements were copiously manufactured in the United States and the subject of much discussion, almost unanimously praised in Britain and in mainland European countries for their quality and performance.

Although leading British journals argued for investment in a renewed, redefined printing industry, Britain remained, for American printers, the heart of what they considered to be the Old World. This distinction between the Old and New Worlds was made very explicit in the pages of *American Model Printer*, by far the most vehement supporter of artistic printing in the United States, which praised American job work for its 'diversity coming from the laudable desire to produce original work' and described its British counterpart as narrow and old-fashioned. The journal's editor, Irish-born William James Kelly, was typical of the well-connected,

Right Chart of primary and secondary colours, *c.* 1890.

Far right John Franklin Earhart, *The Color Printer: A Treatise on the Use of Colors in Typographic Printing*, 1892. Overprinting to gain additional colours became common practice for the American letterpress printer during the 1880s. This page shows the twelve colours from which Earhart demonstrated the thousands of colours possible by overprinting in combination with tints. Earhart laboured for seven years on this book. On publication it was already on the cusp of being overtaken by developments in full-colour printing, achieved through the use of blue, red, yellow and black.

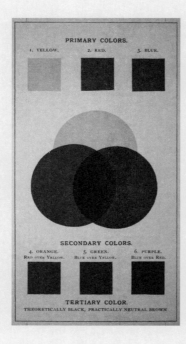

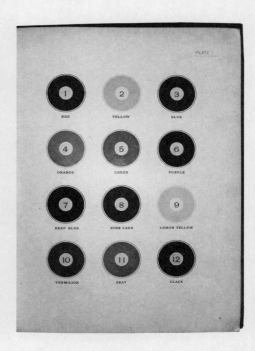

cosmopolitan printer of the time. He was also a consummate self-promoter, contending that he initiated artistic printing while working in New York during the 1860s, and was described in one of his own publications as 'the Homer, the creator of poetry, of fine printing'.[8] Nevertheless, there is no doubt that he made a huge impact on the printing industry through his indefatigable enthusiasm of, and support for, the printer.

Another influential printer of this period was John Franklin Earhart, initially based in Columbia, Ohio, then Cincinnati, where he published the journal *Superior Printer* from 1885. His book, *The Color Printer: A Treatise on the Use of Colors in Typographic Printing*, seven years in the making and completed in 1892, was by far the most exhaustive, practical treatise of its kind. In it he demonstrated the reproduction of over a thousand distinct colour and tint values from twelve stock inks, as well as providing examples of embossing, rainbow fountain printing and special tonal effects, including chaostype, a process of pouring molten metal onto a cold, damp metal plate to create a random-textured surface.[9] *The Color Printer* was consistent with the aspirations of the artistic printing movement but, through the rigour of its analysis and display of results, also reflected the growing interests in science.

Confidence was at an all-time high among American printers, who genuinely felt that they were not only the best in the world but the best ever. American manufacturers of equipment for the print industry were certainly leading the world, but importantly commentators in trade journals such as *American Model Printer* also emphasized differences in attitude: 'American-taught printers have a wider scope of thought, as well as being free from entanglements of old-school fancies and worn-out technical theories. The

American printer is generally a thinking man – and he is, therefore, allowed to exercise this faculty for himself; and right here, perhaps, is the key to his superiority. He is not only willing and ready to test the correctness of new problems, but also able to furnish them for others; so that in practice he is thorough, methodical, and original.'

American printers celebrated their international status and even pitied their Old World competitors (called 'Routinists' by Kelly) for their poor equipment and materials. If the scale and power of the American printing industry were causing international reverberations, so too were its technical prowess and shocking appearance. The concept of newness was, in commercial printing, still new. With the American celebration of individualism, jobbing printing had a role and an identity. There was a genuine sense in both Britain and the rest of Europe that it was essential to conjure up a response.

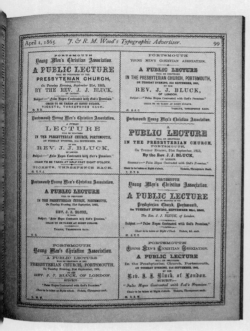

Left Page of the 'Display Typography' competition entries, *Typographic Advertiser*, 1 April 1865. The challenge was to set the copy for a lecture admission card, with the prize of a new composing stick for the three best entries (one of which is illustrated below). Sixty-four of the entries were reproduced in the April and May editions.

Right This winning entry, designed and set by John Barnes of Manchester, was criticized by jobbing master printers for its 'uniformity and adherence to "good" taste'. One commentator made the point that he thought it strange that the winner of a competition called 'Display Typography' could be entirely devoid of display type.

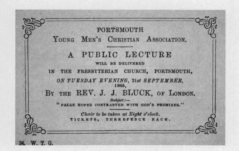

Artistic printing in Britain

The Great Exhibition, held in London in 1851, was a catalyst for an interest in all things 'exotic'. There was a confidence in British design generally (products, furniture, fabrics, etc), and its artistic merit became a topic of conversation for the middle classes. At the same time, the amount and variety of goods flowing from Japan into Paris initially, and then London and the rest of Europe, steadily increased.

Interest in the general standards of jobbing work, and especially how the huge range of display types now available from foundries in England and the United States was being utilized, was the subject of much discussion in trade journals. The changing values of the jobbing printer are reflected in the submissions (and subsequent comments) to a competition titled 'Display Typography', set by the *Typographic Advertiser* in February 1865. Sixty-four of the entries – the challenge being to set the copy for a lecture admission card – were reproduced in the April and May editions. The extent of a large printing house's typographic resources can be gauged by the fact that reproducing these cards entailed the journal's compositors setting each entry from their own stock. Following publication, there were complaints about the lack of invention in the entries. Some complained that the winning entry, set throughout in the same roman typeface with emphasis provided by size and capitals alone, was too restrained, while others used the entries to question the very meaning and function of good taste.

When *Harpel's Typograph, or Book of Specimens* was published five years later, its sole focus on jobbing work and inventive approach to style and colour caused a great deal of interest. Although very few copies were available in Britain,[10] its reputation and undoubted influence on the development of design and printing were assured by the enthusiastic support of English printer-publishers such as Thomas Hailing and Andrew White Tuer. While the American printer's lack of deference to traditional design was viewed by some in England and mainland Europe as the result of ignorance,[11] such views were far from unanimous. George W. Jones (1860–1942), a young compositor at that time, described the thrill of seeing such work, especially its 'brightness and originality … providing a new world to roam in'.[12]

The confidence that emanated from the work of artistic American compositors was infectious, and jobbing printers in Britain and Europe, used for so long to being the poor relation to the book printing fraternity, actively sought to be considered artistic printers. However, as an article in the first issue of *American Model Printer* ('Job Printing as an Art', 1879) indicates, an American assessment of the standards of job printing in Britain, Ireland and the countries of mainland Europe was far from favourable, with England receiving most attention: 'Is there never to be change? Or are the followers of the craft there incapable of originating a new feature? Still these plain faces of letters might be made attractive if they were only artistically arranged… Notwithstanding all this, there is a character to English printing, and that is its painful plainness, lacking nearly all prerequisites pertaining to art.'

The British response was the publication of *The Printers' International Specimen Exchange* from 1880, first conceived by Thomas Hailing and edited by Andrew White Tuer. Tuer, co-owner of the publishing house Field & Tuer,[13] was also editor of *The Paper & Printing Trades Journal*, and it was through these pages that the concept of the *Exchange* was so successfully promoted. Each subscriber, at a cost of one shilling (three dollars for American subscribers), provided a stated number of identical printed specimens – 202 for the

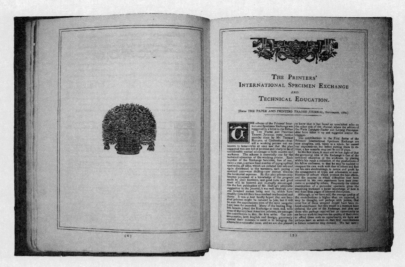

first issue – of a job that represented their best work. These were then collated into sets so that each subscriber received 202 specimens, all different, in return for his own submission. As Hailing explained, the idea was to 'unite a few of us together in the bonds of fellowship and in the worship of the beautiful'[14] – a typically aesthete turn of phrase.

Hailing and Tuer were encouraged by the popularity of a 'specimens' feature included in *The Paper & Printing Trades Journal* since 1874, but the underlying inspiration for the *Exchange* undoubtedly came from *Harpel's Typograph*. Hailing was particularly well connected with events and individuals in American printing. Not only was he the owner of the Cheltenham Printing Company, but he was also an importer of American journals. From 1879, he was also the editor and designer of *Hailing's Circular*, a particularly handsome journal that began as a four-page, self-promotional, quarterly publication, but quickly grew into a journal with an international distribution. The huge demand for the first few issues of *Hailing's Circular* (fuelled by glowing reviews from Tuer in *The Paper & Printing Trades Journal* and from Kelly in *American Model Printer*) persuaded Hailing, in 1879, to publish the first of two books titled *Specimens of General Printing* displaying work from his own company's presses.[15] The timing of these publications placed Hailing at the forefront of his contemporaries within British printing.

Interest in the idea of an exchange of graphic work – of sharing an international stage, as well as the necessity of improving printing standards – grew quickly. In the following issues of the *Exchange*, the number of contributors rapidly increased to 350, then 375 and, eventually, 400. As the number of contributors grew, the pressure on Tuer (especially from Kelly in America) to reject weaker work increased, but Tuer argued that one of the publication's key objectives – raising

standards – would be defeated in following this strict line. 'Is there one amongst the craft's highest geniuses who has not learned something from examples of how *not* to do it?' Far more important was the fact that the *Exchange* carried some of the best examples of work, especially from the United States and Germany, and made these available to all the contributing printers to study.

Following the success of the first few volumes of the *Exchange,* similar ventures were set up in France and Germany, and, in 1886, Ed McClure started *The American Printers' Specimen Exchange*, publishing six issues. Kelly, ambitious as ever, planned his own, strictly vetted *World's Specimen Album*, but nothing came of this scheme.

Tuer sought approval for the *Exchange* from Ruskin. The artistic printing movement, on both sides of the Atlantic, was inspired by Ruskin's argument that life could be whole only when the beauty of nature, art and craft infused everyday life and objects. The presence of printed matter in almost every aspect of society surely gave the printer – and particularly the jobbing printer – a unique responsibility, and Tuer's expectation of receiving Ruskin's support was, therefore, understandable.

However, Ruskin's eventual response suggests reticence at being associated with the project and irritation at Tuer's persistence: 'I assure you again how gladly I hear of an association of printers who will sometimes issue work in a form worthy of their own craft and showing to the uttermost the best of which it is capable… I have the most entire sympathy with your objects.'[16] The word 'sometimes' is important. For Ruskin, 'work in a form worthy of their own craft' refers not only to the appearance of print, but also the purpose for which it was designed. Ruskin deplored mass production in all its forms, and the use of printing to promote such prod-

Opposite, far left *The Paper & Printing Trades Journal*, 1879. Printer-publisher Andrew White Tuer was the proprietor of this influential journal. It was through this publication that *The Printers' International Specimen Exchange*, edited by Tuer, was successfully launched.

Opposite, left *The Printers' International Specimen Exchange*, vol. 1, London, 1880. This book showcased jobbing print specimens from around the world. The idea was that the work should consist of genuine commissioned solutions, but it is clear that many contributed items that were designed specifically for the book. Nevertheless, the result was that compositors and printers went to extraordinary lengths to impress their peers – exactly what the book was intended to achieve.

Top left Detail of an advertisement for the Liberty Treadle Job Printing Press, *The Paper & Printing Trades Journal*, September 1877. The treadle press improved considerably during the second half of the nineteenth century. In its favour, it could be worked by a single person and registration was radically improved (essential for colour work). It was claimed between 1,000 and 2,000 impressions per hour were achievable.

Bottom left Contribution from John Franklin Earhart, Ohio, USA, in *The Printers' International Specimen Exchange*, vol. 1, 1880. This was an extraordinary piece of work for the period, certainly for those working outside the USA, and one of several American contributions whose striking design was much studied and copied.

ucts, regardless of the quality or beauty of the printing, was unacceptable to him. Despite the prominent objectives of improved craftsmanship, a renewed sense of ownership and pride in the work of the artistic printer, for Ruskin there could be no differentiation between craft and purpose.[17]

In contrast, for Tuer mechanization and mass production could be neither ignored nor denied. Moreover, in his view, raising the standards of the jobbing printer's work by giving the compositor and printer the opportunity to use their own initiative and extend their creative potential would benefit not only the printer and the printing industry as a whole, but the society it aimed to inform. The moral obligation for the artistic printer was that every job, no matter how small or insignificant its purpose, had to be done to the very best of the compositor's and the printer's ability.

He was also an enthusiastic print historian, with a particular interest in Caxton[18] and popular reading matter from the previous one hundred years, especially broadsides and chapbooks.[19] His own designs for print reflected these interests and, as a result, his work, and that of those contemporaries following his lead, was termed Antique or Old Style. Because of Tuer's wholehearted support for the ideology of artistic printing, his own work has, understandably but inappropriately, been included within this movement.

The most interesting of Tuer's work was produced in collaboration with Joseph Crawhall, established as an illustrator, designer and publisher of chapbooks in his native Newcastle from the 1850s, and was a deliberate, sophisticated reflection of the technically crude but popular publications of the late eighteenth and early nineteenth centuries. Tuer's publications are markedly different from the 'anaemic regularity of "respectable" book-production at the time',[20] the hand-drawn letterforms being deliberately rough and irregu-lar to provide a 'penny-plain, tuppence-coloured' appearance. Crawhall's bold, playful, yet refined woodcuts exactly matched this, positioned on the page with a carefully considered 'arbitrariness'.[21] The American illustrator and designer William H. Bradley would later be influenced by Crawhall's work with Tuer.[22]

Following the success of Tuer's *Exchange* and Hailing's *Specimens of General Printing*, a number of the leading British printers adopted the practice of issuing their own work-specimen books. These activities reflected a new spirit, born of competition but also of the recognition and approval of individuality. References to the 'art' of composition and printing began to mean more than artisanship. The self-congratulatory rhetoric of the printing trade papers, reinforced, perversely, by the contempt emanating from the upper echelons of the book publishing houses, fuelled the notion that perhaps this shocking new movement might, indeed, be art. For the ambitious young compositor, this very public attention was recognition of his newfound creative role in the business of printed communication.

In 1887 the *Exchange* changed hands. Under Tuer's editorship, much of the work on both the *Exchange* and *The Paper & Printing Trades Journal* had been delegated to his assistant, Robert Hilton. The extent of Hilton's involvement in the *Exchange* was well known, and when he threatened to start his own version (possibly with the encouragement of his new employers, the printing company Raithby & Lawrence in Leicester), Tuer sold Hilton the rights. Hilton did not approve of Tuer's Antique predilections and, from volume nine, changed the *Exchange*'s white, Antique-style binding for a cover of red cloth half-bound in red leather. Hilton broke all ties with Tuer, resigning as his assistant on *The Paper & Printing Trades Journal* to become

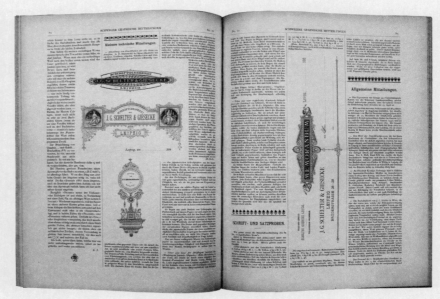

editor of a new trade journal, *The British Printer*, with Raithby & Lawrence.

The inaugural issue of *The British Printer* (January/February 1888) was designed by George W. Jones, who was also working for Raithby & Lawrence. Jones left the company shortly afterwards to work for the Darien Press in Edinburgh but remained on amicable terms with Hilton. Initially influenced by artistic printing, Jones adopted the asymmetrical arrangements also favoured throughout the 1880s by American artistic printers. However, his work was less complex, giving his type conspicuous amounts of space, providing a quieter, highly assured appearance. His arbitrary choice of vignettes – most commonly illustrating country scenes – subdued colours and off-centre arrangement of type is stylistically suggestive of the Art Nouveau movement that would become so influential during the 1890s.

After Jones left Raithby & Lawrence, his influence there continued through the work of the new works manager, Robert Grayson, whose efforts (not surprisingly) were given unstinting support by *The British Printer*. Both Jones's and Grayson's work was recognized as a particularly British mode of typography. Its pared-down appearance certainly caught the attention of, and was much admired by, printers in both the United States and mainland Europe. In Germany, it was called *der ungezwungene Leicester Stil* – 'the Leicester free style'.[23] With this development, and in particular the work of Jones, the initiative in artistic typographic design passed briefly from the United States back to Britain and the Raithby & Lawrence company in Leicester, which remained a centre of influence for British printing into the twentieth century.

A defining feature of the artistic printing movement was international collaboration. Its influential figures formed a mutual support group, writing for the new printing journals, especially those in New York and London during the 1880s, swapping printed samples and criticizing each other's latest work. Sometimes, when discussing general standards, criticism could be scathing, especially on the American side, but all gave unwavering support to any venture that aimed to further the cause of the art of printing, whatever its source.

The artistic movement, so assured of its purpose, became a celebration of itself, a joyful experiment that its exponents assumed would continue ad infinitum. Having experienced the sense of release from historic precedents, there was surely no going back? However, by the mid-1890s, *The British Printer* was already reporting that the 'higher branches of jobbing' were making way for a 'quieter and perhaps less elaborate style',[24] no doubt a reference to the Leicester free style (also referred to as 'mature artistic').

More importantly, other demands caused print buyers to be critical of printers who, in their opinion, placed too high a priority on printing values and not enough on selling value. As competition between manufacturers increased, the function of advertising and the service provided by advertising agencies were becoming more diverse and sophisticated.

Opposite, far left *The Paper & Printing Trades Journal*, edited by Andrew White Tuer, letterpress, 1879. The compact setting and mean margins give Tuer's journal a lacklustre appearance compared with *American Model Printer* (page 172) and *Schweizer Graphische Mitteilungen* (*opposite, left*).

Opposite, left *Schweizer Graphische Mitteilungen*, Swiss print trade journal, letterpress, 1882.

Top left Magazine insert, chromolithography, late nineteenth century. Based on a photograph, this image has been drawn using a mixture of hatching, stippling and other techniques.

Top right Vignette transfer, Rock & Company, UK, *c.* 1870s.

Bottom right Photograph of a sheet of photographs, part of a police file alerting officers of known 'confidence trick men', London, 1899.

Photography and printing technology

Photographic processes had been used to reproduce black-and-white illustrations (with no tone) that had been transferred to metal plates. But in 1880, *The New York Daily Graphic* became the first newspaper to print a reproduction of a photograph with a full tonal range. A more sophisticated result, essentially an adaptation of the same process, was devised by Georg Meisenbach, a copperplate engraver from Nuremberg, Germany. His halftone process, called autotype, patented in 1882, enabled photographs, including a full range of tones, to be printed using letterpress printing technology.

The method he devised required two sheets of glass, each with a series of parallel lines, engraved by machine, running diagonally across it, to be glued together with the engraved lines at right angles to each other. When the image was projected through the glass screen onto a light-sensitive surface, the engraved lines changed the gradated tones of the photograph into a series of dots. Where the tones were dark, the dots on the light-sensitive surface appeared larger and, therefore, closer together. The light-sensitive metal plate receiving the image was then etched to provide the halftone image in relief and mounted onto wood to bring it up to the same height as the type, enabling type and image to be printed simultaneously.

Halftone reproduction of photographs and tonal drawings revolutionized both the appearance and the production of newspapers and magazines. An engraver required about ten hours to cut a 5 × 6 centimetre (2 × 2⅜ in.) wood block, or a week to complete a full-page illustration. In contrast, *The Pacific Printer* reported, in 1909, 'If everything goes well, a picture can now be ready for press in thirty minutes.'[25]

An influential early use of photography was a sequence of eight images reproduced in the German journal *Illustrirte*

Zeitung, taken from a fixed position and recording a choreographed procession, providing one of the first photographic reports. This series demonstrated what was unique to photography: a seemingly objective record – free of the engraver's interpretation. Many sequential photographic essays followed, often celebrating the ordinary and everyday. Photography offered a new realism, the potential of which was immediately recognized by those whose job it was to advertise ordinary and everyday products or services.

As mentioned earlier, photography was also used extensively in transferring black-and-white illustrations from an original drawing to a metal plate, which was mounted onto wood (a line block). By the late 1870s, there were companies, generally called photoengravers or blockmakers, specializing in this field. John Calvin Moss of New York was an early example. The huge advantage of photoengraving over, for example, wood or copper engraving is that the illustrator's own line is transferred, photographically, to the metal

Left Detail of a self-promotional halftone photograph from an engraved copperplate by Garrett & Walsh, reproduced in *The British Printer*, June 1897.

Right *Chromo Waltz* sheet music cover, Cincinnati, USA, *c.* 1885.

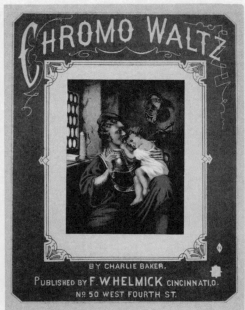

block rather than an engraver's interpretation of the illustrator's line. English illustrator Aubrey Beardsley's work in 1893 for an edition of Sir Thomas Malory's *Morte d'Arthur* was planned and drawn specifically to be printed from photoengraved line blocks.

The earliest photomechanical illustrations were printed for the Christmas edition of the French magazine *L'Illustration* in 1881, and by the end of the decade this process was radically changing the appearance of popular reading material. British journal *The Graphic* made good use of colour halftone illustrations, often taking up whole pages either as a single image or as a sequence of images to provide a humorous narrative.

The appearance of photographs in magazines and advertisements was limited by size and its general grey flatness. As the image was made up of minute raised dots, the printer had to be careful not to over-ink in case the block flooded, filling the areas between the raised dots. The result, invariably, was that early halftone photographs are lacking in clarity.

In 1888, the Eastman Dry Plate Company in Rochester, New York, began manufacturing the Kodak camera. The major breakthrough, however, came in 1900, when the company launched the inexpensive Brownie camera. The availability of this camera changed the purpose of the photograph and encouraged a less formal, more natural image.

Colour printing and advertising

In the last quarter of the 1800s, chromolithography quickly evolved from a relatively slow and expensive process to one able to produce high volumes of multi-coloured graphic work at low costs. The quality of this work and the high number of colours often used to build up the dense, rich, hand-drawn type and image were remarkable. The most significant work was produced in the United States.

Demand for lithographic products during the 1850s had led to the development of the steam-powered lithographic press. Inventing an automated press was difficult because lithographic stones vary in thickness (the surface of each stone is reground before being reused). The first patent for a steam-driven lithographic press was taken out in 1851 by Georg Sigl in Austria, and by 1854 the Imperial Printing office in Vienna was printing up to 1,000 sheets per hour on a Sigl press, the equivalent of four days' work on a handpress.

During the 1860s, a number of American companies boasted about being the first to have automated lithographic presses. By the 1870s, however, their use had become widespread and their output prodigious. The potential of the automated lithographic press for advertising purposes, including posters, packaging, and the nominal branding of products and commodities, was recognized almost immediately. The chromolithographic process offered rich colours and deep tones to produce images that often reflected the American pioneering spirit and a love of nature. Labels might be small, but the images they carried could depict vast panoramas, which came to symbolize the perceived freedom and adventure associated with the United States. The exuberant lettering on these labels was integral to the overall design and reflected not only the influence of the

Far left Illustrated page from *Advertise How? When? Where?*, an early book about advertising by William Smith, 1863. During the 1870s, there was immense interest in the moral and cultural issues regarding advertising as well as its commercial effectiveness. Here, the illustrator demonstrates the merit of word of mouth.

Left Detail of an advertisement for the department store Au Bon Marché, France, late nineteenth century. The merits of a standardized corporate design for packaging are already understood and implemented.

Right Large-scale lithographic printing at the Institute of Graphic Arts, Bergamo, Italy, 1915.

ornate wood type being used by the letterpress printer, but also the close historic association between lithographic artists and engravers.

The technical freedom of lithographic artists did not stop them being influenced by the *trompe l'œil* effects – various surfaces wrapped, folded or interlocked – produced by the letterpress artistic printers. During the 1870s and 1880s, and through to the end of the century, the lithographic Gaslight style became prevalent in the United States and elsewhere, resulting in exceptionally elaborate compositions characterized by multi-layered forms and shadows. More than anything else, these rich and highly sophisticated designs demonstrated the lithographic printer's technical advantages over the letterpress artistic printer.

Vast amounts of lithographed material had been produced for the Philadelphia Centennial Exposition in 1876, showing lithography to be a highly adaptable medium. The use of chromolithography was quickly established for the labelling of branded goods. For example, the production of cigars and other tobacco products grew into a huge and highly competitive industry. Each box displayed a number of labels and seals, using every process at the printer's disposal: multiple colours with varnishes, embossing and debossing, with metallic inks often double- or even triple-printed to maximize luminosity. Cigar makers and their printers projected exclusive status through laurels, medallions, insignia, crests, heroic male role models and the allure of semi-nude female figures.

In this competitive market Louis Prang and other chromolithographers were quick to learn the art of persuasion. Based in Boston, Prussian-born Prang became the most prominent and influential chromolithographic printer in the United States. He produced an enormous range and

variety of material in huge quantities, and yet is renowned for the remarkably high quality of his company's work. After founding his first company in 1856 in partnership with Julius Mayer, just four years later he went into business on his own as Louis Prang & Co. He made his initial fortune producing fine-art prints: copies of paintings, commonly referred to as 'chromos'. These colour lithographs, reproduced in vast numbers, decorated the walls of American homes and apartments as well as brightening up offices, workshops and public places.

Connecting art and mechanization was considered irresponsible and degenerate by the art establishment. Moreover, chromolithography, it was argued, was symptomatic of a general collapse of values inherent in modern American culture. Paintings chosen were certainly populist in nature, depicting pre-industrial landscapes or patriotic scenes, and

Left Label for branded goods, with type and image integrated, chromolithography, New York, late nineteenth century.

Right Trade card for the New Easy Lawn Mower, lithography, printed by Milton Bradley, Springfield, Massachusetts, USA, date unknown.

Opposite Detail from the masthead of the journal *American Model Printer*, the official organ of the International Typographical Union of North America, New York, 1879. Its editor, William James Kelly, made it the voice of the artistic printing movement.

as a result the term 'chromo' was generally associated with sentimentality and ignorance. By the 1890s, the market was so saturated that fine-art prints were being offered as a free supplement with the Sunday newspapers. Nevertheless, in his search for the perfect likeness, Prang raised the quality of chromolithographic printing to the highest levels, exploring every possible manual and mechanical technique using an inordinate number of colours.

Chromolithography was used to great effect in packaging and advertising. In 1860, the earliest colour labels were being used by the dominant American canning industry, despite companies initially having to import tinplate from the UK. The earliest known label on a metal can carried the company name Reckhow & Larne of New York.[26] A hammer and chisel were required to open it. With the lightweight steel can and the invention of the tin-opener, the canning industry expanded with tremendous speed, and labelling was an essential element. For this reason, the 1880s in particular were a boom-time for chromolithographers.

As with any new information technology, the chromo was, for some, a cause for concern because of its ubiquitous presence, but at the same time there was a fascination with where it might lead. 'Universal cheapness' was the critical response, the chromo being just one of many industrially produced items that were said to be homogenizing social taste and destroying individuality. For many critics, the most worrying aspect of this printing technology was its very popularity. At major expositions such as the Centennial in Philadelphia (1876) and the Columbian in Chicago (1893), printers, their mechanized presses and their products drew huge crowds. These large, noisy, spectacular printing machines were, indeed, awe-inspiring to watch: the epitome of power harnessed by human ingenuity. The unveiling of the first

sixteen-sheet billboard poster in Cincinnati in 1878 attracted so many people that a police presence was required.[27] The printer was newsworthy, and a few, such as Prang, became heroic in status.

During the 1880s, experiments with halftones to achieve full-colour images using just three standard colours – blue, red and yellow – were being made. The full-colour process took a number of years to come to fruition, a major problem being a mistaken faith that overprinting just the three primary colours would, or should, produce black: 'Trichromatic printing necessitated the use of a grey tint, which is not necessary if the process is carried out on strictly scientific principles.'[28] Once it had been accepted that black was a necessary fourth colour, full-colour printing using blue (cyan), red (magenta), yellow and black[29] became a commercial standard reprographic process. The letterpress printer finally had the means, when combined with photographic technology, to compete for colour printing commissions with the chromolithographer.

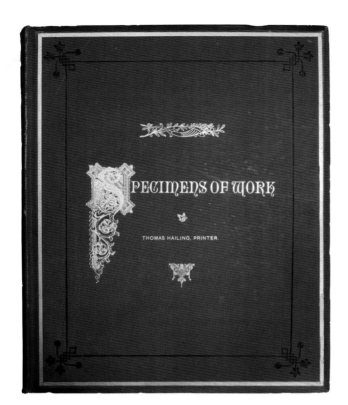

Hailing's Circular

Published Quarterly.   One Shilling per Annum.

No. 5.   Autumn, 1891.   Vol. I.

A Page from Bacon.

ffected dispatch is one of the most dangerous things to Business that can be: it is like that which the Physicians call predigestion; which is sure to fill the body full of crudities and secret seeds of diseases: therefore measure not dispatch by the time of sitting but by the advancement of business: and as, in races, it is not the large stride or high lift that makes the speed; so, in business, the keeping close to the matter, and not taking of it too much at once, procureth dispatch. It is the care of some only to come off speedily for the time, or to contrive some false periods of business, because they may seem men of dispatch; but it is one thing to abbreviate by contracting, another by cutting off; and business so handled at several sittings or meetings goeth commonly backward and forward in an unsteady manner. I knew a wise man that had it for a by-word, when he saw men hasten to a conclusion, "Stay a little, that we may make an end the sooner." On the other side, true dispatch is a rich thing; for time is the measure of business, as money is of wares; for Business is bought at a dear hand where there is small dispatch. The Spartans and Spaniards have been noted to be of small dispatch, "Let my death come from Spain;" for then it will be sure to be long in coming. Give good hearing to those that give the first information in business, and rather direct them in the beginning, than interrupt them in the continuance of their speeches; for he that is put out of his own order will go forward and backward, and be more tedious while he waits upon his memory, than he could have been if he had gone on in his own course: but sometimes it is seen that the moderator is more troublesome than the actor. Iterations are commonly loss of time; but there is no such gain of time as to iterate often the state of the question; for it chaseth away many a frivolous speech as it is coming forth. Long and curious speeches are as fit for dispatch as a robe or mantle with a long train is for a race. Prefaces, and passages, and excusations and other speeches of reference to the person are great wastes of time; and though they seem to proceed of modesty, they are bravery. Yet beware of being too material when there is any impediment or obstruction in men's wills; for pre-occupation of mind ever requireth preface of speech, like a fomentation to make the unguent enter. Above all things, order and distribution, and singling out of parts, is the life of dispatch; so as the distribution be not too subtile: for he that doth not divide will never enter well into business; and he that divideth too much will never come out of it clearly. To choose time is to save time; and an unseasonable motion is but beating the air. There be three parts of business, the preparation, the debate or examination, and the perfection; whereof, if you look for dispatch, let the middle only be the work of many, and the first and last the work of few. The proceeding upon somewhat conceived in writing doth for the most part facilitate dispatch; for though it should be wholly rejected, yet that negative is more pregnant of direction than an indefinite, as ashes are more generative than dust.

PREFACE.

Our fortune rolls as from a smooth descent,
And from the first impression takes its bent.

Dryden.

EVERTHELESS

I persevere, in spite of the envious carpings of self-elected critics, and all the other troubles which surround and harass the daily life of a striving Printer. I endeavour to extract the "sweets" of my "office" as I go along, and I always find an uplifting consolation in the fact that my labour is not entirely thrown away. To those friends who, by their writings and words and example, have helped me forward in my course, I here tender sincere and grateful thanks in acknowledgment of their services, so freely and heartily rendered. Without such help I feel that it would have been impossible to have arrived at the position I am now in and enabled to send forth the Second Volume of my "Specimens of General Printing." Of the merits of the work here exhibited it does not become me to speak. That must be left in the hands of the editors of our trade journals, and I leave it there with perfect confidence, feeling well assured that even their adverse criticisms will exert as beneficial an effect upon myself as upon other readers. I cannot, however, refrain from laying claim to some little amount of consideration: I do my best. No man can do more; and if any one thing more than another gives me courage to persist in the work to which I have put my hand it is the consciousness that I have been, and still may continue in a small degree to be, the means of stimulating my brethren to "go and do likewise."

Thomas Hailing
Based in Cheltenham, UK, Hailing was a printer, publisher and importer of journals. He was a great admirer of *Harpel's Typograph*, claiming that it had 'made more good printers than all the other trade manuals that have been issued either before or since'. He was also instrumental in setting up *The Printers' International Specimen Exchange*.

Hailing's Circular (*opposite, top right* and *below*) began in 1877 as a modest four-page quarterly journal. The design of its inside pages was unremarkable and remained largely unchanged, but each new cover incorporated a different typeface – even extending to the masthead. Hailing seemed to relish using ever more exotic faces as they became available, displaying them at various sizes down the front cover. The twenty-fourth and last issue appeared in 1889.

He also published his own company's *Specimens of Work* (*opposite, top left and bottom*). Others followed suit.

Opposite, top left and bottom
Cover and preface of *Specimens of Work*, published by Thomas Hailing, Cheltenham, UK, 1877.

Opposite, top right *Hailing's Circular*, no. 9, published by Thomas Hailing, Cheltenham, UK, 1881.

Below *Hailing's Circular*, no. 14, published by Thomas Hailing, Cheltenham, UK, 1883.

hailing's Circular

No. 14.   Summer, 1883.   Vol. II.

❃ ANOTHER ∴ FLIGHT ❃

ARTISTIC PRINTING, thanks to the energy and enterprise of American and Continental Type Founders, is daily becoming more and more come-at-able. Nor is this all that we have to be grateful for, inasmuch as there are not wanting signs of the times to show that foreign ventures are beginning to stimulate home productions. ✳ This is much to be desired. We cannot bring ourselves to believe that we lack either the brains or the money to successfully compete with "Our Kin Beyond the Sea," notwithstanding the fact that in too many instances our own Type Founders have been content to import "strikes" of foreign productions, instead of striking out new lines for themselves. Let us hope, however, that this is, or soon will become, a thing of the past. ✳ It is anything but consoling to one's national pride to find that he has to go abroad for types of a telling character. That these types pay those who produce them we are convinced since we have undertaken the agency for the Central Type Foundry, and see how they are caught up. ∴ To give an instance, Messrs. Field & Tuer no sooner saw this series of "harper" than they ordered Fifty Pounds' worth of it! Yet another proof of its popularity is to be seen in the fact that Messrs. Day & Collins, Atlas Works, London, have carried the series into broadside type. ✳ See headline and initial.

171

American Model Printer.

A JOURNAL DEVOTED TO THE TYPOGRAPHIC ART AND KINDRED TRADES.

OFFICIAL ORGAN OF THE INTERNATIONAL TYPOGRAPHICAL UNION OF NORTH AMERICA.

VOL. 1. NEW YORK, OCTOBER, 1879. No. 1.

Subscription Rates.

One Year, in advance,	$3 00
Four Months,	1 25
Clubs of Five, to one address,	13 75
Single Copies,	35

Advertising Rates.

		One Column, one issue, 25 00
One Page, inside, one issue, $50 00		
Half " "	30 00	Half " " 15 00
Third " "	25 00	Third " " 10 00
Quarter " "	20 00	Quarter " " 8 00

Cards, one inch, single column inside, one issue, $3 00.
Special rates on Cover.

Discounts on Advertisements: 3 months, 10 per cent.; 6 months, 15 per cent.; 1 year, 25 per cent.

KELLY & BARTHOLOMEW,
PRINTERS AND PUBLISHERS.

Correspondence and Items solicited from all parts of the world, on matters of interest to the Craft.

Address THE AMERICAN MODEL PRINTER,
22 College Place, New York.

The American Model Printer

WM. J. KELLY, EDITOR.

NEW YORK, OCTOBER, 1879.

PROSPECTUS.

At the urgent request of many practical leaders in the printing profession, we have consented to issue a monthly journal under the above title, which shall be in keeping with the real progress and highest standard of typographic excellence.

The demand for such a journal has not been caused by any dearth of printers' papers, so called, but rather on account of the scarcity of properly edited and printed journals claiming the support of printers and manufacturers of printers' materials. A few creditable technical journals are now published; but at no time has there been one issued that reflected the true practical advancement of the typographic art of this country, and in such a manner as is contemplated in the pages of the AMERICAN MODEL PRINTER.

In view of the foregoing, we are not in doubt as to the want of a thoroughly practical printers' medium, not only as a superior work of reference, but also to aid in more directly developing the taste of the public through their printers, as masters, workmen or apprentices. To this end our publication will introduce a most worthy feature, in the shape of supplementary pages of elegant sample designs,

printed in appropriate colors, which will appear with each number. These designs will be contributed by the publishers and such appreciative brother artists as may desire to enhance the practical value of their art, and thus aid in the advancement and interest of the typographic profession. We shall print all contributed specimens in the best style, and in as many colors as may be deemed necessary, placing the name of the contributor to each design.

The editor is not a stranger to the typographic fraternity, either at home or abroad, but has been identified with that class of thinkers and printers who have made our country celebrated for its wonderful achievements in the art; therefore, no doubt will be entertained as to his ability to give to the craft a journal worthy of their reputation. He will also have the coöperation of the very best talent in the profession, thus making the AMERICAN MODEL PRINTER the peer of any technical journal now published.

SOME OF OUR OBJECTS:

1—The diffusion of advanced and sound practical ideas in typography, and the elevation of the art proper, as a true means of abolishing the disgrace of spawned workmen and the plague of amateurism, which should be strangled as soon as possible.

2—A broader field of practical amicability among printers generally, by opening up fraternal opportunities whereby they can ventilate their opinions, adorn a place with their exquisite handiwork, and thus encourage the more retiring or backward in the profession.

3—The regular production of artistic designs of whatever kind, plain or in colors; together with practical hints and information relative to their execution, etc.

4—An independent and honest criticism on all matters and things pertaining to printing and its accessories.

KELLY & BARTHOLOMEW,
PRINTERS AND PUBLISHERS.

SALUTATORY.

With this number we launch our bark on the wide sea of journalism. To direct its course to usefulness and success will be our zealous endeavor. That we shall meet with difficulties and reverses in many ways is fully apprehended; still, the objects for which we labor shall have our unabated attention, cost us what it may.

How many friends or foes will spring up to assist or assail us, only time will tell. We shall strive to do our duty regardless of either, feeling satisfied that whatever is meritorious in our work will ultimately be appreciated by our foes, as it will be by our friends.

In the publication of such a journal as ours —which, from its character, will undergo the scrutiny of some of the most critical of readers—it will be no easy labor to please all, nor shall we attempt so foolish a task; but we will rather seek out the hidden beauties of the ever-advancing art so dear to us, trusting for the kind sympathy and help of those who, in some degree, know how difficult is our duty.

From time to time we shall speak of things connected with the printing business which may not be pleasant to some of those engaged in it. This will be done without malice or personal feeling—but rather in a spirit of friendliness and a desire to assist in correcting such abuses as we may call attention to.

In whatever labor we may engage, having for its object the bettering of the condition of our fellow-craftsmen, we desire the hearty coöperation of all legitimate technical journalists.

AMATEUR PRINTING MATERIALS.

We wish to say a few words condemnatory of such printers' journals as publish the sale of amateur printing materials, and traffic in them. To us, there can be no semblance of justification for such conduct; and we emphatically question even its expediency, viewed from the standpoint of honest business.

It is too true that printers proper, as a class, are of a most generous and fraternal disposition, seldom looking beyond the *seeming* act of friendship—believing the representations of parties whom they have once accepted as friends. Were it not so, the discreditable trade carried on in amateur goods (to the terrible loss of the legitimate printers all over the land) would have been detected long ago, and its further advance checked, at least so far as being entered into by parties seeking the confidence and money of the fraternity.

We have been more than surprised at the barefaced effrontery of some of the publishers

American Model Printer

American Model Printer (*opposite*) was the official journal of the International Typographical Union of North America. Only twelve issues were printed between 1879 and 1882. Based in New York, William James Kelly, its founder and editor, justifiably described it as 'the most elegant typographic journal in the world'.

Near the front of every issue was a page displaying a selection of trade cards that represented the 'best work in printerdom' (*below, top left and right*), each accompanied by a glowing critique by Kelly. Colour work in journals was still a rarity, and the lavishness of these regular opening pages had a dramatic impact.

Schweizer Graphische Mitteilungen (*bottom*) was launched the same year that *American Model Printer* closed. Its layout and general text-to-page proportions are reminiscent of the latter, but it did not have the same level of campaigning spirit, nor did it carry colour. Nevertheless, it was from the outset regarded internationally as a leader in the field – its influence all the more significant for its longevity.

Opposite *American Model Printer*, no. 1, New York, 1879.

Top left and right Two display pages from *American Model Printer*, nos 1 and 4, 1879.

Bottom *Schweizer Graphische Mitteilungen*, no.1, Switzerland, 1882.

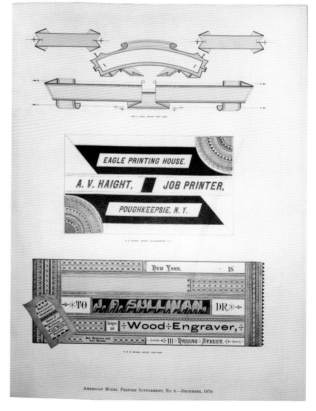

The Printers' International Specimen Exchange

Andrew White Tuer published the *Exchange* (*left*) from 1880, aiming to provide a means by which British jobbing printers could see the advances – both technical and creative – of printers abroad, particularly in the United States. He wrote a brief critique of every entry, some of which could be harsh. This was the case with Doswell's submission (*top right*): 'The effect is by no means commensurate with the pains taken.' The railway and omnibus timetable cover (*bottom right*) fared little better. By comparison, the work in the same volume from the United States was quite shocking in both appearance and technical proficiency (*opposite*).

Left Cover of *The Printers' International Specimen Exchange*, edited by Andrew White Tuer, vol. 1, London, 1880.

Top right Advertisement for John T. Doswell, Winchester, UK, *The Printers' International Specimen Exchange*, vol. 1, 1880.

Bottom right Cover of a railway and omnibus timetable, printed and published by J. R. Beckett, Sheffield, UK, *The Printers' International Specimen Exchange*, vol. 1, 1880.

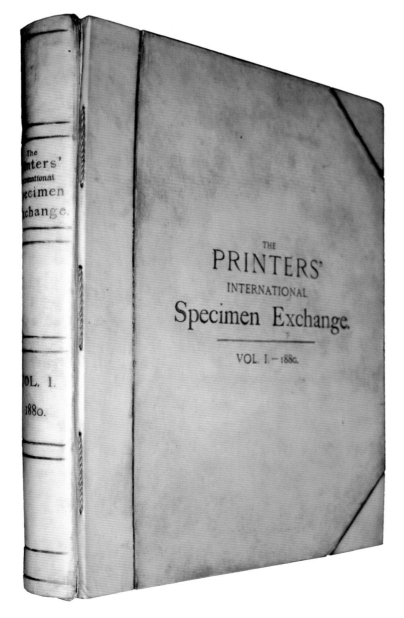

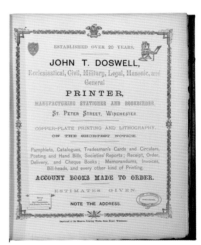

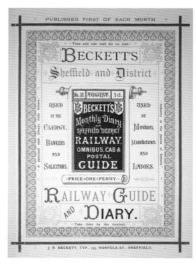

American artistic printing
A page contributed by John Franklin Earhart (*left*) showcasing a business card is the most remarkable specimen in the first volume of *The Printers' International Specimen Exchange*. The card itself epitomizes those characteristics that came to be closely associated with the artistic printing movement: letterpress printed, filled corners, strong diagonals, rules separating (eight) carefully mixed colours and a minimal number of words.

The two typefaces were both recent releases, Glyptic (1878) and Relievo Number 2 (1879) with its drop shadow, both by the Franklin Type Foundry. Equally important, and remarkable for its time, is the way Earhart displays the design, framed by a field of neutral colour. This early work is essentially symmetrical, but asymmetrical arrangements became more common, as demonstrated in the four business cards (*right*), all models of early American artistic printing.

Left Business card by John Franklin Earhart, *The Printers' International Specimen Exchange*, vol. 1, 1880.

Right, from top to bottom Two business cards designed and printed by William Bartholomew of Kelly & Bartholomew (the same Kelly who was editor of *American Model Printer*), New York; two trade cards designed and printed by Haight & Dudley, New York, for the same ink manufacturer.

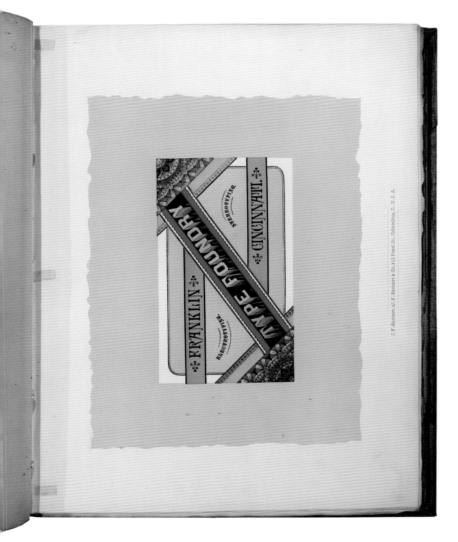

Early American artistic printers depended less on typefoundry-manufactured ornaments, and more on the rule-bending and cutting ingenuity of their compositors. They encouraged each other to be bold and bunk historic precedents (*bottom*). Strong, uncomplicated shapes, particularly circles and diagonals, demonstrated the American artistic printer's determination to break with European perceptions of good taste (*top left* and *top right*).

In the image top left, the compositor C. W. L. Jungloew credits himself as 'artist'. The technical virtuosity in the creation of this composition from brass rules meant it was one of the few examples of artistic printing to be admired throughout the printing fraternity.

There are occasions when the efforts of artistic printers appear distinctly avant-garde in nature. Included in the first volume of *The Printers' International Specimen Exchange*, among the floral

Top left Illustration composed by C. W. L. Jungloew for the Boston Type Foundry, displayed in *American Model Printer*, no. 5, January/February 1880.

Bottom Billhead for P. Inderwick, pipe and tobacco importer, engraving, London, 1873.

Top right Two trade cards designed and printed by Kelly & Bartholomew, New York, for *American Model Printer*, and for M. C. Lynch, manufacturer of printing inks, *c.* 1880–82.

fete programme covers and choral society concert notices, Paul E. Werner's self-promotional piece (*below*) provides a severe jolt to the senses. The choice and diversity of typefaces at the centre of the 'sun' and the wispy, cloud-like borders are the only reminders that this is 1880.

Below Cover of a four-page booklet, designed and printed by Paul E. Werner, Akron, Ohio, USA, *The Printers' International Specimen Exchange*, vol. 1, 1880.

Decorative borders
Decorative border units were designed as sets, enabling the compositor to combine them in various ways. The handbill for the Kingston Freeman printing company (*bottom left*), New York, makes use of MacKellar, Smiths & Jordan's Zig Zag ornamental borders. It was printed with two impressions – black following a multicoloured 'rainbow' pass.

Decorative border sets were designed to help the letterpress printer compete with the lithographic printer, but the effect of commercial competition also worked the other way. On the packaging fragment (*bottom right*), a lithographic printer has drawn panel details that are strikingly similar to Zig Zag.

Top left and top right Thirty-seven Zig Zag border units (*top left*) and a sample make-up (*top right*), produced by an Italian foundry selling sets by MacKellar, Smiths & Jordan, Cincinnati, USA, date unknown.

Bottom left Handbill for the Kingston Freeman printing company, letterpress, New York, 1880.

Centre and bottom right Label and detail from a packaging remnant, lithography, date unknown.

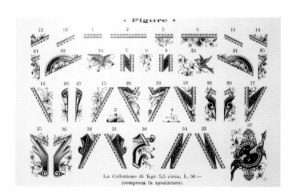

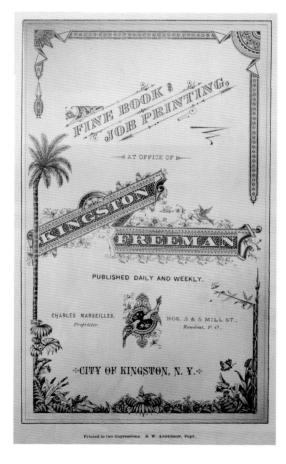

Billheads

The American printing industry took great interest in the standard of work in Britain and the rest of Europe. While English printing was given short shrift, Germany was much praised for its richly textured design, technical accuracy and subtle use of colour.

France, on the other hand, was less enamoured with the burgeoning Arts and Crafts movement and this curtailed its participation in the artistic printing movement. The two billheads below (*centre and bottom*) are models presented in the Berthier Foundry catalogue to demonstrate applications of decorative material and type to printers.

American 'artistic printer' Henry T. Cornett preferred to avoid the excesses of ornament (*top right*). Sans serif type and a more machine-age choice of decorative material reflect a determination to distance himself from European counterparts. Nevertheless, the reverse of the card announces that he has 1,500 styles of type to choose from.

Centre and bottom Two billheads from *Spécimens de travaux typographiques en noir et en couleurs*, S. Berthier Foundry, Paris, 1883.

Top right Trade card of Henry T. Cornett, 'artistic printer', displayed in *American Model Printer*, no. 6, letterpress, New York, 1880.

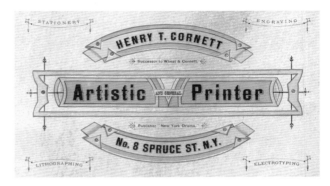

Artistic printing in later trade journals
Typo was a monthly journal first published in 1887 by Robert Coupland Harding in New Zealand. Harding spent his early years working as a compositor, avidly collecting typefounders' specimens and establishing links with the most eminent European and North American printers and founders. It was in *Typo* that his interests in job printing found their fullest expression (*top*), for which he received instant international praise.

The British Printer was designed by George W. Jones in 1888 when he was working for Raithby & Lawrence, UK. This early example (*bottom*) is not typical of the style of work for which he became renowned. It is a blend of the so-called Antique or Old Style made popular by Andrew White Tuer (see page 193) in the use of ragged medieval banners and artistic printing in the choice of typefaces.

Top *Typo*, trade journal, New Zealand, 1887.

Bottom *The British Printer*, trade journal, Leicester, UK, 1888.

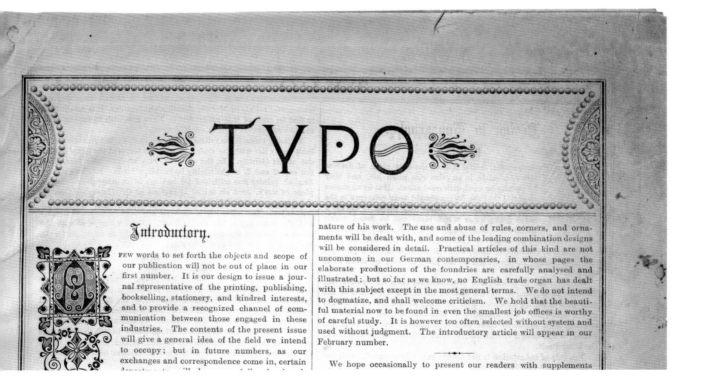

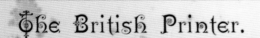

Billheads

The American printing industry took great interest in the standard of work in Britain and the rest of Europe. While English printing was given short shrift, Germany was much praised for its richly textured design, technical accuracy and subtle use of colour.

France, on the other hand, was less enamoured with the burgeoning Arts and Crafts movement and this curtailed its participation in the artistic printing movement. The two billheads below (*centre and bottom*) are models presented in the Berthier Foundry catalogue to demonstrate applications of decorative material and type to printers.

American 'artistic printer' Henry T. Cornett preferred to avoid the excesses of ornament (*top right*). Sans serif type and a more machine-age choice of decorative material reflect a determination to distance himself from European counterparts. Nevertheless, the reverse of the card announces that he has 1,500 styles of type to choose from.

Centre and bottom Two billheads from *Spécimens de travaux typographiques en noir et en couleurs*, S. Berthier Foundry, Paris, 1883.

Top right Trade card of Henry T. Cornett, 'artistic printer', displayed in *American Model Printer*, no. 6, letterpress, New York, 1880.

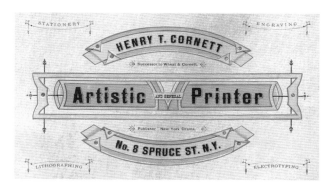

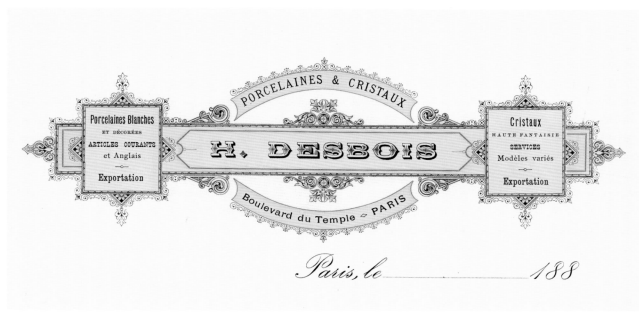

Frankfurt a. M.

zugeeignet

von der

Schriftgiesserei Flinsch

Asymmetrical arrangements

The first volume of *The Printers' International Specimen Exchange* showed clearly that, while American jobbing printers were intent on rocking the print establishment, German printers were displaying a bravado of a different kind. Using a subdued multicoloured palette, they demonstrated exceptional craftsmanship to produce work that had both richness and subtlety (*opposite*).

The rejection of symmetry became one of the key characteristics of artistic printing. Weighted to the left, with decorative borders locked next to fields of texture or colour, the arrangement of type was allowed more freedom. The courtesy card (*top right*) uses an outline typeface called Santa Claus, one of a number of typefaces made by foundries to give the letterpress printer a knowingly unrefined, casual typographic option. In contrast, A. V. Haight's single-colour design (*top left*) is economic but opulent.

The lavish William Cowper book cover (*bottom right*) features an abundance of gold. Such work, common during the late nineteenth century, was the book-printing trade's main contribution to the artistic printing movement.

Opposite Catalogue title page, published by the Flinsch typefoundry, Frankfurt, Germany, reproduced in *The Printers' International Specimen Exchange*, vol. 1, 1880.

Top left Letterhead for an interior decorator, letterpress from an electrotype by A. V. Haight, New York, 1884.

Bottom left Wedding card, W. C. Fabritius & Sønner, Oslo, Norway, 1891.

Top right Courtesy card, letterpress printed by Ellis, Robertson & Company, New Brunswick, Canada, 1886.

Bottom right Casebound cover of *The Poetical Works of William Cowper*, published by George Routledge & Sons, London, date unknown.

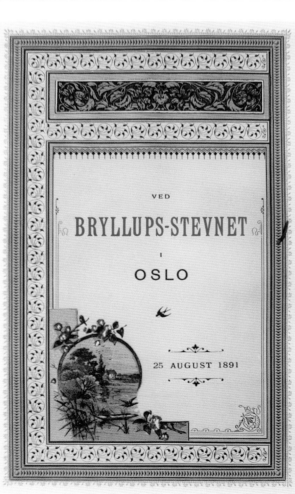

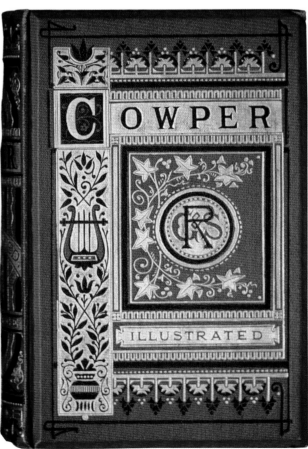

Use of colour in artistic printing
While the sudden explosion in the use of colour by letterpress printers responded to the demand of advertisers and the success of chromolithographic printing, the colour choice might have been influenced by the words of John Ruskin. To quote a lecture he gave in 1858: 'No colour harmony is of high order unless it involves indescribable tints… Even among simple hues the most valuable are those which cannot be defined.'

The similarities between the German-language (*top left*) and American (*right*) advertisements are remarkable since both appeared in the same volume of *The Printers' International Specimen Exchange*. Calkins's use of Relievo Number 2 gives the latter a distinct American appearance. The trade card for Berger & Wirth (*bottom left*) was produced some ten years later and uses a more assertive choice of colours. Ruskin would not have approved.

Top left Advertisement for printer and publisher W. Burkart, Brno, Czech Republic, letterpress printed, *The Printers' International Specimen Exchange*, vol. 1, 1880.

Bottom left Trade card for German ink manufacturer Berger & Wirth, chromolithography, printed by Stiepel Brothers, Liberec, Czech Republic, *c.* 1890.

Right Advertisement for 'general printers' C. W. Calkins & Co., Boston, USA, letterpress printed, *The Printers' International Specimen Exchange*, vol. 1, 1880.

Artistic advertising

By the late 1880s, artistic printing was either maturing, as printers began to concentrate on the message, or filling every last space with extraneous ornament. The example below (*left*) is a carefully constructed arrangement, in which decorative material is non-intrusive and kept clear of the key information. However, the popular spindly new typefaces of this period,

including Alpine (used here and *bottom right*), fail to make an impact and are poorly suited to advertising.

The Swiss company Orell Füssli (*top right*) specialized in security printing of items such as banknotes and sensitive documents. While American printers continued to test the boundaries of good taste, Swiss, German and Austrian printers pulled back, keeping an air of reserve, even in advertising material.

Left Advertisement for Golding's Chromatic Jobber, printed by James P. Burbank, Boston, USA, *c.* 1886,

Top right Advertisement for Orell Füssli printing company, Zurich, Switzerland, 1887.

Bottom right Advertisement for the Photo-Gravure Co., letterpress, Chicago, USA, 1886.

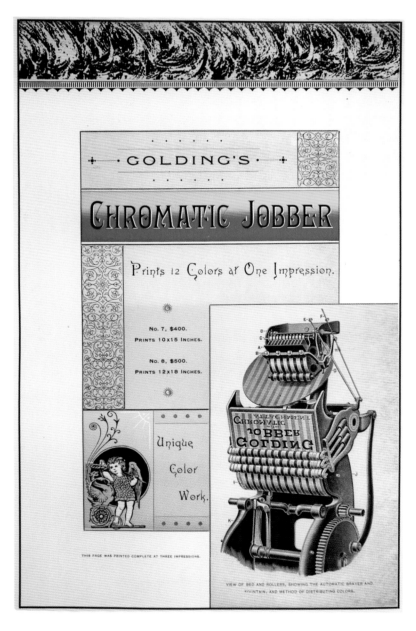

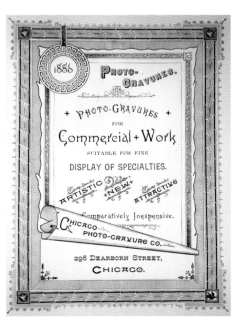

Artistic printing in later trade journals
Typo was a monthly journal first published in 1887 by Robert Coupland Harding in New Zealand. Harding spent his early years working as a compositor, avidly collecting typefounders' specimens and establishing links with the most eminent European and North American printers and founders. It was in *Typo* that his interests in job printing found their fullest expression (*top*), for which he received instant international praise.

The British Printer was designed by George W. Jones in 1888 when he was working for Raithby & Lawrence, UK. This early example (*bottom*) is not typical of the style of work for which he became renowned. It is a blend of the so-called Antique or Old Style made popular by Andrew White Tuer (see page 193) in the use of ragged medieval banners and artistic printing in the choice of typefaces.

Top *Typo*, trade journal, New Zealand, 1887.

Bottom *The British Printer*, trade journal, Leicester, UK, 1888.

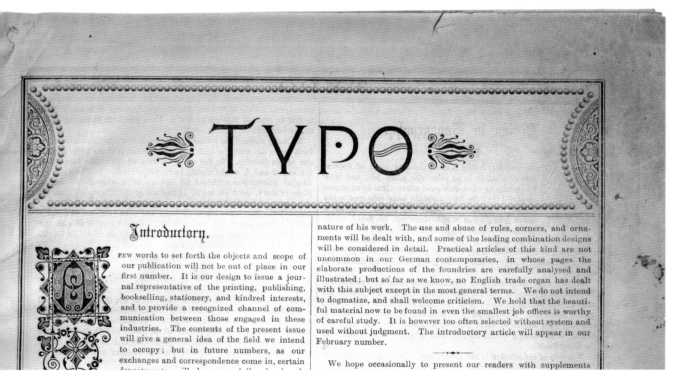

Raithby & Lawrence
This company rose to international prominence due to its close association with *The British Printer* and *The Printers' International Specimen Exchange* when Robert Hilton, then working at Raithby & Lawrence, took over the editorship of the latter from Tuer. Through the efforts of Robert Grayson, who replaced George W. Jones as foreman, the company became renowned for the 'Leicester free style' – or mature artistic printing by another name.

This example (*top*), produced for volume 10 of the *Exchange*, demonstrates the company's willingness to follow American developments, and particularly the work of printer John Franklin Earhart (see page 196).

Top Advertisement for Raithby & Lawrence, *The Printers' International Specimen Exchange*, vol. 10, UK, 1889.

Bottom left Advertisement for Raithby & Lawrence, Leicester, UK, 1880.

Bottom right Advertisement by Raithby & Lawrence, *The Printers' International Specimen Exchange*, vol. 12, UK, 1891.

Gaslight style

The jobbing letterpress printer's introduction of colour and decorative material was an effective response to the lithographic artist. In response, the work of the lithographic studios became ever more detailed and dramatic. The skill with which they described surfaces and forms wrapped around, folded across or interlocking each other was indisputable (*opposite*). Established during the 1870s, this approach to form, space and use of shadow became known as the Gaslight style.

Typical of this style is the booklet cover for the Buckeye Cider Mill (*top right*), featuring a series of undulating panels and scrolls. The design of the small paper change needle packet (*top left*) cleverly incorporates the style into the physical make-up of the envelope. The Robert Crump cover (*bottom left*) is a rather awkward attempt at *trompe l'œil*, the sole point of the coil of paper apparently being the 'C' it creates for 'Crump' or 'colour'. Meanwhile, the label (*bottom right*) is a twentieth-century successor to the Gaslight style.

Opposite Three billheads by Franz Keppler, Aachen, Germany, *The Printers' International Specimen Exchange*, vol. 10, 1889.

Top left Change packet, lithography, printed in a single colour, date unknown.

Bottom left Promotional panel/card, one of a set for the Crump Label Press, lithography, New York, *c.* 1879–82.

Top right Booklet cover for the Buckeye Cider Mill, Springfield, Ohio, lithography, printed by Clay & Richmond, Buffalo, New York, *c.* 1880–86.

Bottom right Label for a box of candles, two-colour lithography, *c.* early twentieth century.

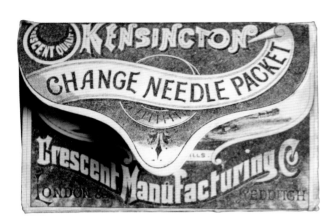

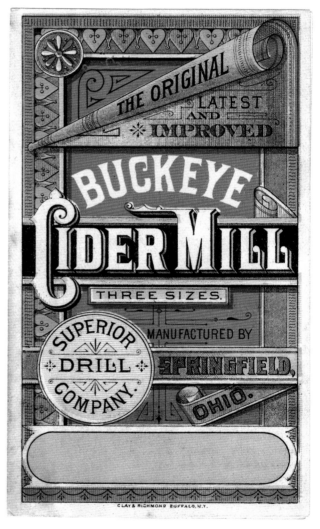

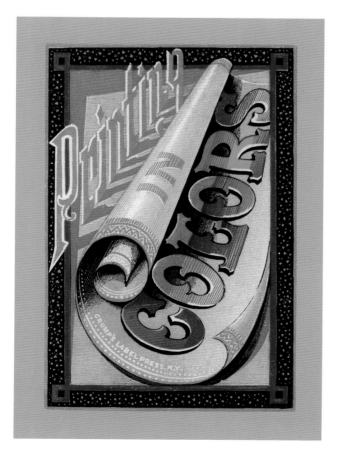

In the cover below (*left*), purples, oranges and greens have been achieved by overprinting, and extra variations created with the use of a ruling machine and additional hand-drawn lines. The intention is to describe the reflective, polished finish of the product.

The lumber advertisement (*bottom right*) was printed by German-born August Hoen. His uncle had been trained by Alois Senefelder, the inventor of lithography, and these links with its early development undoubtedly encouraged Hoen to find ways of improving the process. He explored ways of obtaining gradations of tone through an etching process that he called lithocaustic, using mechanically cut cross-ruled lines through a varnish solution on the stone (see the top left of the handbill). He was later granted patents for a method of producing halftone prints with lithography.

Transport tickets (*top right*) designed in the last quarter of the nineteenth century were often left unchanged for decades, ensuring that remnants of the Gaslight style continued well into the twentieth century.

Left Booklet cover for Seeley Brothers, manufacturers of varnishes. USA, *c.* 1880.

Top right Ticket for city transport systems, Colorado Springs, USA, *c.* 1900s.

Bottom right Handbill and advertisement for timber company Sam Burns & Co., lithography, printed by A. Hoen & Co., Baltimore, USA, *c.* 1880s.

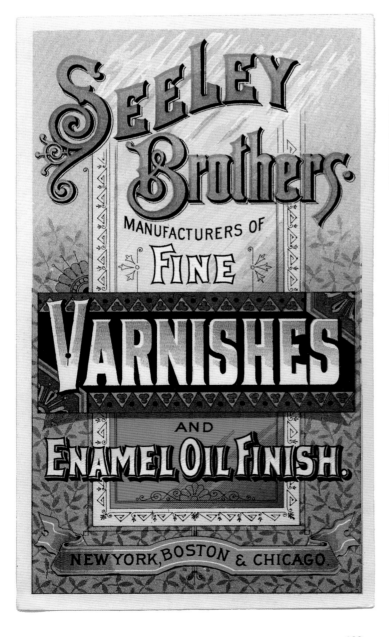

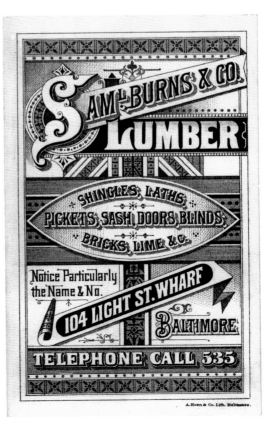

The American firm Mensing & Stecher was started in 1871 but did not arrive at this name until 1875. It specialized in lithographic printing and had a thriving design department handling advertising as well as packaging and showcards. The company became renowned for its colour work, especially the reproduction of fruit and flowers and nurserymen's display signs.

The Gaslight style, with its emphasis on three-dimensional form, lent itself well to the grandiose depiction of a company's factory and encouraged a

brief return of this subject matter (*below*). The back cover of this booklet, however, is far less strident and signals the soft, shallower depth that this style would take during the 1890s (*overleaf*).

Below Cover (front and back) of a booklet for the National Yeast Co., lithography, printed by Mensing & Stecher, New York, *c.* 1878.

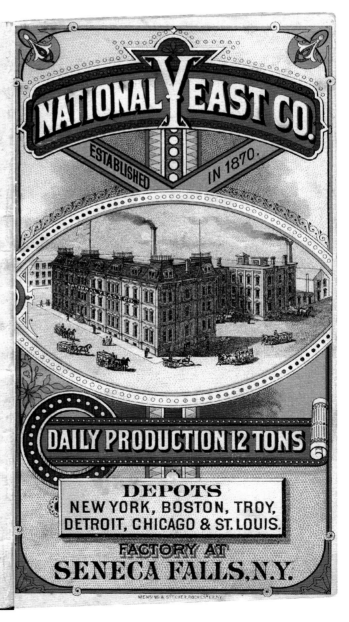

The beginnings of Art Nouveau

The concerns of the Aesthetic movement, which flourished in Britain in the late 1870s and early 1880s, were later absorbed by Art Nouveau. Connecting the two was the potent influence of Japanese art. Japanese motifs had been growing in popularity since the 1860s but reached their zenith around 1885.

The artistic printing movement was keen to embrace such cultural associations, although the reliance of some on foundry-manufactured motifs quickly demonstrated how limited their options were or, more critically, how tentative their true involvement with Aestheticism really was (*below*).

Below Dance card, chromolithography and letterpress, printer unknown, Illinois, USA, 1885.

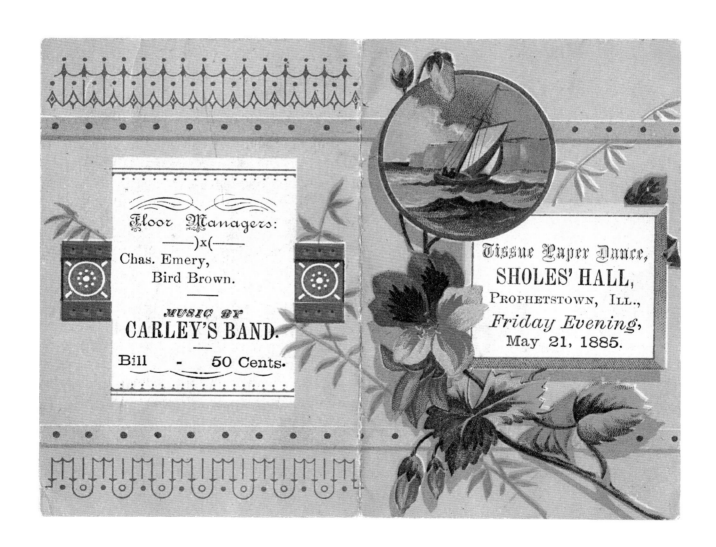

Illustrated advertising envelopes
From the outset, envelopes often bore advertising. Early envelopes were made and sold by printers with their own stationery businesses, so it is not surprising that some featured their name on the envelope (*top*).

Major organizations were quick to realize the potential of the envelope in conveying an appropriate image. The use

of rules on the envelope for the American General Land Office (*centre*) provides a distinctive yet distinguished appearance.

The popular device of linking advertising to major events is demonstrated in the third example (*bottom*). This envelope has a strong patriotic theme and was probably issued during, or shortly before, the Spanish–American War of 1898.

Top Illustrated advertising envelope for G. W. Stacy, printer and stationer, Milford, Massachusetts, USA, *c.* 1870.

Centre Envelope for the General Land Office, USA, *c.* 1880s.

Bottom Illustrated advertising envelope for Seick MFG, St Joseph, Minnesota, USA, *c.* 1898.

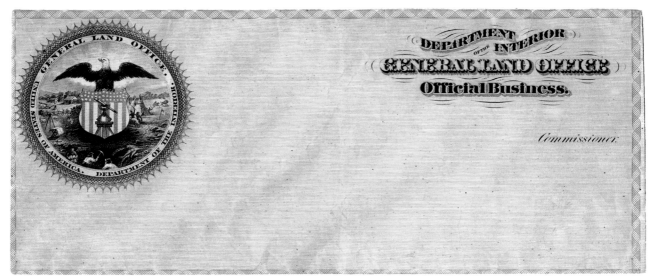

Top left Type specimen, advertising insert, Leadenhall Press (formerly Field & Tuer), London, *c.* 1890s.

Bottom Spread from *Olde Tayles Newlye Relayted*, Andrew White Tuer in collaboration with Joseph Crawhall, letterpress printed with wood engravings by Crawhall, published by Field & Tuer, London, 1883–84.

Top right Cover of *Olde Ffrendes wyth Newe Faces*, letterpress printed with hand-coloured wood engravings by Crawhall, published by Field & Tuer, London, 1884–85.

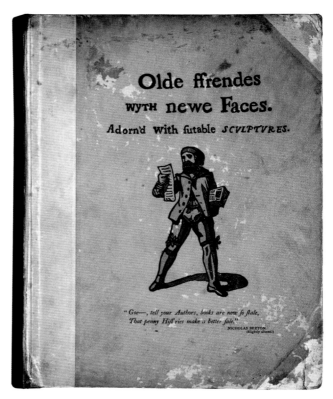

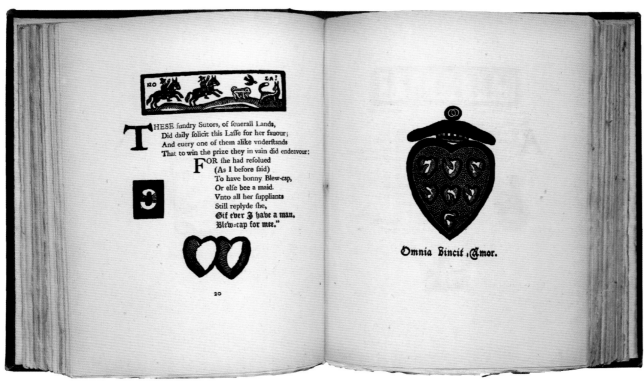

Andrew White Tuer

Tuer was one of the most imaginative printers and publishers of the second half of the nineteenth century. His company took on jobbing work and advertising, but also printed and published a range of items from chapbooks to vellum-bound limited editions. Tuer was also the editor, printer and publisher of *The Paper & Printing Trades Journal*, as well as managing and editing *The Printers' International Specimen Exchange* and contributing to *Punch* magazine.

The two limited-edition books opposite were produced in collaboration with the wood engraver Joseph Crawhall. Crawhall's illustrative style, humour and interest in North Country ballads fitted perfectly with Tuer's antiquarian tastes.

Old London Street Cries provides a record of the calls, songs and other means by which street vendors sold their goods. It is also a portrait of London, including examples of graffiti (*below*) and early Underground railway signage (see page 215) illustrated by artists such as Crawhall and Thomas Rowlandson.

Below Typographic illustration from *Old London Street Cries*, edited and designed by Andrew White Tuer, letterpress printed and published by Field & Tuer, 1885.

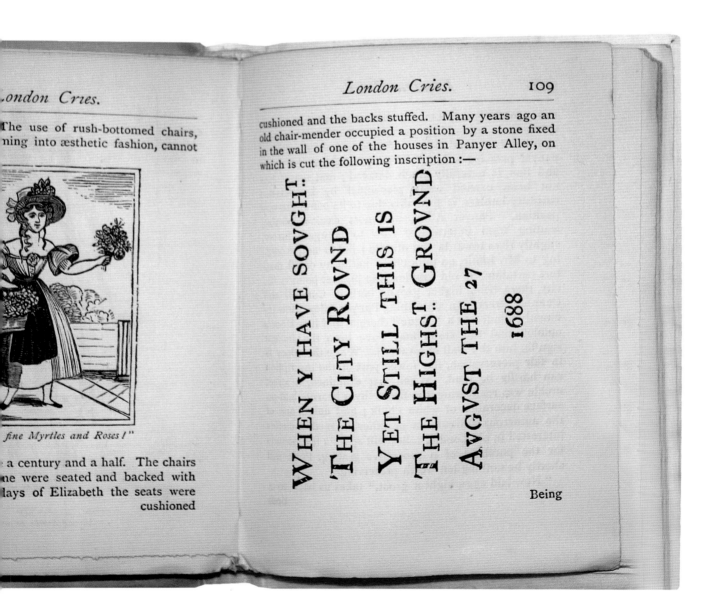

Mementos and greetings cards

During the second half of the nineteenth century, there was a genuine and justifiable concern that essential human values were being lost as a result of industrialization, mass migration to urban environments and factory working conditions. All of this coincided with the development of a regulated postal service, which offered commercial opportunities for printers to develop cards and envelopes carrying religious and/or moral messages. Deriving from

the embossing process, the technique of paper lace-making (*top left*, *bottom left* and *top right*) was commonly used on such items, which were often assembled by mothers and children working from home.

Images of rosy-cheeked children were a nineteenth-century standard. However, in this early Christmas card (*bottom right*) the angelic wings also provide an ominous reminder of the high infant mortality rates during this period.

Top left Souvenir card with paper lace work, chromolithography and white cloth with metallic stars attached, origin unknown.

Bottom left Souvenir card incorporating hinged door and hidden message, embossing, paper lace work and chromolithography, UK, *c.* late nineteenth century.

Top right Paper lace envelope, chromolithography, UK, *c.* late nineteenth century.

Bottom right Christmas greetings card, chromolithography, printed by Tuck & Sons, London, *c.* late nineteenth century.

Novelty advertising
Any form of advertising that might have a secondary use was valued by the advertiser. These bookmarks (*left*), forming a male and female pair, are inventive in design, using elaborately cut dies.

The greetings card (*top right*) has a distinctly Japanese character. The fan and cherry blossom were popular motifs of the Aesthetic movement.

The chromolithographic label (*bottom right*) is an elaborate stock item designed with a space for the buyer to add necessary information. The name of the business has been overprinted in letterpress and finally cut out by hand.

Left Two bookmarks, novelty advertising items for Pears' Soap, chromolithography with die-cutting, *c.* late nineteenth century.

Top right Greetings card, chromolithography with gold embossing and die-cutting, *c.* 1890s.

Bottom right Chromolithographic label, information overprinted in letterpress and cut out by hand, Dijon, France, *c.* 1880s.

John Franklin Earhart
The Color Printer (*centre left and bottom*), which Earhart began in 1885, was the most comprehensive, practical treatise of its kind. In this book he demonstrated the reproduction of over a thousand distinct colour and tint values from twelve stock inks (see page 160).

His chaostype technique, achieved by pouring molten metal onto a cold surface, created a patterned, pitted effect. Depending on the colour choice, it could suggest finished marble, vegetation or otherworldly landscapes (*top right*). The effect is more subtle in Earhart's trade card (*top left*).

Top left Trade card, designed, engraved and letterpress printed by John Franklin Earhart, Columbia, Ohio, USA, 1883.

Centre left and bottom Pages from *The Color Printer: A Treatise on the Use of Colors in Typographic Printing* by John Franklin Earhart, 1892.

Top right Advertisement for chaostype, John Franklin Earhart, New York, 1892.

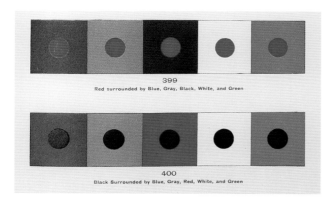

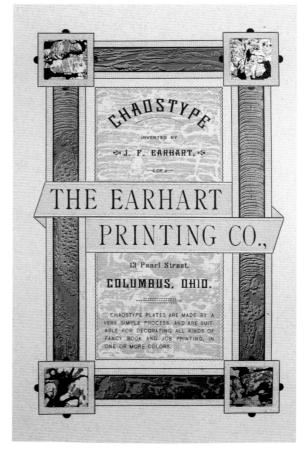

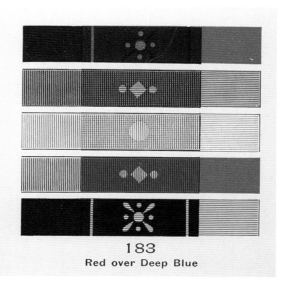

Much of Earhart's book was given over to displaying tints in varying strengths and their resultant combination with other tints. Each was numbered and the results classified (*top*), 'making it easy for the printer to select the best'. This attempt to demonstrate sensory phenomena graphically reflects the growing interest in science and scientific methodology. (Note the names of eminent printers used by Earhart.)

Earhart also provided examples of how these could be applied in practical design solutions. Here (*bottom*), the effects of overprinting using different combinations of three tints are displayed.

Top Detail from *The Color Printer: A Treatise on the Use of Colors in Typographic Printing* by John Franklin Earhart, 1892.

Bottom Map from *The Color Printer: A Treatise on the Use of Colors in Typographic Printing* by John Franklin Earhart, 1892.

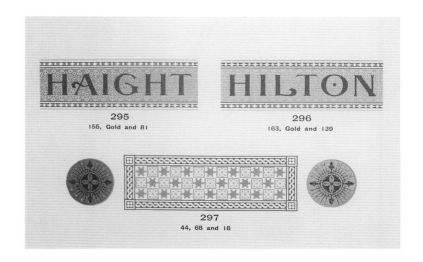

Top Trade card for playing cards, Russell, Morgan & Co., *c.* 1880s.

Bottom Trade card/label, Russell, Morgan & Co., chromolithography with gold, *c.* 1880s.

Russell, Morgan & Co.
The second half of the nineteenth century saw lithographic production become a highly mechanized, low-cost, high-volume process. Lithographic companies became large-scale, highly organized commercial enterprises focusing on mass production of popular prints, labels and a variety of advertising material.

Established in 1867, Russell, Morgan & Co. initially specialized in theatrical and circus posters but was quick to respond to the change in scale and fortune of the lithographic printer. The company's confident, celebratory style and gaudy use of colour were very much the American answer to the softer hues and more subtle tones of their German counterparts. By 1890 they were describing themselves as the largest jobbing printing company in the United States and employing 530 workers. One year later, they went one stage further and changed their name to the United States Printing Company, generally shortened to US Printing Co.

Top left Trade card/label, Russell, Morgan & Co., chromolithography, Cincinnati, Ohio, USA, c. 1880s.

Bottom Letterhead for the United States Printing Company (formerly Russell, Morgan & Co.), chromolithography, Cincinnati, Ohio, USA, 1904.

Right Three trade cards/labels, Russell, Morgan & Co., chromolithography, Cincinnati, Ohio, USA, c. 1880s.

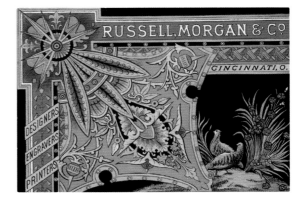

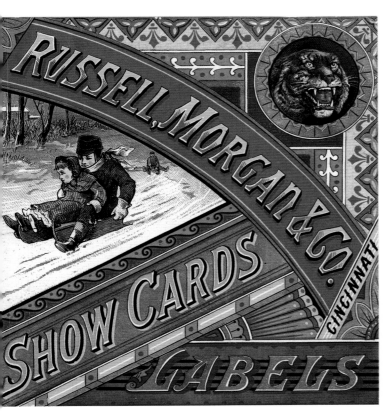

CHAPTER FIVE
THE RISE OF ADVERTISING AND DESIGN

Left Two illustrations from the book *Advertise How? When? Where?* (1863) by William Smith, then acting manager of the Adelphi Theatre, London.

Right A French street. Signs have been painted directly on the wall, while posters can be seen at lower levels, pasted in pairs to maximize impact.

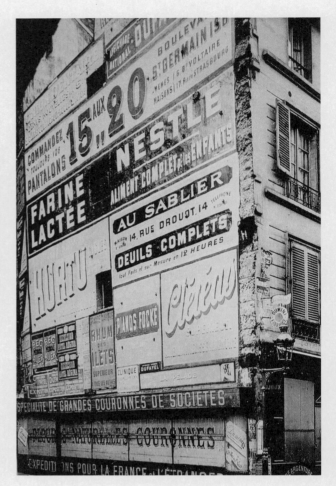

By the 1890s, printing was one of the largest industries in the United States and, through the effectiveness of the advertising material pouring off its presses, was cementing the country's reputation as the 'land of plenty'. While concerns regarding the social, economical and ecological impacts of a fully mechanized print industry continued, print gave visual form to American ambition,[1] accumulating into something akin to a national identity. The J. Walter Thompson Company, in 1909, described America as 'the advertiser's Promised Land, turned into reality'.[2]

Printers such as Prang and others readily acknowledged the importance of advertising revenues and aggressively competed for commissions. The ability of the jobbing printer to respond adequately to the increasingly sophisticated demands of advertising was under scrutiny. Business organizations felt it necessary to remind printers that craftsmanship alone would not suffice: 'The intelligent job printer will never permit himself to forget that printing is allied to advertising, and that almost all of the printing he does depends in some way upon its success as an advertisement or as an advertising medium.'[3] Some advertisers employed people with specific knowledge of print media to take responsibility for print-buying.

From the artistic printer's point of view, pressures to obtain such work were forcing them to cut profit margins, and yet it was also clear that their clients' marketing departments were demanding more. For example, clear visual representations – 'visuals' or 'mock-ups' – of proposed advertising solutions were expected. Such developments were forcing the jobbing printer to think of design as something additional – a service that the compositor or printer had previously not offered. The problem was that visualization required a different mindset and range of skills, as well as

tools and a clean and orderly work space away from the noise of the printing room and the grime of the composing room.

Perhaps it was not only a matter of training, but also of temperament. Edmund G. Gress, editor of *The American Printer*, explained: 'It should be remembered that few typographers have qualifications combining artistic perception and thoro workmanship. It is in a great measure true that a nervous, artistic temperament unfits a typographer for thoro, finished work at the case or stone, while on the contrary, a calm, precise, methodical disposition is often accompanied by lack of imagination. Each workman should have the opportunity to do that which he can do best.'[4]

The idea of setting up a studio dedicated to design – a process previously considered to be intuitive – was something of which artistic printers were wary. And yet the printer, and specifically the compositor, was quite suddenly in danger of having the most prestigious part of the printing process – its origination and intellectual content – taken away. The broad, more liberal, art-school education provided not only the essential skills of drawing, but also the analysis that an increasingly knowledgeable client wanted to hear regarding effective communication. Printers chose not to, or perhaps could not, offer these services from within their own workforce, but nevertheless continued to exclude the art-school-trained designer from the printing office.

Top left *Typographic Advertiser*, March 1864, USA. The rather delicate, effete masthead design was a brave choice for this influential trade journal.

Top right Detail of a receipt of payment for space bought in the *Kentish Gazette*, pre-1850.

Bottom A handbill by L. Hathaway, Boston, USA, displaying readymade styles of acquaintance cards.

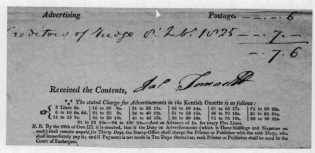

In the early 1890s, it was still uncertain which of several professions would come to dominate the creative processes of advertising and printed promotion. The sophistication, regularity and inherent design controls required by newspapers and magazines were proving a strong attraction for the advertiser. By this time most periodical publications had their own advertising departments whose responsibility it was to liaise with the marketing departments of advertisers or, increasingly, the advertising agency working on their behalf.

The power of advertising agencies increased substantially as they also took responsibility for print-buying and, almost by default, became marketing strategists. Agencies then began setting up their own art departments, initially to enable them to respond on their clients' behalf to small but essential variations in advertising material appearing in different parts of the country. But as co-ordinated, strategic advertising campaigns began to be recognized as a necessity, these quickly became the responsibility of the 'creative department', with those working in them called 'creatives'.

The ability of the advertising agency to control every aspect of a client's advertising matter was isolating the artistic printer, leaving him to pick up the smaller, less sophisticated requirements of local businesses that could not, as yet, afford the services of the agency. The pace of change in printed communication driven largely by the advertising agencies, together with the printing fraternity's protracted system of skill-based, rule-bound training, left even the ambitious printer incapable of responding appropriately. The increasing sophistication of machinery, the financial investment required and the ferocious reputation of the print unions ensured that printing itself remained the mysterious 'black art', but printers were losing control of what they

printed by failing to embrace the processes of design into their training regime.

The creative, working within the advertising agency, and the typographer or commercial artist, working independently, became the printer's clients. With these competitors given the authority of their clients to tell the printer to do precisely as he was told, there followed a painful period of transition as the printing industry readjusted to a radically reduced function within the communications industry.

Right Cover of *Wren's City Churches*, designed by Arthur H. Mackmurdo, UK, 1883. This is one of the earliest manifestations of Art Nouveau, produced at a time when artistic printing was at its height. Mackmurdo was a passionate devotee of the Arts and Crafts, and a close friend of Ruskin and Morris, which makes this design all the more remarkable.

Far right Frontispiece and title page of *Microscopic Fungi* by M. C. Cooke, with illustrations by J. E. Sowerby, London, 1898. The Arts and Crafts movement came under pressure not only from the youthful exuberance of Art Nouveau, but also from an overwhelming fascination with the cool, calculating and very modern objectivity of science.

From Arts and Crafts to Art Nouveau

The Arts and Crafts movement grew out of the writings of Ruskin and was embodied in the furniture, fabric and wallpaper printing, and stained glass work of Morris & Company, which gained an international reputation during the 1870s. The earliest manifestations of Art Nouveau came a decade later with designs by English-born Arthur Heygate Mackmurdo (1851–1942), a passionate devotee of the Arts and Crafts. Both movements sprang from the all-encompassing Aesthetic movement – which focused on fine art and literature, and strove to 'aestheticize' the environment in response to what it saw as the declining standards in contemporary taste – coming to a highly influential fruition in the 1890s.

At its height in the 1880s, the artistic printing movement fitted comfortably under the Aesthetic banner, although its devotees aligned the movement specifically to Ruskin and the Arts and Crafts. It is significant that Art Nouveau and artistic printing shared a common interest in the Japanese artefacts imported into Europe and the United States from the 1850s. Commercial imperatives, along with a penchant for irreverent decoration, also suggest that the artistic printer was an early manifestation of the Art Nouveau movement.

The work of the Arts and Crafts, on the other hand, was essentially Gothic in nature, with a sturdy, heavy sense of structure that exuded rugged usefulness and celebrated the weight and permanence of the material from which it was made. The Arts and Crafts movement had a crusading fervour, believing (as did Art Nouveau) that good design could change the world, and (unlike Art Nouveau) made its serious intent manifest by what was intended to be unaffected design, honest use of materials, and the essential, robust functionalism of the objects made. This, however, did not preclude the use of decorative elements.

Another characteristic differentiating Arts and Crafts from Art Nouveau is that those associated with the latter accepted and assimilated influences from everywhere. Art Nouveau incorporated and celebrated affectation, reserving the right to include or reject style references for no particular reason. It generally masked its socio-political stance behind a façade of colour, pattern and sensual forms, and enthusiastically utilized popular media, such as magazines and posters, to promote its message. It quite consciously dropped Ruskin's moralizing tone, unashamedly aiming to capture the widest possible audience. Art Nouveau and Arts and Crafts certainly blossomed through a shared passion for Ruskin's ideals and, as such, had a strong anti-establishmentarianism about them, but while Art Nouveau was youthful, playful and eclectic, Arts and Crafts remained bombastic and studiously self-important.

William Morris (1834–96) was a founder and leading practitioner of the Arts and Crafts movement and, like so many of his contemporaries, was swept along by the Victorian enthusiasm for historical revivals. Yet the power of Morris's socio-political ideas – so closely aligned to his aesthetic concerns – made him a highly influential figure in the final decades of the nineteenth century. In cities throughout Europe and America, Arts and Crafts Societies became a refuge from the industrialized world and remained significant until the onset of the First World War in 1914.

Morris had trained as an architect but found the routine of office work dull. Critically, he had an income from his family estate sufficient to enable him to do anything that took his interest. He attempted to become a painter, working with his friend Edward Burne-Jones, and both fell under the influence of Dante Gabriel Rossetti. It was during the building of the Red House in Bexleyheath, UK, for which he

Left Bookplate by Frederic Leighton. During the second half of the nineteenth century, the distinction between illustration and fine art remained fluid and many important artists took commissions from publishers. It was also the norm that an engraver would be employed (usually anonymously) to interpret the artist's drawing.

Top right Double-page spread from *Ornamental Decoration*, compiled by F. Scott Mitchell, published by Thomas Parsons & Sons, London, 1909. The number of publications concerned with the application of advertising, illustration and design grew as retail businesses and manufacturing increased. Here, a range of generic design elements are provided for the designer of print and signs.

Bottom right Art Nouveau wood ornaments designed by Luigi Melchiori, Italy, *c.* 1900.

commissioned the architect Philip Webb, and the subsequent search for quality furniture with which to fill it, that Morris began to formulate what would be his vocation. In 1861, he and six friends established the decorative arts firm Morris, Marshall, Faulkner & Company.

Morris proved to be a brilliant pattern designer, creating hundreds of designs for fabrics, carpets, tapestries, stained glass and wallpaper, and hundreds more were produced under his direction. In 1875 the business was reorganized and renamed Morris & Company. Through the success of this company's products, the ideas of the Arts and Crafts movement were well known throughout Europe and the United States by 1880, some eleven years before Morris printed his first Kelmscott Press book.

Morris was driven to set up the Kelmscott Press by what he considered the poor quality of printing, and no effort was spared in his endeavour to rediscover the original means of producing type, paper and ink and re-establish the printing of books as fine as anything in the past.[5] He worked to please himself and took as much time to produce his books as was necessary to achieve his aims. The beauty of his first Kelmscott book, *The Story of the Glittering Plain* (1891) – as with all his books – depends in great measure on the interaction between sharp, well-inked, deep black type and blocks, and strong, textured paper. The impact was immediate and international. By the mid-1890s, the general opinion was that the Kelmscott Press, and in particular its edition of *The Works of Geoffrey Chaucer* – completed just weeks before Morris's death in 1896 – represented the best example of printing since Johann Gutenberg.

While there was a great deal of sympathy for Ruskin's and Morris's ideas in printing trade journals, their rejection of machine production was largely ignored. For those who had

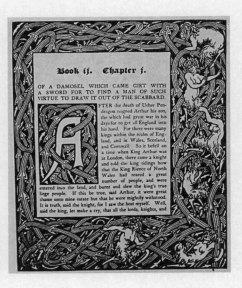

Far left Illustration by Aubrey Beardsley, from *The Savoy*, London, 1896 (cover opposite).

Left Aubrey Beardsley's irreverent version of Sir Thomas Malory's *Morte d'Arthur*, 1893.

spent their working lives in the often brutal conditions of earlier printing workshops, rejection of the power-press was ridiculous. Instead, Morris's attraction for the printing community lay in the promise he held to revive the status of craft and craftsmanship, with the intention of improving standards of printing and, with that, reinstating pride. Commercial printers across the spectrum of the industry were being forced to face the challenge of assimilating new technologies with fine design and traditional craft values. The application of art to industry became a conspicuous theme in printing trade journals, and the results of Morris's explorations of print were much anticipated.

During the 1890s, Morris's books had a huge influence on the appearance of printed matter of every kind. However, the general public would have been most aware of Arts and Crafts ideology through the many home and lifestyle magazines that suddenly came out during this decade, ironically due to more efficient printing and paper-making technologies. Although the editorial content might espouse Arts and Crafts ideals, their compositors mixed visual references with abandon. Liberties were taken, and done so knowingly. The results were what we now call Art Nouveau.

The ideological gulf between the Arts and Crafts movement and Art Nouveau, despite their being intrinsically connected stylistically, can be measured by Morris's furious reaction to Aubrey Beardsley's work for a new edition of Malory's *Morte d'Arthur* in 1893. Beardsley (1872–98) became the *enfant terrible* of Art Nouveau, making an immediate impact with his vibrant, linear, shockingly 'exotic' illustrations. His illustrative design for this book was clearly based on Morris's *Recuyell of the Historyes of Troye*, published the previous year. What incensed Morris was that, to his mind, Beardsley had not just plagiarized but vulgarized the

Kelmscott Press style, with a 'Japanese-like spirit of devilry and the grotesque'.[6] Morris's rational structure of tightly knit, rhythmic bouquets had been replaced by a bolder, chaotic briar border, resplendent with provocatively posing nymphs. The grotesque satirical aspect is impossible to ignore, and all the more poignant because Morris was at his authoritative zenith.

Beardsley's irreverent *Morte d'Arthur* was a popular success and numerous commissions followed, including Oscar Wilde's *Salomé* (1894) and even the editorship of the journal *The Yellow Book* (which he held for just four issues). He represented everything new, youthful and outrageous. Beardsley's achievements, along with his ambivalent attitude to authoritative figures, mark the establishment of Art Nouveau as a separate entity from Arts and Crafts, based on broadly similar principles, but utterly dismissive – even mocking – of Ruskin's and Morris's specific historic references and their perceived sense of self-importance. Later that year, German-born entrepreneur Siegfried Bing opened his gallery in Paris and called it L'Art Nouveau, providing the movement with its most enduring and widely used name.

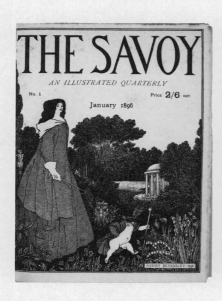

Art, design and the cultural magazine

Cultural journals, generally containing a mixture of satire, politics and social comment, had emerged in France, Germany, Italy, England, Russia and the United States by the mid-nineteenth century. However, it was in France that the earliest and most obstreperous publications, *Le Charivari* and *La Caricature*, were produced. In appearance, these were more akin to newspapers than magazines: tabloid-size, pictorial editions with acidic black-and-white illustrations of *comédie humaine* by, among others, Honoré Daumier, J. J. Grandville and Gustave Doré. The front covers of these French publications featured topical illustrations and a bold masthead, while the text inside was tightly set adjacent to large, often full-page illustrations.

In Britain, the introduction of *The Graphic* in 1869 challenged the strong position of *The Illustrated London News*. The large format of *The Graphic*, but especially its excellent printing on good quality paper, served its illustrators and advertisers well and ensured its dominance in the field. The reputation of its illustrators, such as Randolph Caldecott and Paul Renouard, was renowned, and they were paid accordingly.[7]

During the 1880s, *The Graphic* carried many sequential-style illustrated stories and anecdotes, sometimes in full colour. This was a device that *The Strand Magazine* successfully developed. Set up in January 1891, and edited by George Newnes, this monthly publication took over the prime position among the popular magazines by attracting writers such as Arthur Conan Doyle, as well as featuring lively use of illustration and, a little later, photography.

Full-page advertisements had begun to appear in *The Graphic* and elsewhere, and this trend was increasing. These advertisements were sometimes lavish productions, designed to hold attention and exude integrity. A sense of propriety was essential, and the more outlandish the claim for the product, the greater the degree of propriety required. References to subjects such as religion, cultural icons and even royalty (almost always spurious) would be made with remarkable assuredness.

Literature concerning art and design also became a subject of popular interest at this time, including the political and moral objectives of its practitioners. Writers, designers and printers collaborated not only to document cultural issues, but also to explain them in the context of everyday life.[8] Many influential publications emerged in support of Art Nouveau during this period, including the German magazines *Pan* (1895) and *Jugend* (1896), and the British magazines *Dial* (1889), *The Studio* (1893), *The Yellow Book* (1894–95) and *The Savoy* (1896–98), which also took the movement's aims and visual style very effectively to the United States and influenced American designers and illustrators such as William H. Bradley, Margaret Armstrong and John Sloan. French Art Nouveau, meanwhile, was promoted largely through poster design.

The most important magazine was the Century Guild's *Hobby Horse* (1884–94), the first finely printed publication devoted exclusively to the visual arts. Produced with painstaking care under the direction of Emery Walker, this quarterly magazine sought to proclaim the philosophy and goals of the Century Guild, which mirrored those of the Arts and Crafts movement, and its influence carried these to an international audience. It was also one of the first arts magazines to treat printing as a serious subject in its own right. Walker was master printer at the renowned Chiswick Press and Mackmurdo, the editor of the magazine, later suggested that Morris's interest in printing had been ignited

Left Personal emblem for the London publisher William Heinemann, designed by artist and illustrator William Nicholson, wood engraving, *c.* 1890s.

Centre Cover of the book *Ornamental Decoration,* compiled by F. Scott Mitchell, published by Thomas Parsons & Sons, containing sample solutions for commercial artists and sign-writers.

Right Illustration by Ronald Anderson supporting an article in *Art Printer* reminding the printer that his professional status relied on him broadening his responsibility to his clients, Cambridge, Massachusetts, USA, 1913. Images such as this, depicting the printer in an office, wearing a suit and discussing potential solutions with a client, were intended to present printing as a profession – akin to advertising – rather than a trade.

by Walker's design of *Hobby Horse.*[9] It was certainly after attending a lecture on type design given by Walker that Morris decided to set up his own press. Walker was invited to be a partner but declined and agreed instead to act as advisor.

In the United States, several journals introduced the public to the work of the Aesthetic movement. *The Crayon: A Journal Devoted to the Graphic Arts* (New York, 1855–61) was one of the earliest and has the distinction of having contributions by Ruskin. Many others followed, but *Art Age* (New York, 1883–89) is of particular interest in regard to the emergence of graphic design. Its co-publisher and editor, Arthur B. Turnure, was a great admirer of the Arts and Crafts movement and recognized that its moral and technical interests were shared by the artistic printers. Indeed, he devoted the first issue of *Art Age* exclusively to artistic printing, making it arguably the earliest example of what today might be called a graphic design journal.

The fall of artistic printing

During the 1880s, the jobbing printer successfully established a large, growing and potentially lucrative area of activity. The best and most ambitious printers were also growing in sophistication and technical expertise. Some printing companies were becoming more than printers; they were advising clients about design, copy-writing, illustration and even marketing. In other words, they were providing an increasingly consultative service. The compositor's craft in particular had been revolutionized by the nature and demands of jobbing work. The printing office revolved around him, his work was individually credited and wages reflected his newfound status.

However, voices critical of artistic printing within the printing fraternity had never entirely died away. The dislocations and redefinitions that took place within the industry between 1875 and 1900 caused concern for many, and consternation, even despair, for others. During the final decade of the nineteenth century, as the dominant position of the compositor began to be eroded by growing competition – the result of rapid technological developments in typesetting, the irrepressible rise of the art-school-educated commercial artist, and the growing influence of the advertising agency for what had previously been the printer's clients – the ability and very purpose of the artistic printer were being called into question.

The impact of Morris's Kelmscott Press was instrumental in this regard. The combination of moral argument, immaculate craftsmanship and critical success cast a long shadow over every aspect of the printing industry in England and further afield, causing it to reflect not only on its technical standards, but also its function – with artistic printing, by now a distinct activity positioned at the forefront of commercial enterprise and entrepreneurship, particularly vulnerable to criticism.

There grew a significant market for 'art' book and magazine publishing supporting the ideals, broad historic associations and moral aspirations of the 'Kelmscott style'. Nowhere was this more evident than in the United States, and there, no one was more vocal, or more persuasive, than Theodore Low De Vinne (1828–1914). De Vinne had begun his career as a journeyman compositor under Francis Hart, one of the leading jobbing printers in New York City, rising very quickly to foreman. In 1858 he became a partner and, when Hart died in 1877, he gained ownership of the company, changing its name to Theodore L. De Vinne & Company. With De Vinne's nurturing, the company grew to become a book-printing house of grand proportions – its reputation sealed when it was commissioned to print the journal Century. The prominence of his printing business in an era when print was the medium of choice made De Vinne a household name in the United States.

In 1887 De Vinne became the president of the United Typothetae of America, a New York-based association of master printers whose primary interest was in sharing business issues, new technologies and the promotion of practical ideas. At the sixth annual convention, in 1892, he presented a paper titled 'Masculine Printing', in which he discussed the attributes of Morris's printing, comparing these to the industry standards, and argued for a return to traditional values of craftsmanship, describing the current 'promiscuous overload of useless ornament' as being not only bad aesthetically, but also – and this is where his emphasis lay – bad for business. This was an argument he had made previously, in 1883, reminding his own company's compositors that 'the business of the house is done for profit … the office cannot allow one-quarter of a day for the composition of a card for which it receives but fifty cents'.[10] Like so many others at that time,

De Vinne applied the moral weight of Arts and Crafts to his own, sometimes quite contrary concerns.

In De Vinne's view, contemporary printing was suffering from a malaise, the symptoms being a 'feebleness' that he characterized as 'feminine': the lack of rationality in the composition of type and image on the page; decorative patterns from ornaments that defied traditional construction or reason; the use of colours, often in pastel shades; a cultivation of complex, fine-line intricacy and fancy types. The strong, heavy pages of Morris's Kelmscott Press were, De Vinne suggested, the antidote – the essence of 'masculine printing'. He urged his fellow printers to rouse themselves from their 'aesthetic beguilement', to forsake notions of self-consequence and return to typography that was 'noticeable for its readability, for its strength, and absence of useless ornament', arguing that good printing must be a response to the needs of the reader, not the compositor. This call for a simpler, more direct means of communication would resonate throughout the print industry and make De Vinne a (rather dubious) cultural marker for the modernists some twenty years later.[11]

While such criticism was aimed primarily at the publishing fraternity, it also had a sobering effect on the jobbing printer. The idea that the jobbing printer had lost touch with

Left William Morris, *The Story of the Glittering Plain*, 1891. This much anticipated book was the first to be printed by the Kelmscott Press, which Morris set up after becoming frustrated by the poor standards of commercial book printing. The Kelmscott Press brought into question not only technical but also moral issues, especially for the jobbing printer, who was suddenly under critical scrutiny for his collaboration with mass production.

traditional standards of good work was a stylistic and, importantly, a moral criticism. What the artistic printer undeniably did, on a daily basis, was to help sell products and services, many of which, in Morris's view, were petty, unnecessary and even morally detrimental to society. The world of the Kelmscott Press was a very different one from that of the commercial artistic printer's office, even for those who, regardless of purpose, were passionately committed to the highest possible standards of craftsmanship.

The arrival of Morris's books, with their fierce severity of purpose and contempt for all things contemporary, was, at the very least, disconcerting, and probably shocking to most of those artistic printers who admired Ruskin and advocated Arts and Crafts ideals – men such as Andrew White Tuer, Thomas Hailing and George W. Jones. Jones explained the sensation of seeing his first Kelmscott book thus: 'Many of us, even those who had for many years been more or less single-mindedly giving time and strength to the advancement of our calling, will never forget the day when the first of Morris's books was placed in our hands. For myself I realised how little I knew, how great a fool I was, and how much I had to learn even after so many years of serious work.'[12]

In the twentieth century, and particularly following the First World War, there emerged an overwhelming sense of shame within the printing fraternity for the work of the artistic printers, even among those who, at the time, had been committed to its aims. An anonymous apologia[13] appeared in *The Linotype Record* of August 1922: '[Artistic printing was] usually a conglomeration of typefaces, many of them crude in design, incongruous in association, and so bewildering in effect as almost to defeat their object.' If anything, the sense of regret was greatest in the United States.

Samuel E. Lesser wrote in 1929: 'Despite all the ingenuity exercised, it must be admitted that Artistic Printing was all "love's labour's lost" in so far as lasting worth was concerned... If this be an American contribution to typography, none can be found today to be proud of it as such.'[14]

Self-flagellation of this kind is understandable when set within the context of a post-war new order in which universal support was afforded to modernism. Clearly the most effective way to demonstrate allegiance with the new wave of science and progress was to turn against historic precedent, and especially everything associated with the flamboyance of the Aesthetic movement.

Left An illustration from Andrew White Tuer's *Quads Within Quads, c.* 1884.

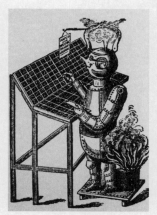

Right Monotype keyboarding room, *The Times* newspaper, London, date unknown. While presses were becoming increasingly automated, typesetting continued to be done by hand. It was a comparatively slow process and could only be speeded up by employing more compositors. Many attempts to mechanize the process had been made during the nineteenth century (satirized, left), but it was not until the 1880s that a successful and commercially viable typesetting machine was devised: one of these was Linotype, invented by Ottmar Mergenthaler; the other was Monotype, introduced by Tolbert Lanston.

The mechanization of type composition

Throughout the nineteenth century, attempts were being made to mechanize typesetting operations. The first patent for a composing machine was registered in 1825. Early versions used a keyboard arrangement connected to existing, foundry-cast metal type that had been pre-loaded into the machine. Then, at the press of a key, the type characters dropped from their storage-channels into position as required. *The Times* newspaper in London had one of the more successful machines of this kind: a Kastenbein, installed in 1872.

In the 1880s, Ottmar Mergenthaler and Tolbert Lanston both devised composing machines – two very different solutions, but both incorporating the production of type from matrices (brass character moulds) within the machine. Both systems were developed in the United States and relied on the molten type-metal turning solid within a second or so of casting.

The Linotype came first in 1886. Mergenthaler (1854–99) was a German immigrant working as a mechanic in Baltimore. His typecasting machine cast a 'line-o-type' as one solid piece (called a 'slug'). When the operator had keyed in a line of text, the machine released the corresponding brass matrices, which dropped into position in the correct order along with the required word spaces. Once a complete line of matrices was in place, it was justified by the use of inter-word wedges and then set in molten metal as one piece. After the slug had been made, the brass matrices and space wedges were returned to their channels ready to be reused. A Linotype caster was first installed by the *New York Tribune* in 1886, and by the turn of the century Linotypes had replaced handsetting in virtually every newspaper office in the United States and many parts of Europe.

The Monotype was introduced by Lanston (1844–1913) in 1889. The Monotype machine controlled the typesetting by means of a series of 'valve-holes' punched into a reel of paper tape. The perforations were created as a result of the keyboard operator typing, or keying in, the copy. The Monotype keyboard (unlike Linotype) adopted the Universal arrangement already established on typewriters such as the American Remington model of 1874. Another important difference was that with Monotype, the keying-in was done quite separately from the casting. The perforated paper reel would be taken from the composing room to the casting room and fed into the caster, which read the perforations as characters and spaces and, using matrices, cast these from molten metal and dropped them into position as individual characters in lines. This made corrections or fine adjustments easy because individual characters or spaces could be substituted by hand, an activity that also maintained a comforting link with craft-associated skills of the past. With Linotype, the whole line, or slug, containing the mistake would need to be reset on the machine. Both Linotype and Monotype allowed the type, after use, to be melted down and reused.

Initially, both the Lanston Monotype Corporation and the Linotype Company provided 'types similar in appearance to ordinary types and of commercial character'.[15] They viewed these typefaces as little more than fodder for the caster. Little pretence was made to originality, and type patents taken out by foundries in an attempt to protect their designs proved hopelessly inadequate. Among the early typefaces offered by Monotype was Modern, a style of typeface similar in appearance to Bodoni's types, copies of which had remained the standard choice for all kinds of printing during the nineteenth century.[16] Once Monotype

Left Monotype 'hot metal' casting room, *The Times* newspaper, London, date unknown. The effect of Monotype and Linotype technology on typefoundries was initially catastrophic. However, the increased speed and efficiency of the process caused a significant growth in the print market and many of those made redundant were able to rejoin the industry and, in fact, embraced the new technology.

Bottom A Pantograph, FTC Fonderia Tipografica Cooperativa, Peschiera Borromeo, Milan, Italy, date unknown. By 1885, the American Linn Boyd Benton had improved the pantograph, an instrument for copying a drawing at a different scale based on a system of pivoted levers, for use in type design. Here, the operator follows the outline of an uppercase pattern held in place by magnets.

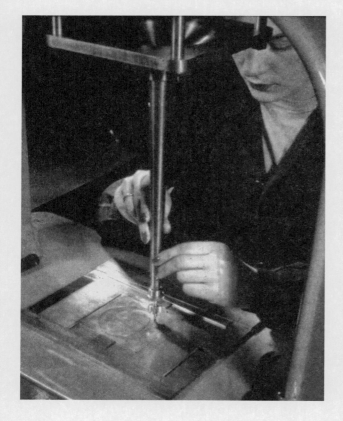

(returning used type to its case) was obviated because the used type was simply recycled via the 'hellbox' and melted down. Type, therefore, was created anew for every job, giving the printer clean, crisp letterforms for each task.

Type composition machines quickly and negatively affected the individual typefoundries. Uniform price scales were broken as smaller, individual foundries attempted to stave off bankruptcy, but the resulting price wars drove many to ruin anyway. Amalgamations were a logical alternative and, in 1892, the American Type Founders Association (ATF) was set up, which included large companies in Boston, New York, Philadelphia, Cincinnati, St Louis and Chicago, along with twelve smaller companies.

In the newspaper-printing industry and book-printing houses, the effect of the mechanization of typesetting on hand-compositors was initially devastating. Mergenthaler's Linotype machine could do the work of seven or eight men. Its rapid deployment replaced thousands of highly skilled hand-typesetters, resulting in strikes and violence at many new typecasting installations. However, this new technology also caused an unprecedented explosion of graphic material by reducing the cost of newspapers, magazines and books, which, over time, created thousands of new jobs. As a result, many hand-compositors were able to retrain as keyboard operators.

Great effort went into establishing the status of machine compositors as a 'step up' from the hand-compositor. It was emphasized that they needed to be better educated and trained in order to deal with the mathematical and technical aspects of what was a complicated system. Operators were offered prize scholarships to attend training, called 'postgraduate' courses, where they were offered gold medals for attaining set standards.

and Linotype realized that the range and quality of typefaces available with their machines were factors in the printer's decision concerning which system to buy, both embarked on a programme of research, development and design of fonts, historic and contemporary in origin, to match the commercial needs of the printer.

For the larger printing office, the advantages of mechanized typesetting were considerable. The machines increased the output of the retrained compositor (now a keyboarder) significantly, and the time-consuming task of dissing

Left A wood engraving in the chapbook style, from *Old London Street Cries*, edited by Andrew White Tuer, Field & Tuer, London, 1885.

Right The American illustrator William H. Bradley was an important influence in the introduction of European styles to the United States. The image on the right is his copy of a late nineteenth-century woodcut by Joseph Crawhall, who in turn was influenced by earlier chapbook illustrations.

The Monotype Users' Association was formed in the UK as a means of exchanging technical information, while in the USA, the International Typographical Union (ITU) set up schools to train their members in mechanical composition. In this way, both Linotype and Monotype successfully gained the support of machine compositors by creating 'an elite of workers within the trade'.[17] In the case of Monotype, the system separated the compositor, or keyboarder, from any physical contact with metal type. His was now a clean job, allowing him to wear smart clothes, which added considerable prestige to the role. The result, almost uniquely, was that pride in craftsmanship for the compositor did not end with the introduction of mechanization.

Meanwhile, for the jobbing compositor, little changed. When smaller amounts of text were required, it remained far easier, quicker and cheaper to do this in-house by hand. The jobbing printer was more likely to be asked to provide price lists, timetables, catalogues, handbills and the like, all requiring complex practical judgments using blocks, rules and textual matter. The necessity of drawing up a detailed type specification, from which a keyboard operator working for a different company might provide the required setting, did not make economic sense. For these reasons, hand-composition would remain an essential skill and continue to function in the expanding jobbing market of the print industry well into the twentieth century.

The commercial artist and the poster

Photography, and the mechanically produced halftone block by which it was printed, had significantly reduced the demand for engraving by the end of the nineteenth century. Those still employed found they were now cutting through a photographic image printed directly onto the surface into the wood block. This activity, though still highly skilled, required little imagination.

For anyone newly entering the field of illustration, there was no definable career path. Most had attended art schools or colleges and, doubtless, aspired to become artists. Working for the commercial printing, publishing or advertising sectors was generally perceived as a temporary means of earning money to subsidize their true vocation. Anyone who continued to do this, therefore, was just as likely to be called a failed artist as a commercial artist.

The status of commercial artists was not helped by the attitude of many of those from whom they sought commissions. *The British Printer*, for example, in 1893, made a distinction between 'artists and illustrators, Art and art', describing those involved in commercial art as the 'small fry' of the art world, for whom the disappointment of having to seek commercial work was tempered by 'the comparative [higher] remuneration … than in painting unsold canvases'.[18] Such derogatory attitudes were common within the printing industry, and commissioning art editors within magazine publishing houses and the art directors employed by advertising agencies, renowned for being rudely dismissive of moral or aesthetic ideals, were often little better.[19]

The status of the commercial artist during this period can be gauged by the approach taken by the respected academic painters James Pryde and William Nicholson. When these brothers-in-law decided to collaborate on the design of

posters (between 1894 and 1899), they created a pseudo-name for themselves, Beggarstaff Brothers, in order to keep their academic fine art reputations intact.

During the 1890s, the growth in the number of magazines and illustrated books being published, as well as advertising agencies, at least provided the possibility of employment as an illustrator, although it would always lack any form of personal, financial security. There appears to have been a readily understood hierarchy of work among commercial artists, the highest value being attached to book illustration, followed by magazine illustration and, lastly, advertising. This was not a reflection of financial remuneration, in fact quite the reverse, but one of cultural status. It was also linked to working practice. The longer gestation period required in book production meant that illustrators not only had time to ruminate and discuss ideas, but also generally received a more considered, more reasoned editorial response than in magazine work where the turnaround had to be rapid.

There were, however, exceptions. The American publishing company Harper & Brothers of New York was able to attract the best illustrators of the day to work on its magazines. Despite the remarkable speed with which images had to be created and cut, Harper's had a reputation for encouraging and mentoring illustrators. In 1863 Charles Parsons was given the job of overseeing the illustrative content of the company's output and became the archetypal art editor, much admired for his ability to discover and nurture young talent such as Edwin Austin Abbey, Charles Dana Gibson and Howard Pyle.

This new generation of American illustrators was generally art-school-trained and, following the example of Pyle, established what became known as the golden age of American illustration, from 1890 to 1920. Britain's golden period for illustrative work was during the second half of the nineteenth century, although this focused on book illustration. Randolph Caldecott, Walter Crane and Charles Ricketts were leaders and, significantly, at a time when cultural differences were still acutely important, considered themselves professional illustrators rather than artists condescending to allow their drawings to be reproduced. Rich in narrative character and detail, such work did not, however, transfer to the larger scale required of poster work, where a simpler, more immediate impact was required.

The large-scale poster had been in existence for much of the nineteenth century in various guises, promoting theatres, circuses and other forms of entertainment. These had come to epitomize the newfound confidence of the jobbing printer, making good use of his large-scale types, often in combination with stock engraved wood blocks. But in the final decade of the century, there was a rather sudden change of emphasis in poster design, from typographic to image-led design, and the few words that remained were often integrated into the illustration. Lithography was the process by which this material was being printed, the scale was increased and its impact profound, making those responsible, such as Jules Chéret and Alphonse Mucha, international celebrities. A characteristic of these and many of the other 'poster artists' is their lack of a structured, prescriptive training.

Perhaps the best example of the inherent advantages of unrestricted training was the American William H. Bradley (1868–1962) who, while remaining within the industry, was able to move from one position to the next in order to develop his skills and knowledge as his interests dictated. He began in the conventional way by working as a printer's 'devil' (assistant) in Boston, Massachusetts, where he saved

Left Poster for luxury biscuits, chromolithography, France, c. 1900s.

Right Two information signs relating to the London Underground system as reproduced in *Old London Street Cries*, edited by Andrew White Tuer, letterpress printed and published by Field & Tuer, 1885. The signs were composed by a compositor and so are possibly not an accurate representation of the original.

enough money to accept an unpaid position with J. Manz & Company, an engraving firm in Chicago, before taking an unpaid six-week internship in wood engraving at Rand McNally. He decided to stay with Rand McNally to train and work as a compositor for two years, then worked for the printing company Knight & Leonard for another two years before, finally, renting a studio of his own and becoming a freelance designer in 1890.

The contrast between the freedom of movement and choice available to an independently minded commercial artist such as Bradley and the system of apprenticeship within the printing industry itself, in which a young man was indentured (tied to a single master printer for a period of seven years) is stark. However, it appears that the intrinsic qualities of the lithographic process – fluid, unrestricted image-making and lettering – were reflected in a flexible attitude to working practices that was quite different from the letterpress printing office.

The idea that art and commerce, artist and artisan, and culture and commerce might be reconciled resurfaced. There was certainly no barrier in terms of who might create these posters – renowned artists such as Édouard Manet, Henri de Toulouse-Lautrec and Pierre Bonnard all designed posters – and the democratic nature of this medium was much discussed. The designer A. M. Cassandre later described the situation thus: 'The young painters ... could easily, like so many others, show us more still-lifes, nudes and landscapes which should perhaps be thrown into the sea... They have preferred, however, the open air of the streets and roads to the rarefied air of museums and galleries. They have left the academies and gone instead to the printers. And, while they have lost contact with some aesthetes, they have made contact with men.'[20]

Although the art poster was hugely influential, its use was largely limited to entertainment and cultural activities. The business community was suspicious of its connections with the art world: 'There is the temptation, which many artists cannot resist, to press the point "high art" (so "high" that the common people do not appreciate it!) beyond the boundary of good taste, and thus the announcement loses its force.'[21] In contrast, there was much discussion about the moral and educational advantages of posters which, it was argued, brought art into the streets. Posters were very popular, demand being such that special editions were often printed for the general public to buy, while poster exhibitions were held in Paris and other European cities as well as in the United States.

The letterpress printer, unable to compete with the lithographer, also regarded poster art with suspicion. A common criticism was that its purpose appeared to be to promote the artist rather than the product or service. These posters certainly have a distinctly youthful, sensuous, care-free (or what critics called 'care-less') approach to colour, type and composition. They were life-affirming, and celebrated the opportunities offered by an urban lifestyle. Cherét has even been credited with helping the cause of the women's suffrage movement with his images of confident, proactive women. However, within the letterpress trade such imagery was criticized as irrelevant, perhaps even subversive, and it was questioned whether the needs of the client were being served at all.

The effectiveness and notoriety of art posters influenced the design of other printed material, especially cultural and lifestyle journals. But also influential in the continued growth of this market were improvements in print technology, especially colour halftone work. Harper & Brothers

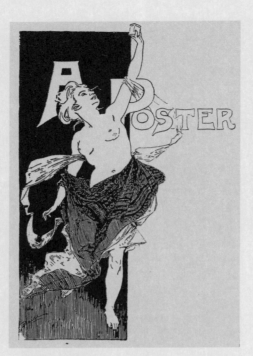

ning of an 'artistic' style that was to dominate not only American poster design, but also magazines, journals and book covers well into the twentieth century.

In 1895 Bradley set up his own Wayside Press in Springfield, Massachusetts. Working from a printing workshop rather than an art or design studio demonstrated the designer's acknowledgment of those recognized craft activities of the printer and gave the process of design a degree of gravitas. However, Bradley gave up his printing business in 1897 to concentrate on design, embarking on a remarkably varied and successful career. For example, he worked as a consultant for the American Type Founders, for whom he wrote and designed a set of booklets/journals called *The Chap-Book* (1904–5), and as art director of a number of magazines, including *Century*. In the final phase of his career he was employed by businessman and newspaper publisher William Randolph Hearst and given responsibility for art and typographic assignments involving the broadest range of media, including the movies. The concept of the independent designer of print had been established.

became particularly successful in this field during the 1890s with Edward Penfield, then head of the art department. Between 1889 and 1892, some of the *Harper's Bazaar* covers had been commissioned from Eugène Grasset in Paris, where they were printed before being shipped to the United States and bound into the magazine. In 1893 Penfield designed a one-off promotional poster for the April issue of *Harper's Magazine*. His design depicted a man standing in the rain obliviously reading his magazine. Its simplicity, emphasis upon composition and few words – 'Harper's for April' – made it similar in appearance to the art posters proliferating in France at the time.[22] The impact of this poster, perhaps because of its association with a popular American institution, was immediate and marked the begin-

THE ·:· Artist Printer

A JOURNAL FOR THE PROGRESSI

JANUARY, 1892.

The William Morris effect

Morris was publicly critical of commercial print standards and responded with the establishment of the Kelmscott Press. His first, much anticipated book, *The Story of the Glittering Plain*, was hugely influential in this regard, initiating a period of intense introspection and self-criticism in the jobbing printing industry, not only of its aesthetic solutions but

also the moral implications of servicing the commercial print requirements of mass production.

After the success of the Kelmscott Press, a physical link between designing for print and actual printing was pursued by designers, especially in America, seeking authenticity and authority in their work. The typeface Satanick (*opposite, top right*) was an unauthorized version of Morris's Troy

Below *The Story of the Glittering Plain* by William Morris, Kelmscott Press, London, 1891.

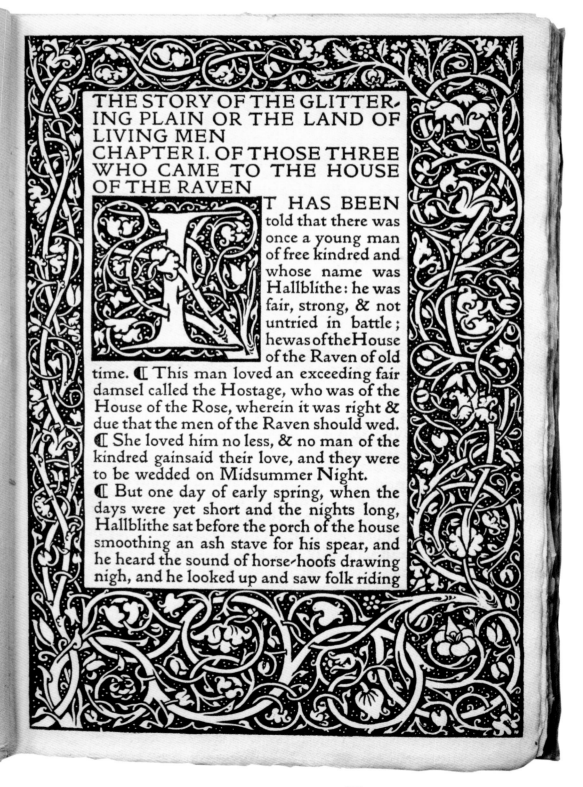

(1891), made by the American Type Founders (ATF) in 1896.

A number of new journals sprang up around 1900. *The Printing Art* (*top and bottom left*), first published in 1903, reflected the views of Morris and the Arts and Crafts through its cover design and editorial stance. Targeting commercial artists and illustrators as well as compositors and printers, it included examples of work by leading designers of the day, bound in as inserts or mounted onto dark papers.

In comparison, *The British Printer*, although editorially respected, was poorly designed. In the example below (*bottom right*), displaying influences such as Tuer's still popular Antique style (note the sign for 'Ye Printerie') and Morris's championing of medieval craft values, the archaic design jars with the journal's contemporary subject matter.

Top and bottom left Cover and page from *The Printing Art*, Cambridge, Massachusetts, USA, 1913.

Top right Prospectus cover for the typeface Satanick, American Type Founders, 1896.

Bottom right Cover of *The British Printer*, Leicester, UK, 1906.

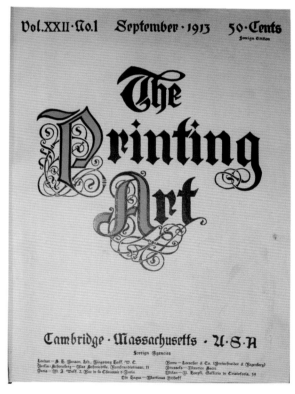

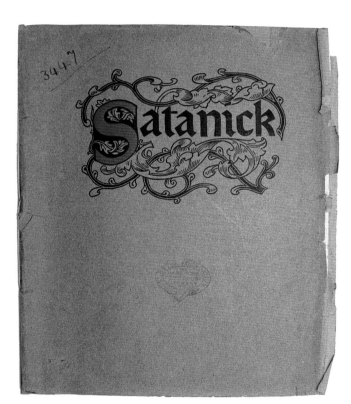

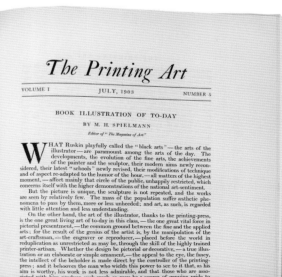

Of the hundreds of typefaces featured in the catalogue of the American Type Founders, the association decided to use William H. Bradley's font adapted 'from medieval sources' on its opening page (*below*) – such was the influence of Morris and the Arts and Crafts movement in the USA. The font had been designed two years earlier for *The Inland Printer* (*opposite, bottom left*). Bradley then licensed the design

to the American Type Founders, an amalgamation of typefoundries formed in reaction to the invention of automated setting and casting of type. The ATF cut the complete font family, the 'Bradley Series', introduced in 1895.

Below Title page of a type specimen catalogue, published by American Type Founders, 1896.

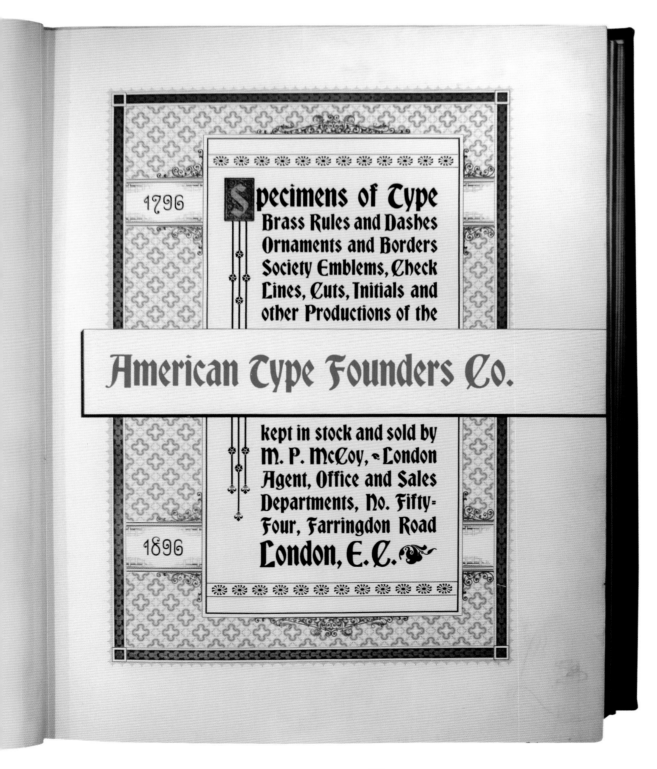

The emergence of Art Nouveau
The design of the London Society of Compositors trade union membership card changed annually. Many incorporated predominant styles of the time and (as intended) were the source of much debate among members. Here (*top, from left to right*), the transition from the late remnants of artistic printing (with reference to Morris) through to Art Nouveau and beyond can be discerned.

Such a transition was more confidently stated with *The Inland Printer* (*bottom left*). This American journal, which began in 1883 as a 24-page publication, had, by 1900, become a 200-page monthly, highly respected for its editorial content, technical information and ever-changing cover designs. More typical, *The Artist Printer* (*bottom right*) maintained a single cover design, reflecting the dominant interest in Art Nouveau.

Top Membership cards for the London Society of Compositors. From left to right: 1898, 1907 and 1912.

Bottom left *The Inland Printer*, Chicago, USA, 1896.

Bottom right *The Artist Printer*, published in Chicago and St Louis, USA, 1892.

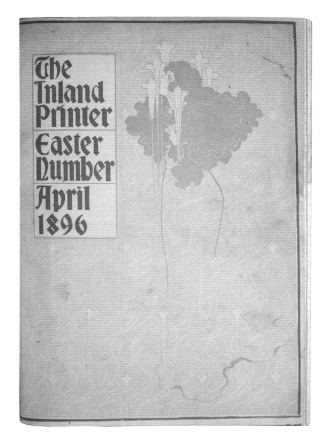

Business stationery

Art Nouveau shared certain characteristics with the Gaslight style, including an eclectic mix of stylistic references and a general lack of restraint, as the examples below show to effect. The billhead for Martin Billing, Son & Co. (*top left*) incorporates a detailed description of the company's range of activities, from printing and the manufacture of paper products to the publication of its own almanac. The billhead for Morris & Jones (*top right*) is in a similar style to Martin Billing, Son & Co.'s example and also provides an interesting contrast with the highly efficient, almost perfunctory letterpress-printed receipt attached.

In the carte de visite of the photographic studio Rugg & Company (*bottom left*), the clarity with which the company name is presented – even its use of serrated edges – is strikingly individual. The billhead for the timber importer and slate merchant John Eede Butt & Sons (*bottom right*), meanwhile, was printed onto a thin veneer of wood.

Top left Billhead for Martin Billing, Son & Co., lithography, Birmingham, UK, 1903.

Bottom left Carte de visite (reverse of a photo mount) for Rugg & Co., Minneapolis, USA, *c.* late nineteenth century.

Top right Billhead (with receipt attached) for wholesaler Morris & Jones, lithography, Liverpool, UK, 1898.

Bottom right Billhead for timber importer John Eede Butt & Sons, lithography, Brighton and Littlehampton, UK, *c.* late nineteenth century.

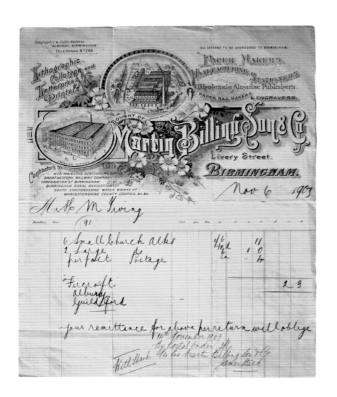

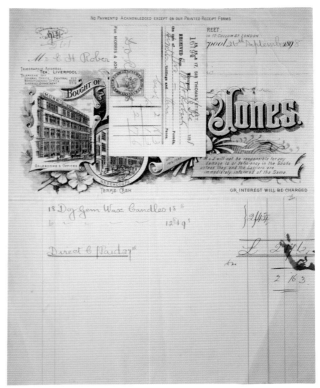

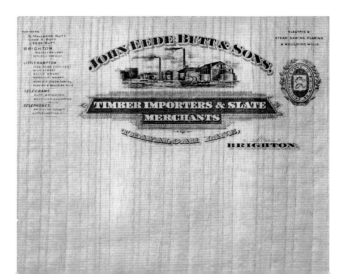

Although the two billheads below share similar lettering styles and the use of a banner to detail business activities, the earlier example (*top*) contains much more elaborate decoration. The later example (*bottom*) reveals a considerable loosening of the elements, creating a less formal, more transparent impression.

Top Billhead for builder and decorator Frank Corbett, engraving, London, *c.* 1890s.

Bottom Original artwork (detail) for a billhead for footwear wholesaler Lewis P. Ross, New York, *c.* early 1900s.

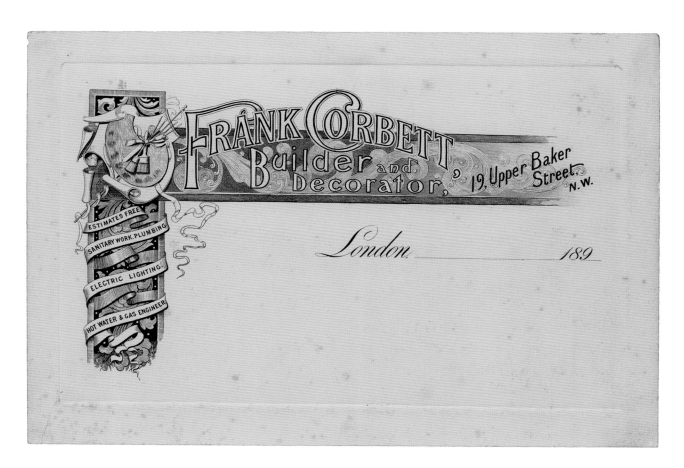

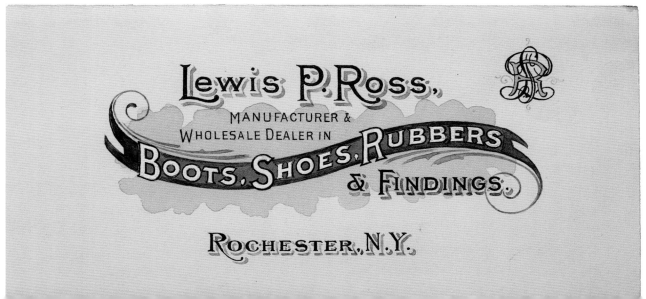

Top left Medicine label for Hunt's Remedy Co., lithography, designed by William E. Clarke, *c.* 1880s.

Top centre Label for Helmbold's Chemical Co., engraved steel, New York, *c.* 1900.

Top right Printed cardboard box for the Dana Sarsaparilla Co., Belfast, Maine, USA, 1891.

Bottom left Two matchbox labels, Russia, date unknown.

Bottom right Wrap-around label (detail) for Price's Battersea Sperm Candles, lithography, London, *c.* 1900.

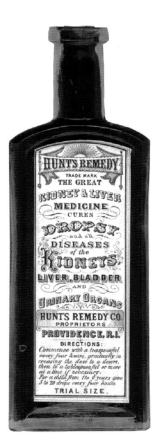

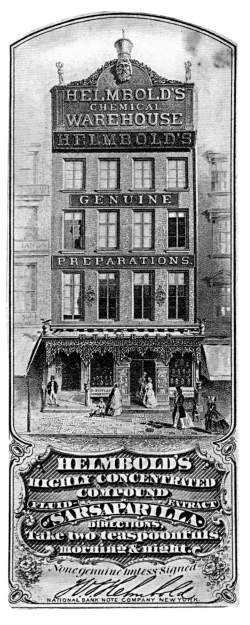

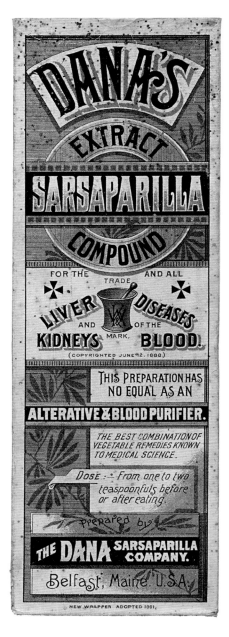

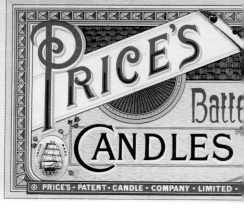

Packaging materials

Glass bottles had been used for wine since about 1630. Initially, 'marking' a bottle was achieved by stamping a seal of glass, usually onto the neck, with the owner's initials. When quantities increased, it became far cheaper to have labels printed. The bottle included a recessed area in which the printed paper label would be glued (*opposite, top left*).

Before the mid-nineteenth century, containers were made by hand from wood or card for dry goods, usually reserved for expensive items such

as jewelry. However, by the 1890s, cardboard boxes were being mass-produced and used for all sorts of goods, from pills to matches (*opposite, bottom left* and *top right*).

The first canning factory was set up in England in 1813. By 1900, automated production of cans had been introduced, although can lids still had to be soldered by hand after the food had been put in. This advertisement (*below*) is early enough for the can itself to be sufficiently interesting as the focus of attention.

Below Advertisement showing a can of ox tongues, McCall & Co. Ltd, London, *c.* late nineteenth century.

Children's reading material
Improvements in printing quality, especially the introduction of colour, had the effect of attracting a higher calibre of illustrators to children's books. Once established, the illustration of children's literature became a much sought-after commission because of the considerable creative freedom it allowed.

The French ABC primer (*top right*) provides a series of unlikely animal pairings, represented with a disturbing semi-human appearance. The muted colour adds to the sense of unease.

In the final quarter of the century, the development of chromolithography transformed children's reading material as it burst into rich colour (*top left*). Nevertheless, children's single-colour 'newspapers' such as *Munro's Girls and Boys of America* (*bottom*) were highly popular and remained so until the mid-twentieth century.

Children became a greater focus of attention in print as the notion that

Top left Cover of a children's book, *The Farmer's Boy*, illustrated by R. Caldecott, published by Frederick Warne & Co., London, *c.* 1890s.

Bottom *Munro's Girls and Boys of America*, published by Munro, New York, 1876.

Top right ABC primer, chromolithography, France, *c.* late nineteenth century.

children should be 'seen but not heard' gave way to a celebration of childhood. Images of children became common in advertising as a means of conveying humour, innocence or delight (*bottom left*).

The *Boy's Own Paper* (*top left*) was first published in 1879 by the Religious Tract Society, followed a year later by the arguably more influential *Girl's Own Paper* (*top right*). Although regular subjects included Bible study, fashion, sewing, cookery and music,

the latter also printed fictional accounts touching on social problems such as long working hours and poverty. Importantly, it also took a lead on women's education and encouraged girls to be more independent.

It was common for matchbooks to carry images of pertinent social issues and news. This illustration (*bottom right*) is perhaps unusual in providing a positive image of the burgeoning suffragette movement.

Top left *The Boy's Own Paper,* letterpress, London, 1900.

Bottom left Lid for a box of Christmas crackers, three-colour lithography, *c.* 1890s.

Top right *The Girl's Own Paper,* letterpress, London, 1887.

Bottom right Matchbook, London, *c.* early twentieth century.

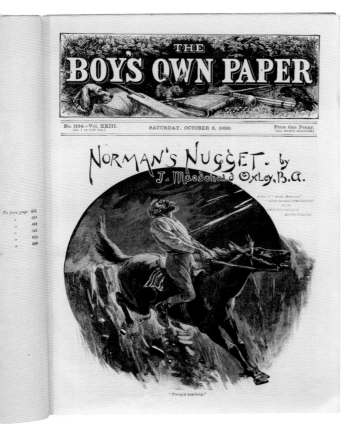

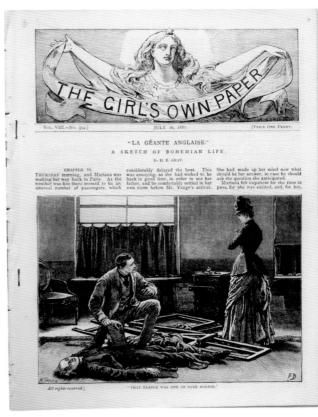

Advertising

Advertising was emerging as a subject in its own right. The illustration (*left*) is taken from *Advertise How? When? Where?*, an early book explaining the benefits and perils of advertising by William Smith, then manager of the Adelphi Theatre, London. The later illustration from *Punch* (*top right*) depicts the various ploys used by theatre management in attracting the general public to their latest productions, including sensational subjects.

Advertising in journals was an imprecise activity, and the general appearance chaotic. In *The Graphic* (*bottom right*), for example, there is also little evidence of any real sense of design in the individual adverts beyond fitting the information into or around much-used and often worn stereotypes.

Left Illustration from *Advertise How? When? Where?* by William Smith, 1863.

Top right Illustration titled 'How we advertise now', *Punch*, London, 1887.

Bottom right Double-page spread from the Christmas special of *The Graphic*, London, 1887.

Advertisements in magazines were heavily taxed, a calculation based on size until the mid-nineteenth century when the 'tax on knowledge', as its opponents called it, was repealed. A number of journals emerged to take advantage of this new stream of income. Larger advertisements became more feasible, although full-page (*left*) remained relatively rare.

Many magazines restricted advertising to a standard column-width, which caused some simply to fill the space by repeating a product name (*right*). This crude solution eventually compelled the magazine's proprietors to give advertisers more freedom in how they could utilize the space they were buying.

Left Full-page advertisement for St Jacob's Oil, *The Graphic*, London, 1887.

Right Advertisement for Nubian Blacking shoe polish, *The Graphic*, London, 1887.

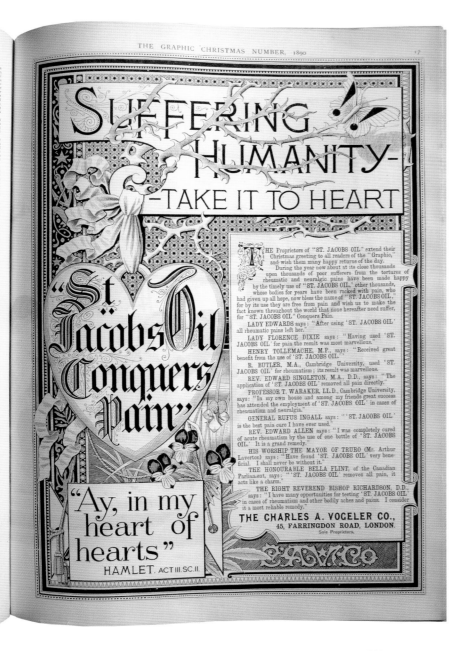

Narrative illustration
The arrangement of the illustrations in the full-page advertisement (*left*) effectively gives the reader a tour of the bank's facilities. The design of the text and images is, essentially, symmetrical, but the use of perspective not only accentuates the scale of the bank's premises, but also adds considerably to the overall drama and interest of this advertisement.

The Graphic was a pioneer in the use of sequential illustrations. The example below (*top and bottom right*) shows a close rapport between the illustrator and the compositor, the result of an art editor's planning. The illustrations have been positioned to work in harmony with the text, their shapes helping to create a sense of flow as the reader is taken around the house and outbuildings showcased.

Left Full-page advertisement for a bank's safe-deposit facilities, *The Graphic*, London, 1887.

Top and bottom right Illustrated page and detail, *The Graphic*, London, 1890.

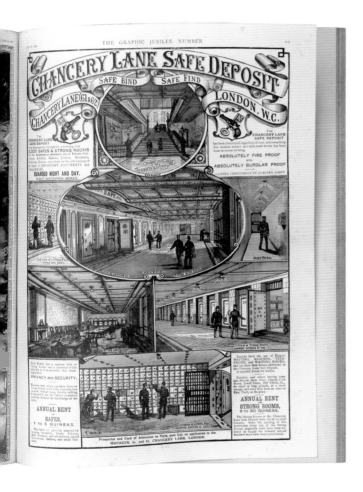

The arrival of *The Graphic* in 1869 challenged the dominance of the leading image-led publication, *The Illustrated London News*. The ability to demonstrate fine tonal work (shown in its masthead) was *The Graphic*'s forte from the outset. Each issue had a different cover illustration. The example below (*top left*) is a copy of a painting by the Royal Academician J. W. Waterhouse. Typically, the engraver is not credited.

Improvements in process work during the 1880s allowed the magazine to venture into colour.

Tit-Bits (*bottom left*), meanwhile, carried advertising on its cover. Even in these early days, this generally indicated a cheaper product – just one penny for *Tit-Bits*, compared with sixpence for *The Graphic*.

Top left and bottom right Cover of *The Graphic*, featuring a copy of a painting by J. W. Waterhouse, and detail of the masthead, 1875.

Bottom left Cover of *Tit-Bits* (full title: *Tit-Bits from All the Most Interesting Books, Periodicals and Contributors in the World*), London, 1892.

Top right Colour spread from *The Graphic*, Christmas number, chromolithography, London, 1888.

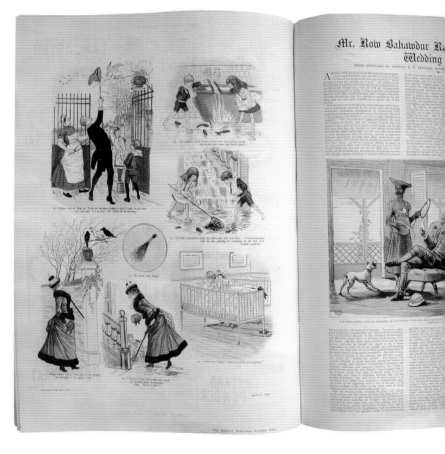

Picture composition

Foundries such as MacKellar, Smiths & Jordan (*below*) sold sets of combination borders in styles called, for example, Japanese, Assyrian and Egyptian. Each comprised perhaps twenty or more pieces, some of which were discreet readymade illustrations such as a boat, a fan or a dragonfly, while others could be fitted together in numerous variations to compose decorative boxes or borders.

The universal availability of foundries' decorative border material undermined

the integrity of the compositor and highlighted his limitations. Clearly few compositors had the skills or the wherewithal to design their own material. The result was that popular decorative border sets became a common sight throughout the world.

Two of the trade cards (*opposite, top left and right*) make use of the same combination border series from the MacKellar, Smiths & Jordan foundry. Both depict Japanese-themed scenes and feature the same character holding

Below Catalogue issued by the typefoundry MacKellar, Smiths & Jordan Co., Philadelphia, USA, 1888.

EXERCISE IN COMBINATION BORDERS, BY CLIFFORD COMLY, WITH MACKELLAR, SMITHS & JORDAN CO.

a parasol. The advertisement for the
jeweler (*bottom left*) uses the foundry's
Egyptian decorative set.

The three trade cards (*bottom right*) for
a furniture upholsterer, a fuel merchant
and a sewing machine retailer all use the
same stereotype block – a practice that
certainly undermined the ambition of the
printer to become an agent for design.
It was easy for advertising agencies to
use such work against the printing trade
as an indication of the latter's marketing
naivety and creative shortcomings.

Top left Trade card designed by
George Sutherland, foreman at John
Baxter & Son, letterpress, Edinburgh,
UK. It was included in *The Printers'
International Specimen Exchange*, no. 4,
using a combination border series
from the MacKellar, Smiths & Jordan
foundry, 1883.

Bottom left Trade card for a jeweler,
letterpress printed using the MacKellar,
Smiths & Jordan Egyptian combination
border series, 1883.

Top right Trade card designed by
William W. Jackson, letterpress using
a combination border series from the
MacKellar, Smiths & Jordan foundry,
New York, *c.* 1880s.

Bottom right Three trade cards designed
by Caulon Print, New York, *c.* 1890.

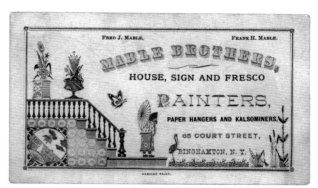

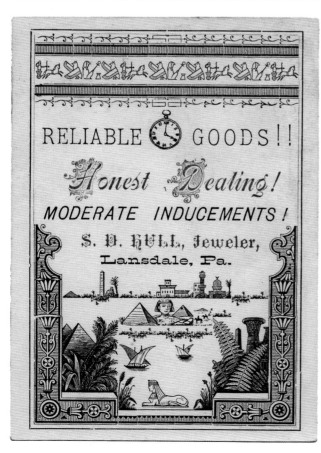

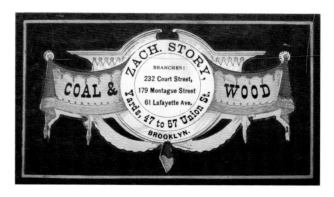

233

Below Poster for the Northern Pacific
Railroad Line, black with rainbow printed
background, lithography, USA, *c.* 1890.

The late Gaslight style

The Gaslight style, rather surprisingly, had drawn little comment or analysis from the trade press, and its name only began to be applied as it was overtaken by Art Nouveau. In its maturity, the Gaslight style retained many of its key elements – banners, ribbons, layered panels and turned-up faux page corners – but became heavier and less animated. Letterforms became increasingly experimental and idiosyncratic to compensate. The trade card (*top left*)

and advertisement (*top right*) celebrate their multiple affectations and reflect the Art Nouveau work emerging at the same time.

The rare cover of the 1876 *Centennial Exposition Guide* (*bottom right*) is an earlier example of the Gaslight style and, therefore, all the more remarkable for its energy and complexity. The swirling, interlocking forms make an interesting comparison with the Art Nouveau-style *Philadelphia Record Almanac* (*bottom left*), designed twenty-five years later.

Top left Trade card for McClain Bros., engraving, New York, *c.* 1890s.

Bottom left Cover of *The Philadelphia Record Almanac*, USA, 1901.

Top right Advertisement for the printers of *The Baltimore Sun*, Denver, USA, date unknown.

Bottom right Cover of *The Centennial Exposition Guide*, Philadelphia, USA, 1876.

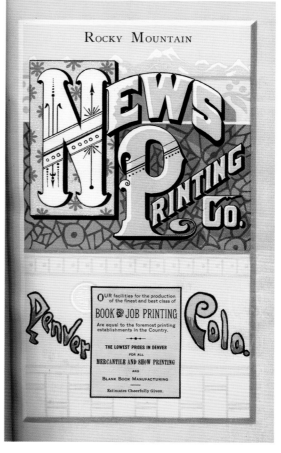

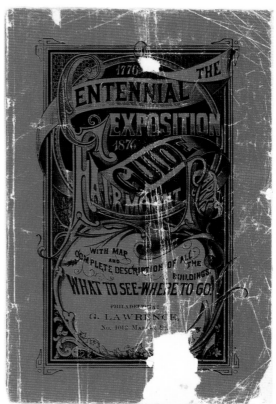

Manifestations of Art Nouveau
The shadowed titles, arched panels, floral fill-ins and trademarks carrying interlocking letterforms are all reminiscent of the Gaslight style, but in these examples the type billows and floats. Bright colours are also repeatedly featured. Some of the most distinctive work of this period – the Liquore Strega label (*bottom*), for

example – remained largely unchanged throughout the twentieth century. Button labels (*top left and right*) were used on display box-lids and on the back of button cards (a small card designed to have a set of buttons sewn onto it).
Designed in the Gaslight style, these Squirrel Brand labels (*opposite*) do not rely on elaborate printing techniques and finishes, but rather on the inventiveness

Top left and right Two labels, used variously on display box-lids and on the back of button cards, UK, *c.* 1900.

Bottom Label for Liquore Strega, three-colour lithography, Rome, Italy, *c.* 1890s.

and drawing skills of what appears to be a single designer. The clarity achieved – given emphasis by the lack of colour – provides a particularly distinctive appearance. The brand carried around fifty products, but the lithographic artist designed appropriate letterforms for each product.

The final decade of the nineteenth century saw a coming together of styles, generally applied in an ad hoc manner. The eclectic nature of this period is characterized by the use of rococo and neoclassical references (*overleaf, top*) together with a fascination for complexity of pattern.

Based in the United States, the inventive printer Conrad Lutz relished being unconventional and experimenting with new processes and products.

Below Three labels for Squirrel Brand, lithography, London, *c.* 1890s.

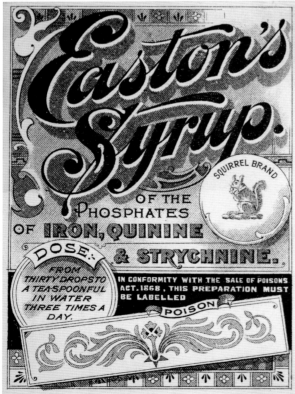

The yellow and blue marbling effect on the job band (*centre*) was achieved by the chaostype process (see page 196). His 'signature' (*bottom left*) required five passes through the press: two each for yellow and blue; the fifth was an adhesive medium onto which Lutz sprinkled gold dust.

The letters on the 'teas' trade card (*bottom right*) are constructed from combination borders that form part of MacKellar, Smiths & Jordan's Chinese series 91.

In middle-class Victorian England, the giving of change, from hand to hand, was considered rather uncouth and the preference was to seal it in a paper packet. However, when the amount of change was particularly small, an alternative was to give the customer

Top Card, purpose and printer unknown, Italy, *c.* 1890s.

Centre Band by Conrad Lutz, Burlington, Ohio, USA, *c.* 1890s.

Bottom left Signature (detail) by Conrad Lutz, Burlington, Ohio, USA, *c.* 1890s.

Bottom right Trade card for a tea merchant, printer unknown, *c.* 1890s.

a packet of pins instead. These packets were often extravagantly designed. The Citizen packet below (*top left*) makes much of the product's 'Britishness', with imagery referencing the Boer War. The Rococo packet (*top right*) is more abstract, relying on decorative form and colour.

European chemist labels, especially in France (*bottom*), tended to have a more refined and certainly more elegant quality than their American or British equivalents.

Art Nouveau did not take hold in the UK and USA as it did in Europe, but its presence is prominent in the Wilkie & Soames label (*overleaf, bottom*), in which arching panels derived from flowing ribbon or parchment are reduced to a flat, abstract form.

Top left and right Two change pin-packets (or pin-papers), UK, *c.* 1900.

Bottom left Label (detail) for cod-liver oil, France, *c.* 1890s.

Bottom right Label for face powder, France, *c.* 1900.

239

The billhead (*top*) shows the kind of visual reference from which the Wilkie & Soames label derives.

The professional penman's extravagant use of calligraphic 'flourish' (see page 44) was revived during the late nineteenth century, and in the 1880s a number of magazines specialized in the subject. It was inevitable that some of these newly trained penmen would transfer

their skill to print media, and the oft-repeated combination of bird, angel and scroll began to appear in engravings and lithographs (*opposite, top and bottom left*). Occasionally, when these flourishes were added to letterforms, the result would be all but unreadable (*opposite, bottom right*).

The advertisement for C. Potter Jr & Company (*opposite, top right*) is a

Top Billhead for the Preston Soap Company, lithography, UK, 1899.

Bottom Label for soap manufacturer Wilkie & Soames, London, *c.* 1900s.

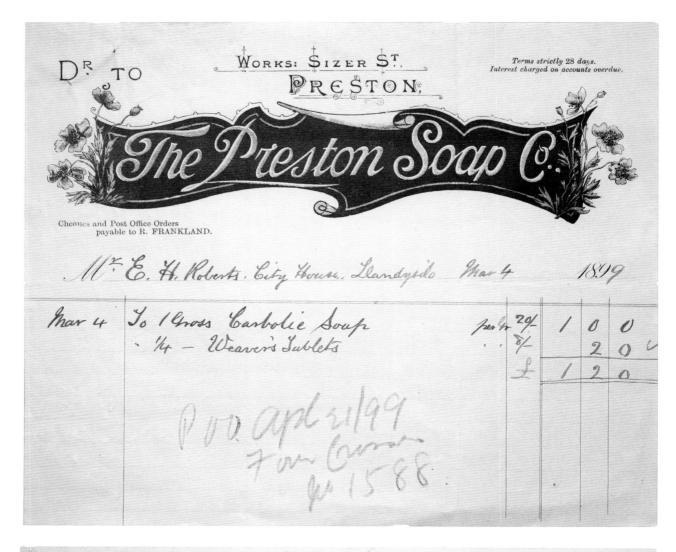

240

reminder that the fascination with past handicrafts was also making a comeback during the 1880s. Although a manufacturer of automatic printing presses, this company chose to present itself through the form of a leaded stained-glass window, albeit in the Gaslight style.

Top left Trade card for 'artist and penman' Henry C. Kendall, photo-engraving, Boston, USA, *c.* 1890s.

Bottom left Advertisement for the Arc Engraving Co., taken from *The Penrose Annual*, London, 1902–3.

Top right Advertisement for C. Potter Jr & Co., manufacturer of power printing presses and steam engines, New York, printed by Fahnestock & Co., Boston, *c.* 1880s.

Bottom right Carte de visite detail (reverse of a photo-mount) for Crosby & Swett, lithography, Lewiston, Maine, USA, *c.* 1890s.

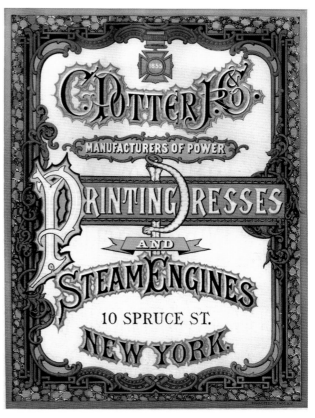

Freeform lettering
Louis Prang built his reputation on chromolithographic work, but when that market began to shrink he diversified into other products. For example, he was one of the innovators of greetings and Christmas cards. He also printed and published a range of books containing inventive letterforms (*top and centre*), which were designed for the aspiring

professional sign-writer or graphic artist to copy.

Although Prang's decorative alphabets might appear remarkable, there were already far more eccentric letterforms being created and used in a commercial context. The Van Houten showcard (*bottom*) and the advertisement for Hübel & Denck (*opposite*) are striking examples of freeform lettering from the 1890s.

Top and centre Two details from *Prang's Standard Alphabets*, designed and published by Louis Prang & Co., Boston, USA, 1878.

Bottom Showcard (detail) for Van Houten's Cocoa, probably printed in the USA, 1892.

Opposite Advertisement for Hübel & Denck bookbinders, artwork by Max Dutzauer, reproduced in the book *Die Graphischen Künste der Gegenwart* by Theodor Groebel, Stuttgart, Germany, 1895.

Top Page from *Ornamental Decoration*, lithography, printed and published by Louis Prang & Co., Boston, USA.

Bottom Page from the Fonderie Générale catalogue of type specimens, Paris, 1900.

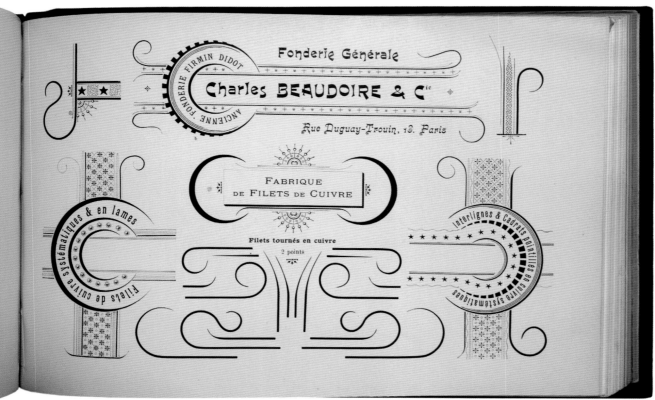

Art Nouveau

With their bright colours, flowing lines and lavish use of gold, Prang's decorative letters (*opposite, top*) have an unmistakable medieval flavour – something American Art Nouveau, in deference to Morris, was reluctant to shake off.

It was difficult for the letterpress printer to partake in the Art Nouveau movement, which was far better suited to the freedom of the lithographic artist. However, typefoundries did respond, especially in France. The example opposite (*bottom*) shows a set of readymade decorative swirls and curls. Tools enabling the compositor to create curved lines from brass rules

had been available for some time, but the letterpress printer preferred to buy readymade stereotypes. The result was corruptive. The print manager thought he gained in efficiency of labour, and the compositor learned that 'design' was bought from foundry catalogues.

In France, especially in poster work, freeform lettering became relaxed to the point of formlessness (*bottom*). Here, the free spirit of the brushwork describing the flowing material is extended to the lettering, which is drawn with breathtaking nonchalance. In contrast, British Art Nouveau was generally less animated and rather more solid than in mainland Europe (*top right*).

Top left Two cartes de visite, Sweden and Germany, *c.* 1900.

Bottom Poster after Pal (Jean de Paléologue), printed by E. Delanchy, Paris, 1897.

Top right Cover of *The Art Annual: The Life & Works of John Tenniel*, London, 1901.

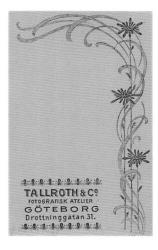

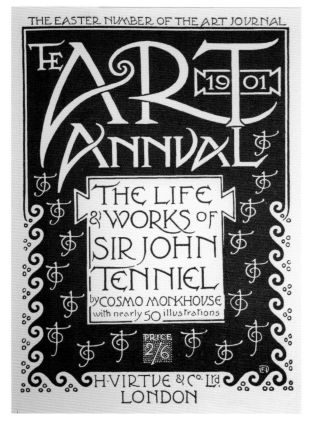

Advertising inserts
The style of these advertising inserts (essentially a small version of a poster inserted in popular magazines) demonstrates how illustration was becoming less concerned with naturalistic detail, focusing instead on narrative and visual impact. Two of the examples below (*top and bottom left*) remain, essentially, charming illustrations of precocious children, with a title

casually included in case the viewer misses the point.
The modelling of every part of the Lux insert (*right*) has been virtually flattened. Reality is suspended, allowing a yellow sky to be presented and enabling the blue shirt to be the focus of attention. There is already a sense that advertising has to work harder, emphasized by the addition of words.

Top and bottom left Two advertising inserts, one for Sunlight Soap, the other for Heinz, chromolithography, *c.* 1900s.

Right Advertising insert for Lux Washing Powder, chromolithography, *c.* 1900s.

The decline of the printer

The pages of this sketchbook (*below*) by Walter Bunn, who was a letterpress apprentice in 1891, incorporate printed matter collected and rearranged to suggest the design of a menu or theatre poster. While design remained largely self-taught, the apprenticeship scheme began to creak, not only under the pressure of new technologies, but also from students leaving schools of art and design to join advertising agencies or to work as independent designers.

What happened to Bunn later in life is not known, but it would be his generation of printers that would feel the brunt of this new competition. Its practitioners were variously called commercial artists, layout men and typographers, but importantly they were all determined to function quite separately from the printer.

Below Makeshift sketchbook page by Walter Bunn, letterpress apprentice, Norwich, UK, *c.* 1891.

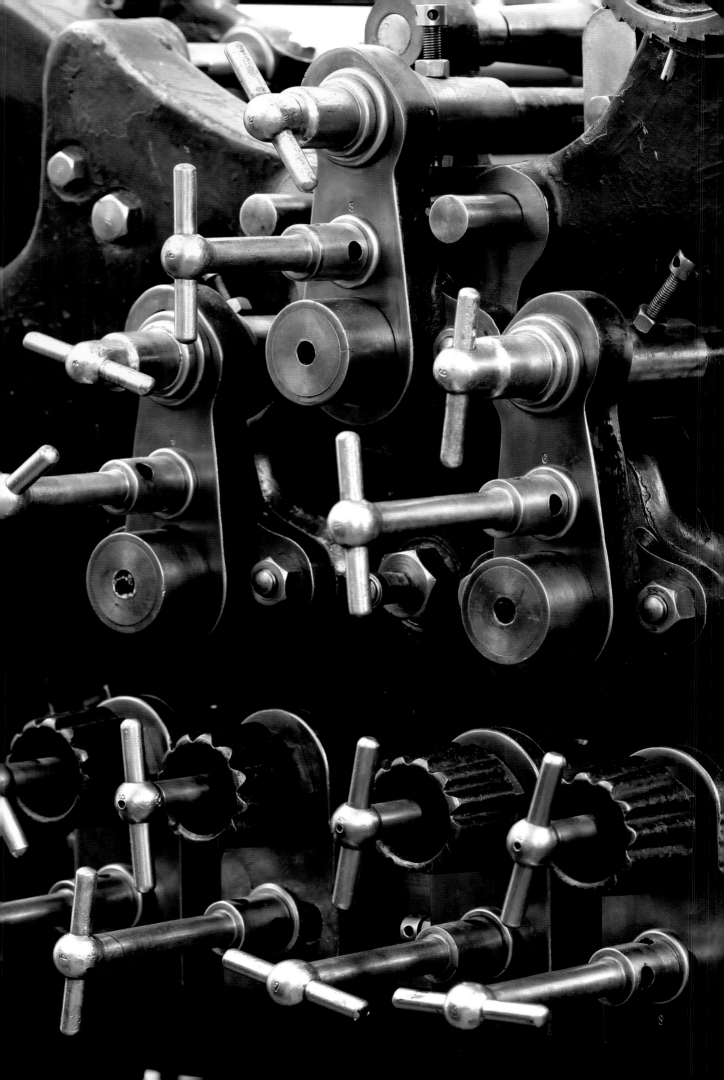

CHAPTER SIX
PRINTING AT THE SERVICE OF DESIGN

The early twentieth century was a complex period for the commercial printer. In some quarters, nineteenth-century concerns regarding mechanization and urbanization were losing support. Industrialization and the resultant abundance of cheaper commodities were changing how people lived, worked and used their leisure time. However, the Arts and Crafts movement remained a potent cultural force, its ideals often quoted, while cultural journals continued to carry its social and aesthetic arguments for a natural, truthful and socially responsible consciousness.

One of the legacies of Morris's Kelmscott Press was the private press movement. The much admired work emanating from such establishments as the Doves Press in the UK and the Cranach Press in Germany remained principal cultural references, not only for craft-conscious trade printers but also artists and designers. Like Kelmscott, these presses were chiefly run by idealists whose background was not in the printing trade; typically, T. J. Cobden-Sanderson at the Doves Press and Count Harry Kessler at the Cranach Press. But while the private press movement maintained a certain status, its achievements became increasingly remote, even irrelevant, to the daily concerns of the jobbing printing trade.

The attention of the jobbing printer began to focus on a different front. The battle with 'outside forces' – advertising agencies, commercial artists and independent typographers – for control of the design of print was not yet lost, at least according to the numerous printing trade annuals, catalogues and journals. *The Penrose Annual* (published by Lund Humphries from 1895 until 1982) contained articles appropriate not only to the printing trade but also the designer. The early issues accentuated the dilemma of the printer by offering sycophantic reviews of work by the private presses while, at the same time, extolling the printer to 'be bold', 'keep abreast of modern business practices' and service their customers with 'something unique'.[1]

But the 'unique' was exclusively coming from those outside the printing trade. There were two almost simultaneous waves. The first was the Deutscher Werkbund (founded in 1907), a group inspired by the social ideals of Ruskin and admirers of Morris but less concerned about the utilization of mechanized production so long as it enabled them to take art into everyday life. They achieved this by applying artistic sensibilities to the design of products and print.

At the same time, a younger generation of avant-garde artists, incorporating radical tactics but with the similar ideology of merging art and life, were gaining notoriety. Rejecting the preciousness of the hand-crafted solution epitomized by the Kelmscott Press, they had a specific interest in the harnessing of print in order to democratize art. The common link between the Futurists in Italy, Spain and Russia, the Vorticists in England, the Constructivists in Russia, the Activists in Hungary, and the international Dadaists was a contempt for rational outcomes. And there can be few activities more rational than the design of a page of text. These avant-gardists resisted the establishment and had little interest in standard practices advocated by the trade, except when conventions provided a familiarity that could be harnessed to further their cause. Magazines, for

Top left Label for Motorist cigars, chromolithography with gold and embossing, Chicago, USA, 1922.

Bottom left Label for Edison Gold Moulded Records, National Phonograph Company, lithography with halftone photograph, London, c. 1905.

Right Diagram of a four-colour web or continuous paper-feed printing press. Rotation brought speed, and mass production printing flourished.

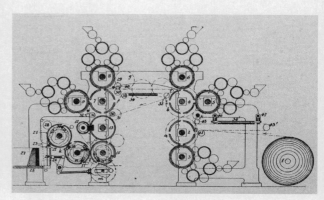

example, complete with poor printing on cheap paper, provided art in a form that could be bought at a news stand and carried in a coat pocket to be viewed on the tram, or at the kitchen table – in fact anywhere except on the walls of an art gallery.

While print was the medium of choice for these interconnected, high-profile and influential cultural movements, the commercial printer was in danger of becoming irrelevant as a cultural force. When material to be printed required a creative input – an increasingly common request – the printer, if asked, preferred to hire the services of the new art-school-educated freelance artist rather than adapt or broaden his own skill base. Commercial printing was establishing itself as an industry bereft of imagination and, despite the mammoth efforts of a few notable individuals who attempted to restore propriety and respectability, was failing to respond to the new demands.[2]

The situation in Germany, which had only recently come out of economic recession, was the cause of a unique enthusiasm for the improvement of communication between the manufacturer and the consumer, a task calling for expertise in linking the activities of art and business. The use of creative solutions in the service of commerce was not new, but in twentieth-century Germany the technological and economic developments addressed by the Werkbund would galvanize

these ideas and turn them into a national cause. This formidable group – comprising artists, industrialists, economists, sociologists, and at least one printer (Carl Ernst Poeschel) – recognized that when art was applied to business tasks, it had to be done in a business-like manner. They argued that the language, etiquette and ambition of the business world had to be met and understood if art were to function as an integral part of a modern society.

France, proud of its international reputation for the high level of individualistic craftsmanship, especially in the fields of furniture and products, was increasingly aware that apprentices had to make additional efforts if they were to obtain a comprehensive knowledge of their trade. Generally, this could only be achieved by attending evening classes – after a ten-hour working day. Worse still, attendance at these classes encouraged some patrons to relinquish their own responsibilities further. The number of fully trained craftsmen in France, and many other countries, was falling.

In contrast, Munich held a huge exhibition in 1908, 'Die Ausstellung München', intended to establish the city's competitive position as a centre of modern German design. The international ramifications of this event, in which the advantages of linking training, design and industry were stated clearly, were felt Europe-wide, but nowhere more acutely than in France. An official report, prepared for the Conseil Général du Département de la Seine by Rupert Carabin, explained: 'There was not a single room in which the smallest detail was not studied in terms of the decorative whole, from the windows, the iron-work, the wall hangings, the curtains and the lighting, to the hot-water heating apparatus.'

In England, contrary views on the way forward were being debated. For instance, while William R. Lethaby at the

Top left Design studio of a French advertising company, date unknown.

Bottom left Illustration by Ronald Anderson for *Art Printer*, supporting a number of articles that urged the printing fraternity to regain creative control of print design from a burgeoning advertising industry, Massachusetts, USA, 1913.

Right Illustration by Thomas Fogarty for an article in *The Printing Art*, 1916. Despite the pioneering work by large printing establishments at the centre of major American cities, there were thousands of small printers eking out a living with antiquated equipment in rural townships across the United States. This nonchalant scene suggests that in rural America, where union influence was less keenly felt, female compositors were a common occurrence in print shops.

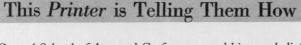

This *Printer* is Telling Them How

Central School of Arts and Crafts promoted his own belief that education must come from the handling of tools and materials in a workshop environment, just a mile away at the London School of Printing, the view of its Principal, J. R. Riddell, reflected a distinctly modernist, more scientific approach. Clearly with Morris and Lethaby in mind, he was critical of printing and typography courses that 'blindly comply with the views of "visionaries", who may be genuinely interested in education, but do not understand what is required in a modern printing office'.[3] Riddell's criticism was a sentiment with which members of the Werkbund would surely have empathized.

Writing styles experienced an analogous shift away from elaborate, self-consciously literary or flowery excesses. Magazine editors were asking for a simpler style that communicated ideas in a straightforward manner. The new opinion was that an absence of decoration, whatever the medium, gave a message of transparency and, in so doing, not only made it more accessible but also more trustworthy.

The same ideas were simultaneously being applied to graphic communication. Illustration was still very much to the fore, but the shapes and forms were less complex, less literary, bolder and simpler. At the same time, advertising strategies were becoming more subtle and cunning. Manufacturers were tactfully persuaded that portraits of the company founder were 'sops to vanity [that] hindered the work of advertising'.[4] Likewise, images of vast factory buildings, previously perceived as representing 'heroic progress', were now associated with child labour, blight and hardship. Instead, advertising agencies organized strategies to convey messages intended to connect with consumer interests. As a result, major manufacturing companies began to recognize that their printed material required far more expertise than even the most craft-conscious printer was capable of.

Left A drawing class at the Central School of Arts and Crafts, London, *c.* 1910. The design of this purpose-built school, with its high ceilings and exposed beams, gives the work areas a bohemian ambience that was a model for British regional art schools and design studios alike.

Right Illustration by Herry Perry (Heather Perry) revealing the activities undertaken within the Central School of Arts and Crafts, London, *c.* 1910. The prominence of female students is demonstrated both here and in the drawing class (*left*).

Craft, science and revival

In 1906, a decade after the Central School of Arts and Crafts had opened, a course for printers was established requiring attendance of two evening classes a week. John H. Mason (1875–1951), then working as a compositor at the Doves Press, was invited by the Principal, Lethaby, to take responsibility for them. Although called 'printing', these classes were almost exclusively concerned with typography. The 1906 prospectus explains: 'Printing. A class will be established in typography...[5] This class, which is intended solely for apprentices and journeymen actually engaged in the trade, aims at supplying instruction in the highest type of bookwork to the exclusion of mere advertisements, trade cards etc. It is felt that in view of the recent revival in printing, the establishment of such a class, which would co-operate with classes in bookbinding, lettering, black and white design etc, to form a complete school of book production should do great service to the craft generally.'

This brief description highlights a number of issues regarding the training of printers, and resistance on cultural grounds to the changes that had taken place in the printing trade – specifically, in the reference to advertisements and trade cards, in other words jobbing printing. This critical attitude would later soften through the School's association with the new wave of post-Morris commercial printers such as Harold Curwen of the Curwen Press, and Gerard Meynell of the Westminster Press, a change reflected in the journal *The Imprint* (1913). The restriction to apprenticed boys would be dropped in 1909, thus finally making the mysteries of the black art available to anyone. The reference to 'the recent revival in printing' alludes to the notion that Morris's technical and moral idealism was achievable by those working within the printing industry.

Mason's experience of the general printing trade was limited to his years working at the Ballantyne Press in London, where he had been an apprentice. Ballantyne printed a wide range of material, including jobbing work, but also, from 1895, reserved a press and a pressman to work exclusively on limited-edition Vale Press books.[6] To Mason, this proved that the finest printing was, indeed, possible within the general trade if sufficient time and care were forthcoming. When the Ballantyne Press was destroyed by a catastrophic fire in 1900, Mason moved to the newly formed Doves Press, the most impressive of the private presses to be set up in the wake of the Kelmscott Press.

In 1909 Mason was offered a full-time post by Lethaby to organize day-time classes in Printing.[7] To Lethaby, Mason's knowledge and experience of working within the private press movement were important, bringing not only the highest technical standards but also a historical context for the craft of printing. Mason's intention was that his day-time course should instil those aspects of a craft-conscious knowledge and a recognition of moral standards that the

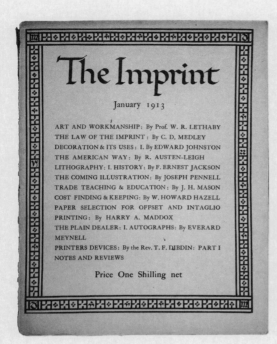

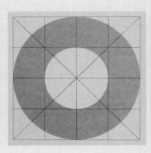

apprentice could no longer expect to receive in a commercial printing context.[8]

Despite their cultural debts to Morris, Lethaby and Mason belonged to the second generation of Arts and Crafts, which confronted the practical and ideological issues inherent in applying the ideals of Ruskin and Morris to commercial imperatives. The revival in printing, vigorously proffered by Lethaby and Mason, would not become modernist, but it certainly shared the same disdain for the printing trade's attempts during the previous two decades – culminating in the artistic printing movement – to harness the new demands of commerce and industry to their medium. In 1913 Lethaby described in *The Imprint* his approach (and a critique of artistic printing) as follows: 'Art is not a special sauce applied to ordinary cooking; it is the cooking itself if it is good. Most simple and generally, art might be thought of as the well-doing what needs doing'.[9] This attitude permeated the Central School.

The work of the Central School of Arts and Crafts attracted international attention, and visitors from Germany, France and Italy came to inspect its methods. Of particular importance was Lethaby's appointment of Edward Johnston (1872–1944) to teach writing and illumination. Johnston's influence was enormous. His students included Harold Curwen and Eric Gill. Foreign pupils such as Anna Simons from Germany[10] returned to their home countries to lecture and set up open classes in the way that Johnston had done. His involvement with the private press movement was also important.[11] Johnston's career, from his early study of medieval manuscripts to the designing of his sans serif alphabet, begun in 1913 for the London Underground and characterized by simple, legible letterforms, reflects the general evolution of design thinking, its appearance and perceived purpose during the first two decades of the twentieth century.

Around 1907, Lethaby also began to espouse a more pragmatic approach to the ideals of the Arts and Crafts movement. In a letter to the English bookbinder Sydney Cockerell he wrote: 'If I were learning to be a modern architect, I'd reject taste and design and all that stuff and learn engineering with plenty of mathematics and hard building experience. Hardness, facts, experiments – that should be architecture, not taste.'[12] Lethaby's growing acceptance of the construction engineer's influence was shared by many and is reflected in the number of significant buildings, at that time collectively called 'engineering architecture', designed for modern purposes such as railway stations, factories and exhibition pavilions.

Some people, among them the Belgian architect, designer and artist Henry van de Velde (1863–1957), saw parallels between the work of the engineer-architects and the designers of industrially manufactured products using new, man-made materials – ideas that would also be applied to the design of print. Van de Velde, who had worked as an independent designer of packaging, general printed material and industrial products (notably for the food company Tropon) during the 1890s, was also integral in the establishment of a school of arts and crafts in Weimar in 1905. This enterprise, together with other similar schools in cities such as Berlin, Düsseldorf, Hamburg and Nuremberg, proved to be highly influential in establishing Germany with the reputation as a cultivator and promoter of design.

Students in the graphic art classes at these arts and crafts schools before 1914 were generally taught lettering, drawing and ornament. This was achieved by copying historical examples together with book design, typography and book-

Left Cover of *The Inland Printer*, July 1896, New York. Each cover was entirely different and the range of styles and influences varied remarkably. Compare this with the cover on page 221.

Right Trademark of the German electric company AEG, designed by Peter Behrens, 1908. The interlocking honeycomb pattern alludes to the diligence and industry of the honeybee. As well as devising and coordinating all the printed material for AEG, Behrens also designed their factory building and many of the products they manufactured. Together with Van de Velde and Bernhard, he played a key part in establishing the role of the designer of print to the detriment of the printer.

binding – not dissimilar to Mason's classes in London. However, German students were expected to use their analysis of traditional designs to develop new designs for application to packaging, posters, press advertising, trademarks and the like – something Mason would not have contemplated. Also, while Lethaby's intention was to instil a clear understanding of the shared values of different crafts, in German classes this interdisciplinary appreciation was put into practice, enabling design initially intended for a book cover to be extended and applied, for example, to pressed metal sheets, fabrics or rugs.

These schools, certainly in their early years, often had few or no printing facilities. The result was that the students, naturally, considered themselves designers of print, quite distinct from the activity of printing itself. Meanwhile, the training of printing apprentices in Germany was supported by attendance at excellently equipped technical trade schools (*Fachhochschulen*) and institutes of higher education (*Technische Hochschulen*). The possible ramifications of such a situation – a technically naive design profession, and an aesthetically naive printing industry – were discussed at length.[13]

In France, supplementary education of apprentices was unregulated. In 1912 only one tenth of apprentices in all fields attended professional courses to supplement their apprenticeship.[14] It was also recognized that, such were the standards of the average patron, most apprentices had little hope of becoming skilled design practitioners. As a result, printing apprenticeships were being rejected in favour of full-time art and design college education. This drift, mirrored across Europe, effectually cemented the separation of design for print from printing itself.

In Germany, however, the technical trade schools, in which liaison between college and workplace was fully integrated, well organized and appropriate, continued to provide the printing profession with a workforce that was not only highly proficient, but also imbued with an understanding and appreciation of good design. At the same time, the schools of applied arts also maintained close working links with the printing industry and manufacturing and commercial enterprises. The influence of the Werkbund in these developments was significant.

Lethaby resigned from his role as Principal of the Central School of Arts and Crafts in 1911 and changes were quickly instigated there. The previous restriction of classes being exclusively for those involved in craft industries was now opened up to include a broader range of students. But changes in policy were most clearly demonstrated by the arrival, in 1912, of a new discipline, 'scientific management', in the syllabus, including lectures on the 'science of salesmanship' and the 'science of negotiating', while practical work now included 'commercial art' with subjects such as 'display techniques' and 'lettering for advertising'[15] – all a far cry from Ruskin and surely recognition of the successes of the Werkbund.

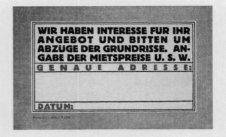

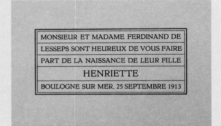

The independent designer

The first thing commercial artists and independent typographers had to do was persuade potential clients that their skills could contribute to profit margins: that design in itself had a value. However, within the printing trade, design and craft were still considered one and the same thing, and grouped together as part of an intuitive activity so that design was not even itemized on the printer's bill. For the customer, therefore, the idea of paying for the design of printed matter was still rather novel and many wondered what, exactly, they would be getting for their money.

The common perception was that design was an extension of art; art applied to a specific commercial requirement and, as such, the practitioner was called an 'applied artist' or 'commercial artist'. But the growing use of the term 'designer' signalled a recognition that this was, in fact, a separate activity from art. The break with art was resisted by some who highlighted the skills and imagination required, to say nothing of shared cultural inspiration (the term 'artist' in the context of design remained in use well into the twentieth century). After all, the huge majority of designers were still educated in art schools, where the line between art and design remained deliberately blurred.

It is not surprising, then, that the designer was approached with caution. Moreover, there was no recognized code for professional design ethics or its practice. Prior to 1900, there was little agreement regarding appropriate qualifications or even what might be required for basic education or training. Indeed, there was a sense that the success of the independent print designer depended as much on his social networking skills, charm and 'silken tongue' as his creative, intellectual or technical abilities. Difficulty in defining the core activi-

ties of the independent designer, as well as the complexity of the market in which he functioned, meant that his modus operandi had a vague, even suspect character.

To all of this must be added the very deep resentment that was felt within the print trade towards the growing interference by the independent designer. With the exception of the illustrator, who was tolerated because his (or, by now, increasingly her) skills were entirely different from those in the print trade, the print designer was seen, quite correctly, as a direct threat to the printer's livelihood as well as the integrity and pride of the trade. A more direct complaint was that the independent designer was taking money away from the print trade, although this was unlikely to be the case. Printers were not charging less for not having to plan or 'design' work and, besides, the compositor had to decipher the designer's type specification – not always an easy task.

To establish functions and intentions, most professions form an authoritative body to provide a focus for identity, sharing of information, and a platform for their commercial and cultural achievements. Printers, typographers, advertisers and illustrators had all previously done this. The problem was that the print designer could quite easily join all of these and still not adequately cover what his role entailed.

The distinction between designer and printer had been established to some extent within the jobbing printing industry during the first flush of artistic printing, causing the skills and responsibilities of the compositor and printer to become quite separate, to the advantage and status of the compositor, and detriment of the printer. The printer had been described as merely a mechanic. Now the same was being said of the compositor, who was reduced to following the instructions of the designer.

Opposite, far left The back of a cabinet card (a stock card on which a photographic print would be mounted), designed by J. Schmidt in the Art Nouveau style, Germany, *c.* 1890s.

Opposite, centre Catalogue cover for stock electrotypes, Frankfurt, Germany, 1907. Compared with the earlier cabinet card, although some semblance of natural forms remains, the decorative elements are essentially abstract.

Opposite, top right Label, Germany, 1913. This label was one of several examples of German printing included in the American journal *The Printing Art*. The caption reads: 'How a German printer advertises.'

Opposite, bottom right Announcement of a birth, set in Hollandsche Mediaeval, France, 1913.

Left Spread from the Dutch journal *Typografische Mededelingen*, featuring a series of close-up photographs to show the effect of different paper and ink combinations on legibility, July 1913.

Of the early independent designers[16] who started working before or during the time that the Kelmscott Press was in full production, George W. Jones in the UK and Daniel Berkeley Updike in the USA were important in establishing the 'normality' of separating design from printing, although both achieved this within printing companies they owned. The same could be said of many artistic printers, including Harpel, Haight, Kelly, Earhart, Tuer and Hailing. Other, truly independent, freelance designers, for example Henry van de Velde (Belgium) and Peter Behrens (Germany), as well as Bruce Rogers, Frederic Goudy, William A. Dwiggins, Will Ransom, Thomas M. Cleland and Frederic Warde (all Americans and collectively known as the 'heroic generation'), would follow.

Jones, as the newly installed Head of the Art Printing Department at the Darien Press in Edinburgh,[17] was reported in *The British Printer* in 1888 to be 'devoting himself exclusively to designing'.[18] In June of the following year, he moved to London where he set up his own printing office and compositors were employed to set type to his instructions. Jones's international reputation for the quality of both design and printing was remarkably high (perhaps this was linked to his notorious reputation for being unable to meet deadlines). His work was admired by American contemporaries such as Updike and Rogers, and his outspoken views made him a popular speaker.

Updike (1860–1941), who 'started with no training, not much health, and little money',[19] began his career by chance, working as an errand boy for the publishing company Houghton Mifflin, Boston. Having flourished there, in 1893 he set himself up as an independent typographer designing books and established his own printing company, Merrymount Press, shortly afterwards in partnership with

John Bianchi, who took responsibility for print production. The work of this press, closely aligned with Morris but utilizing commercial printing processes, was later celebrated in major exhibitions in New York and Boston. However, Updike's biggest legacy results from his writing. He taught at Harvard's Graduate School of Business Administration and the lectures given there, between 1911 and 1916, concerning the technique of printing became the basis of his two-volume *Printing Types: Their Histories, Forms, and Use*, first published in 1922, which remains a standard text today.

The most significant of the early independent designers, however, was Rogers (1870–1957) who, like Updike ten years earlier, had started his career working for Houghton Mifflin. Rogers took art classes as part of his studies at Purdue University and on graduation spent a brief period as a commercial artist working for advertising and newspaper publishing companies in Indianapolis. At this time, Rogers was working essentially as an illustrator, but on seeing his first Kelmscott Press books decided instead to follow the interest he had always had in typography and the materials that provide the book with its physical form.

Houghton Mifflin was a model book-printing plant. In the 1890s, its composing room employed between 40 and 50 men, 6 apprentices and an estimated 15 women. There were as many as 20 proofreaders, while the presses were worked by 30 printers assisted by 36 feeders. Initially, when Rogers joined the company, he was designing trade books and advertisements. But in 1900, a separate department was established by the senior partner, George H. Mifflin, for the design and production of limited-edition books. That a large American printing company would place its resources, together with funds for experiments, at the disposal of a young designer was without precedent, and especially remarkable given the sceptical attitude towards design in book printing at that time. A book compositor expected to be instructed by 'elders and betters'.

Nevertheless, over time, the impact of Rogers's work at Houghton Mifflin was significant enough for him to be given, in 1903, a separate studio complete with the exclusive

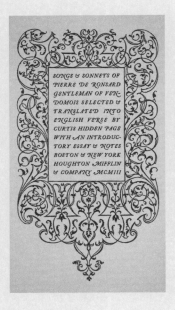

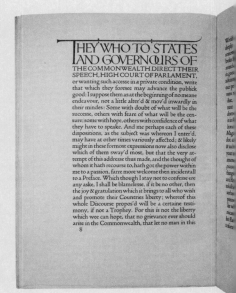

use of the elderly but reportedly malevolent pressman, Dan Sullivan. With George Mifflin's support, this became the department for the production of Riverside Press Editions. Thorne typesetting equipment was installed, although much of Rogers's work was still set by hand, which even extended to punch-cutting and casting of special characters and ornaments. Custom-made inks and the finest papers were ordered. In all, forty-seven Riverside Press Edition books were published. Managerial change eventually brought the work of the department to an end in 1912.

Rogers's subsequent international freelance career as a book designer was remarkably successful. He became renowned for the infinite pains he devoted to the detail of typographic design, a process recorded by a trail of successive marked-up proofs demonstrating his reverence for typography, his fascination with the process and the fine judgments required in its setting. This use of the type specifications followed by a sequence of proofs, each with a succession of directive amendments in red ink for the compositor to implement, would be the template by which independent typographers would function deep into the twentieth century.

The type specification heralded the beginning of a new era, for both designer and compositor. To many, it very effectively demonstrated the skills, knowledge and sensibilities required of the designer, the unfortunate assumption being that these same skills, knowledge and sensibilities were lacking in the compositor. This was unfair. Rogers was making visual what good compositors had always done, without comment or credit, since the fifteenth century. Fine judgments concerning the balance and proportions of a page of text, its margins and distribution of hierarchic elements, down to the finest detail of specific inter-character spacing,

had been the very essence of the compositor's craft. With the arrival of the independent designer, what could the compositor do but follow instructions, whether, in his opinion, they were correct and appropriate, or not? And who could blame the compositor for wondering where everything had suddenly gone so wrong?

Rogers, like many American designers of his generation, was awe-struck by the achievements of the Kelmscott Press, but what separated him from his contemporaries was that he looked beyond the Kelmscott books themselves to study the work that had originally inspired Morris. His great achievement lay in successfully transferring the artistry and finesse of handcraftsmanship to the mechanical processes of machine production.

Frederic Goudy (1865–1947), like Rogers, began his career in commercial art and was drawn to typography by the work of the Kelsmscott Press. He moved from Chicago to the East Coast and set up the Village Press. Although never important from a financial viewpoint,[20] this press did provide an appropriate context, a historic reference to the craft and purpose of his main activity, which became the design of typefaces. Goudy was prolific in his output, primarily producing display faces for use in advertising. These letter-forms sometimes have the swagger that characterized the American wood-letter fonts of fifty years earlier and, as such, were criticized by designers such as Updike and Rogers, for whom Goudy's 'peculiar looking types' were coarse and even naive.[21] The criteria that would later define the differences between 'graphic' and 'advertising' design were already being established.

Opposite, left *Songs & Sonnets of Pierre de Ronsard Gentleman of Vendomois*, designed by Bruce Rogers for Houghton Mifflin & Co., Boston and New York, USA, 1903.

Opposite, centre Cover of a booklet promoting the typeface Hollandsche Mediaeval, designed by S. H. de Roos, 1912. This was De Roos's first typeface, designed for the Dutch typefoundry Lettergieterij Amsterdam. It was a remarkable success, becoming a standard typeface in Dutch printing.

Opposite, right The opening page of *Areopagitica* by John Milton, Doves Press, with calligraphy by Edward Johnston, London, 1907. The Doves Press was the leading light of the private press movement, designing, handsetting, printing and selling limited-edition books with very few decorative elements.

Right *The Art and Practice of Typography: A Manual of American Printing* by Edmund G. Gress, New York, 1917. This page is from a chapter titled 'The Layout Man', whom Gress describes as a compositor with an 'artist temperament'.

Designers working with printers

'Every well-regulated [printing] office has its own "rule-twister", "fancy man", or "artist", if you please, and he is paid a salary in proportion to his ability – or should be,' *The British Printer* reported in 1892.[22] This was the print trade's response to the employment of art-trained staff by advertising agencies. American journal *The Inland Printer* stated in 1907, 'the tendency is for larger [printing] offices to have an artist to lay out the work'.[23] The expectation was that this person would be an experienced compositor with sufficient 'artistic inclinations' to be able to devise a layout (also called a 'mock-up' or 'visual') by which a customer could judge the appropriateness of the printer's intended solution.

In contrast, advertising agencies employed a whole department of layout artists who did nothing else. These would normally have received an art-based education and achieved a high standard in drawing and lettering skills. Their responsibility was to provide a realistic visual interpretation for the client of what the job would look like when printed. Most important, it had to sell an idea. Only after the idea had been accepted would the layout, together with additional detailed typographic instructions, be passed to the printing company who, ultimately, passed it to the compositor.

A layout might be a pencil sketch or, if the size of the client's budget demanded it, it could be highly detailed, including all headlines, straplines and copy, and illustrations drawn with sufficient detail to make their style and content clear. The finished layout was generally mounted on thick card and protected by a sheet of translucent paper folded over the top and attached to the back.

The presentation of the advertising layout to the client often had a theatrical aspect. It would take place in a room allocated for the purpose, with the advertising company's greatest achievements framed on the walls. Holding the layout in front of the client, a senior company representative (not the layout artist) would set the scene by explaining the concept behind what was about to be unveiled. The cover sheet would then be lifted with a flourish and, having paused for a second or two, the representative would guide the client through the layout, explaining its salient points. All of this would be conveyed in a charming but authoritative tone. Whereas such display smacked of artifice to many in the printing fraternity and even to those in the jobbing sector, for whom addressing the expectations of clients was a daily occurrence, advertising agencies recognized the art of selling as a central plank of their business.

Trained entirely within the confines of the printing office, the calm, methodical, often self-effacing disposition of the printer did not fare well against the slick advertising executive. Advertising agencies were dominated by educated men with university degrees[24] who had every intention to steer the profession away from the discredited 'chromo-culture' of patent medicines and circus posters. Advertising, as practised by the advertising agency, was now a science rather than art: rational, and if correctly researched and planned, its results (and profits) predictable. This, of course, was exactly what clients wanted to hear.[25] Despite the creativity offered by the jobbing compositor and his transformed status over the previous twenty years, the overall design service provided by the printer compared to that of the advertising agency was falling short, and the gap was quickly widening.[26]

The American Edmund G. Gress, in his book *The Art and Practice of Typography* (1917),[27] argued that printers must resist the 'responsibility for typographic layout passing to men outside the printing office'. But to achieve this, the printer had to find the means to communicate his intentions to his

clients before any type was touched. In a chapter titled 'The Layout Man', Gress advised: 'In printshops extensive enough to allow the expense, one or more layout men should be employed, and in the smaller concerns the head job-compositor or foreman could do the work... From the composing-room force take the most artistic and practical job-compositor and install him at a desk. If there is not sufficient desk work to occupy his full time, arrange with him to fill in spare time at the case... His work will be expedited if he has an assortment of good crayons; hard, medium and soft pencils; a pair of shears, a T-square, a gelatine triangle, a type-line gage, a table for giving a number of words to an inch in the various size type bodies; and a library of books and periodicals on printing, especially those showing examples of type designs.'[28]

Gress describes the layout man as being an apprentice-trained compositor rather than an art-college-trained designer, maintaining the official line of restricting entry to the printing office to those with union membership. The reality was that art departments within printing companies were increasingly manned by 'outsiders'. Union rules were circumnavigated by physically separating art departments from the print shop. Designers were told not to enter the designated print areas, although such rules were impractical and, over time, relaxed. Nevertheless, animosity in the print trade remained rife, and the designer's presence was, at best, tolerated.

Hollerbaum & Schmidt in Berlin was one of many printing companies promoting itself as providing a 'complete reproduction service ... guaranteeing effective artistic standards and advice against unnecessary expenditure for a commission of between five and ten per cent'. But rather than establishing an in-house art department, the co-director,

Ernst Growald, contracted Lucian Bernhard, the most celebrated poster designer in Berlin before 1914, to use Hollerbaum & Schmidt exclusively for printing; in return Growald commissioned artwork from Bernhard.[29] Such innovative contractual agreements between designer and printer were much discussed in the printing trade press but remained relatively rare.

The status of the commercial artist in Germany was rather unique in that it was recognized as a profession in its own right and, indeed, seen as a national strength. This was due in no small part to the pioneering work of the Werkbund, which established a distinction between the function of art and the function of 'applied' art. Because of this, advertising agencies were slower in being established in Germany and, instead, poster and press campaigns were generally orchestrated by commercial artists working independently of both advertising agencies and printing companies. As a consequence, while American advertising placed much emphasis on the power of the printed word, in Germany advertising developed an emphatically pictorial style.

Specialist magazine printing and publishing establishments had probably been among the earliest to recognize the advantages of having their own art departments. The range of expertise, as described by the advertisers' journal *Printers' Ink*, included lettering artists, 'one to create "unusual lettering or freak fonts", and another "capable of rendering more refined, copper-plate lettering"'. 'Decorative designers' were also necessary to 'pull the design together'. The growing influence of photography is demonstrated by the reference to an airbrush retoucher, while other specialists included illustrators, a colourist and, of course, a layout man.[30]

Opposite, far left Ideas from *Type for Books and Advertising* by Eugene M. Ettenberg, New York, *c.* 1937. Aimed at printers, advertising agencies and production departments of magazines and newspapers, this book focuses on design rather than technical processes, explaining: 'The average designer will fill a page with these postage-stamp-sized ideas, putting them down in rapid succession.'

Opposite, centre One of a series of more refined thumbnail layouts from *Layout in Advertising*, written and illustrated by William Addison Dwiggins, published by Harper & Brothers, USA, 1928.

Opposite, right Hand-drawn 'rough' layout for a direct mail company, simulating what the client would receive from the printer, London.

Left 'How to design advertising', *Print User's Year Book*, 1934.

Top right An example of a typographic specification – drawn by the independent typographer to provide the compositor with all the information required to set the job – and the first proof, from *Printing Design and Layout* by Vincent Steer, 1934.

Bottom right A page of competition entries, *The Printing World*, UK, 1910.

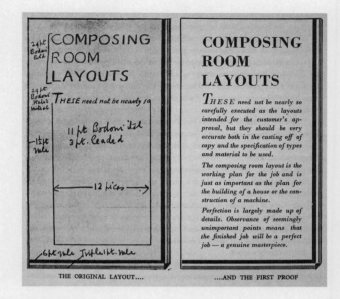

THE ORIGINAL LAYOUT....   ....AND THE FIRST PROOF

Establishing credibility for design

In order to participate fully in 'progress', advertising agencies, along with ambitious business entrepreneurs, believed it essential that modern business practices and attitudes be incorporated. Modernism required a scientific, pragmatic approach, and larger business organizations rallied behind the cause. Advertising agencies also fell into line but, simultaneously, had to find a way of accommodating creativity. When and how to control creative activity, and then measure its success or failure, became something of an obsession, not just for the advertising agencies but modernist thinkers generally.

From 1900, the discussion over whether advertising was an art or a science had major implications for education and training as well as for commercial organizations. If advertising was to be viewed as a science (a far easier notion to sell to business than art), then its necessary expertise had to be studied in theoretical as well as practical terms, preferably at the most prestigious institutions. The traditional, ad-hoc method of training on the job – the approach championed by the printing industry – was being rejected by the advertising industry.

Advertising, still a relatively new profession, required and sought public esteem. Put bluntly, the public 'had to be taught to trust them'.[31] The answer, at least in part, was the incorporation of institutional training: diplomas in applied art and design, and university degrees in anything from literature, psychology and sociology, to business studies, marketing and law. It was argued that academic qualifications gained at nationally recognized institutions, independent of the advertising industry, would not only raise the credibility of advertising with its clients, but improve its public esteem and, indeed, self-esteem.

These views were diametrically opposed to those of the printing industry, which sought to remain as independent as possible from institutional interference and maintained the line that only it knew what the required standards were and how to achieve them. Even attendance by apprentices at technical college was considered by many to be a damaging concession to modern ideology. In fact, the focus of such courses was often parochial and formulaic, the ultimate aim being 'to protect their "art and mystery", and confine it to those legitimately entitled to its possession, and to [show] opposition to any device, educational or otherwise, which threatened to break down the privilege and exclusiveness of the journeyman craftsman'.[32]

In this way the printing industry was losing its autonomy by failing to respond to the changing purposes of printed

Modern Demands

media.[33] The energy generated by that loose but highly effective international coalition of jobbing printers during the 1880s was now not just over, but despised. In its place were a series of post-Morris 'print revivals' championed in England, Germany and the Netherlands. Such a revival was also in the minds of a group of American professionals based largely in printing for publishing houses but with interests in the broader graphic arts. They called themselves the Graphic Group and met at the National Arts Club, New York, during the winter of 1911–12. An enlightened range of lectures was arranged on subjects that included photography (Alfred Stieglitz), typography (Frederic Goudy), advertising campaigns (Earnest Elmo Calkins) and poster design (Max Weber).

Associations such as the Graphic Group, as well as the United Typothetae of America (1862), the Grolier Club (1884) and the Society of Printers (1904) before it, were often established by, and drew their membership from, the middle and upper classes living and working in the larger metropolitan areas. Importantly, they were non-union, and often viewed themselves as organizations primarily for employers. United Typothetae concerned itself with practical and economic issues, while the Grolier Club membership was made up of book collectors interested in the non-commercial aspects of publishing. The Society of Printers, meanwhile, consisted of those inspired by Morris and actively engaged in the private press movement, including Rogers and Updike. What these organizations shared was an interest in books and publishing. In contrast, the broad interest-base of the Graphic Group was a major break with tradition.

In November 1913, the Graphic Group was effectively incorporated into the newly formed American Institute of Graphic Arts (AIGA) whose subsequent national member-ship campaign was further broadened. John G. Agar, president of the National Arts Club, New York, announced the founding of the AIGA thus: 'The Institute will include engravers, etchers, the Typothetae, lithographers, illustrators, panel painters, mural painters, and generally, all arts and crafts to make ideas visible', its aim being to 'raise the standard and aid the extension and development of the graphic arts in the United States.'[34] The emphasis on ideas, extension and development gave impetus to the designer, to the detriment of the printer. The printer was not only losing his status as a craftsman but also as a businessman.

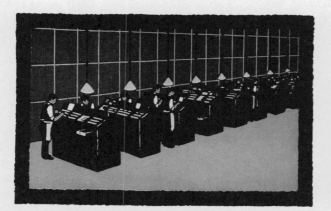

Graphic design and the graphic designer

William Addison Dwiggins (1880–1956) was only twelve years younger than William H. Bradley, but the differences in their early careers reflect the fast-changing status and nature of design within the graphic arts. Like Bradley, Dwiggins initially felt impelled to work in a printing environment in order to become a designer of print. But unlike Bradley, thanks to an uncle's generosity he was able to obtain an education in art. From the age of nineteen, he attended the Frank Holme School, Chicago, where one of his classes – lettering – was taught by Frederic Goudy. On finishing his studies, Dwiggins sought freelance advertising work before deciding to establish his own printing workshop in Cambridge, Ohio – a short-lived venture. After a brief spell at Goudy's Village Press, Dwiggins left printing behind to set up his own, very successful studio designing layouts and producing artwork for advertising agencies and for customers directly.

The allure of the artisan workshop to Dwiggins, Goudy, Bradley and others reflected the continued influence in the United States of the Kelmscott Press. The need of the print designer to demonstrate the craft skills and maintain the cultural references of the printer remained potent. It also provided independence for the designer from the vagaries of a print profession. Having sole responsibility also meant that the designer-printer wore overalls and got ink on his hands, while his uncompromising passion – demonstrated by long hours refining even the smallest of jobs with little regard for the cost of time – further isolated him from the print trade, which considered this behaviour naive.

Such estrangement would, no doubt, be considered honourable by the designer-artisan, but Dwiggins decided to break with the print workshop to concentrate on design, confident that he could apply his artisan principles from outside the print trade. More than that, he chose to explore and understand the mechanisms of the advertising industry – and to master them. Between 1904 and the mid-1920s, while working in the most demanding of commercial conditions, Dwiggins demonstrated a principled approach and a social conscience by, in his own words, aiming at 'honorable merchandizing' and avoiding the 'kind of leverage that no person with a rudimentary sense of social values is willing to help apply'.[35] His experience spent in advertising was summarized in his book *Layout in Advertising*, published in 1928.

Dwiggins's article 'New Kinds of Printing Calls for New Design',[36] written in 1922, contains echoes of the discussions recorded by the Werkbund regarding the necessary separation of art and design, for example: 'When placards are put at the corner garage announcing the current price of gasoline they do not need fine art. They do their work just as they are. All the main purposes of printing can be served without calling upon the help of art.' Later, in the same article, he uses the term 'graphic design' to describe that aspect of advertising – design for print – most effective in communicating to the widest possible audience: 'Advertising

design is the only form of graphic design that gets home to everybody.'

Dwiggins was a modernist, although he admired the work of Edward Johnston in England and Rudolf Koch in Germany and, like them, considered a shared passion for craftsmanship to be essential in the symbiotic relationship between designer and printer. He was also a pioneer of the revival of calligraphy in the United States. But, like the membership of the Werkbund, he was also comfortable embracing the commercial maelstrom and was forthright in encouraging others to do the same. In this respect, Dwiggins did much to define what a graphic designer did and, equally important, demonstrated the intelligence and integrity that the role could bring to advertising and to print design generally.

Postscript

The *Bauhaus Manifesto and Programme* (1919), under the heading 'Principles of the Bauhaus', explains that 'there will be no teachers or pupils in the Bauhaus but masters, journeymen, and apprentices'. However, by 1923 the idea of a 'new guild of craftsmen'[37] was being dropped to focus on the modern world of machines, radios, telephones and cars. The 'masters' were now 'professors', as the concept of the medieval-inspired master, together with journeymen and apprentices, was abandoned.

The print trade, hampered by its own internally regulated training scheme, could not so easily abandon its guild-based roots. Many argued that by distancing himself from these discrete roots, the printer would lose what little integrity he had left. Artistic printing, it was argued, had been the embarrassing legacy of such folly. Morris's critically successful return to medieval basics was seen by many as a devastating indictment of a print trade that had lost its moral compass.[38] Few had the stomach to take on the conspicuously indiscrete business of advertising.

As the status of the designer grew, so the function and prestige of the printer diminished. In an article for *The Printing Art*, J. Horace McFarland describes the low esteem in which the American jobbing printer was now held within the business community: 'No one now cares for the printer as a business man. He is the football of the publishers and the doormat of those who have large relation to his work. He no longer wears the sword which once proclaimed him a man of consequence … unless he is one of the happy dozen or more who have fought themselves into knowledge of their pursuit and then into such comparative wealth as will make them nearly equal to the average plumber in commercial importance.'[39]

Art Nouveau

Luigi Melchiori (*left*) began his business in 1880 and quickly gained a national reputation for his wood types. Only a small number of type specimen catalogues were made with this remarkable cover and reserved for esteemed customers. The central panel is made from wood and was achieved using a pantograph.

In France, one of the best-known products of Art Nouveau was developed for the Paris Métro. The original station entrances and lettering, characterized

by elaborate, organic forms, were designed by Hector Guimard from 1900 (*top right*).

Art Nouveau reached its height in Europe, where it touched virtually everything, and its influence can be detected in illustrative work deep into the twentieth century (*bottom right*). However, its free-flowing lines did not suit letterpress technology and caused the compositor to become increasingly reliant on foundry-manufactured readymade stereotypes (*centre right*).

Left Cover of *Premiata Fabbrica Caratteri e Fregi in Legno* by Luigi Melchiori, Veneto region, Italy, *c.* 1910s.

Right, from top to bottom Signage for the Paris Métro, designed by Hector Guimard, *c.* 1900; stereotype from *Album d'Application*, Fonderie de G. Peignot & Fils, Paris, 1901; cigarette card (front and back) from the series 'Eastern Proverbs', illustrated by René Bull, Imperial Tobacco, full-colour lithography, *c.* 1930s.

Below Catalogue cover for pencil
manufacturer Koh-i-Noor Hardtmuth,
lithography with gold and embossing,
London, *c.* early twentieth century.

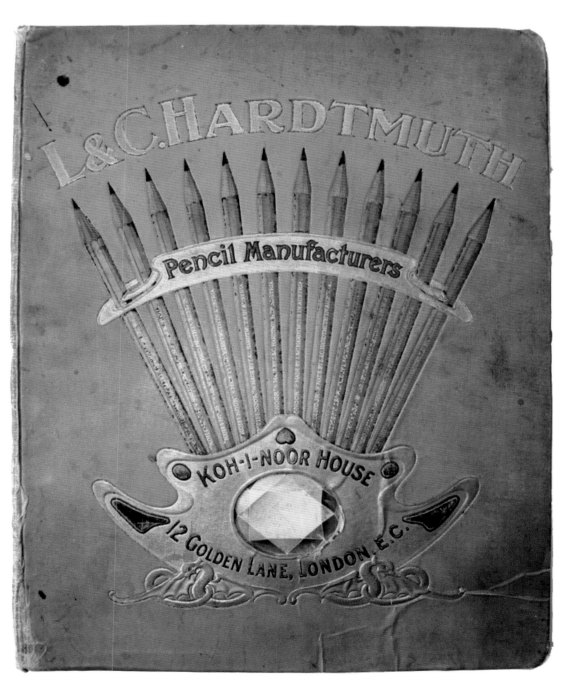

Print revivalism

By 1900, the remnants of various nineteenth-century stylistic preoccupations had been absorbed into the Art Nouveau movement. Some argued that the appearance of print had become ill-disciplined and pointlessly complex, its production inefficient and its effectiveness compromised.

The response – the print revival movement – was a concerted effort to revive traditional standards and principles but with the use of the best automated presses. In Germany, its earliest supporters were based in Leipzig. Among these was Tauchnitz, whose book covers during the 1900s were reassuringly utilitarian (*top right*) and praised by the print revivalists for their lack of ostentation.

The print revival, while favouring a return to a simpler and more efficient form of graphic communication, was certainly not anti-decoration. In fact, there was a resurgent interest in the

Top left Page from Schriftgießerei Ludwig & Mayer (typefoundry), Germany, 1910.

Bottom Letterhead for the Association of German Bookshop Agents, St Gallen, Switzerland, *c.* 1914.

Top right Cover of *The Eternal City* by Hall Caine (paperback), letterpress printed and published by Tauchnitz, Leipzig, Germany, 1902.

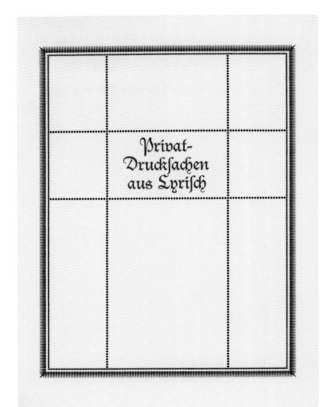

use of 'flowers', a traditional part of the compositor's skill set, by which individual decorative units were used to build up areas of pattern (*opposite, bottom*).

Bruce Rogers played a leading role in the print revival movement in the United States, drawing on Morris's well-documented exploration of late fifteenth-century Italian printing. Because of the link with Britain, the resultant interest in early American printing and its European roots was more commonly referred to in American trade journals as the

'colonial' or 'post-colonial' style. Out of this also grew a theatrical writing style inspired by European manners (*top left*).

Those working in the colonial style were self-consciously serious about their work. Others such as Dwiggins, seeking not only a more American but also a more human voice, utilized a home-spun, whimsical humour. The title page of his book *Layout in Advertising* (*bottom left*) is typical, featuring the torch of knowledge in a frame loosely based on various cultural styles.

Top left Invitation, Boston, USA, *c.* 1904.

Bottom left Title page of *Layout in Advertising* by William Addison Dwiggins, Harper & Brothers, New York, 1928.

Right Cover of *Scum o' the Earth and Other Poems* by Robert Haven Schauffler, designed, printed and published by the Houghton Mifflin Co.'s Riverside Press, Boston, USA, 1912.

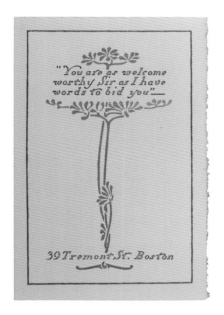

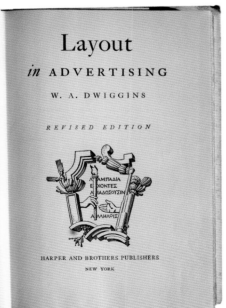

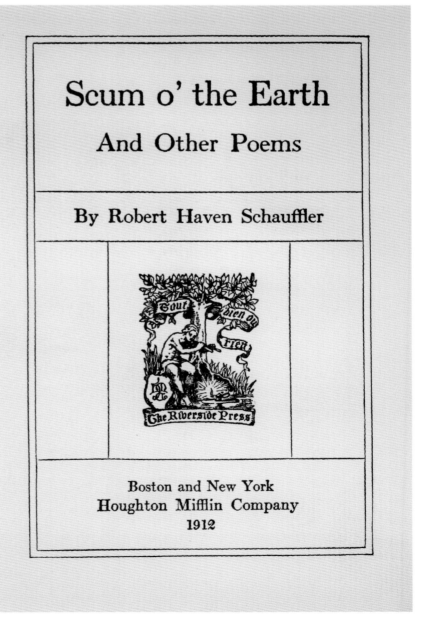

Germany entered a period of printing that was positively bright in colour and warm in form. Renewed focus on commercial imperatives was not seen as a counter argument to humanistic values – quite the opposite. Maintaining the 'hand of the artist', Behrens argued, provided the emotive link between the advertiser and the public (*top left*). The printer-publisher Insel Verlag, an important supporter of the print revival movement in Germany, produced one of the most potent

examples of the simpler, distinctly vernacular approach with its Insel-Bücherei series of books (*right*), begun in 1912.

Insel Verlag certainly impressed Harold Curwen during his stay in Leipzig in 1906. At his own Curwen Press in London, he successfully applied Arts and Crafts ideology to the design and production of advertisements, which set the Press apart. The advertisement (*opposite, top right*) lays out his intentions.

Top left Cover of a type specimen catalogue, *Behrens Schrift und Zierat*, for Rudhard'sche Gießerei, Offenbach am Main, Germany, 1902.

Bottom left Entry ticket to a gardening event in Schaffhausen, Switzerland, designed and printed by Buchdruckerei Zollikofer & Cie, St Gallen, 1913.

Right Cover of *Die Minnesinger in Bildern der Manessischen Handschrift*, published by Insel Verlag, printed by Poeschel & Trepte, Leipzig, Germany, date unknown.

Flowers, intricately built into decorative patterns, had been reintroduced in Germany to great effect from about 1908, most commonly by typefoundries on their catalogue covers. *Die Zierde* (*centre right*) is dedicated to ornaments available from the J. G. Schelter & Giesecke foundry in Leipzig.

Decoration would decrease as German designers, influenced by the arguments of modernism, rediscovered the power of letterforms alone both to attract and communicate (*bottom*). The mistrust of

decoration was an incentive for foundries to produce a new wave of distinctive typefaces – this time with the high levels of visibility required of advertising (see page 280).

Top left Cover of *Apropos the Unicorn* by Joseph Thorp, designed by Macdonald Gill, letterpress printed and published by the Curwen Press, London, 1919–20.

Bottom Letterhead for a Swiss electrical engineering company, designed by Anton Blöchlinger, Berne, Switzerland, *c.* 1914.

Top right Advertisement for the Curwen Press, letterpress, London, 1913.

Centre right Cover of *Die Zierde*, J. G. Schelter & Giesecke foundry, Leipzig, Germany, 1913.

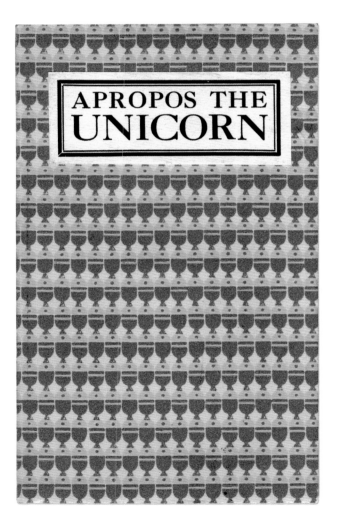

SCHWEIZ.LANDESAUSSTELLUNG BERN 1914. GRUPPEN 33 u.36
GMÜR CO. SCHÄNIS
ELEKTROMECH.WERKSTÄTTEN.
TELEPHON N.º13. / GEGRÜNDET 1884 / TELEGRAMME: GMÜRCO – SCHÄNIS.
BETRIFFT:
IN DER ANTWORT ANGEBEN!
SCHÄNIS.
ST.GALLEN.
RORSCHACH.
SCHAFFHAUSEN.
VILS/TIROL.

Impact of the Deutscher Werkbund
The newfound strength of German industry – above all its thriving exports – caused every other major economy to study the methods of the Deutscher Werkbund. Initially influenced by the Arts and Crafts movement, this formidable group of artists, industrialists, economists and sociologists moved towards a simpler, unadorned form of communication that became the hallmark of German design and was much admired in the United States.

The card below (*top left*) was among several examples of German printing showcased in American journal *The Printing Art.* The ability of the

German printer to compete with advertising and design companies in this way was cited in America and Britain as evidence of a far superior training system in Germany.

In the United States, the design company Bertsch & Cooper, set up in 1904 by Fred S. Bertsch and Oswald (Oz) Cooper, represented the competition. His famous Cooper Black, designed in 1921, is clearly discernible in the hand-drawn letters of 1915 (*centre left*).

Top left Card for the printer and bookseller Otto Elsner, Berlin, Germany, 1913.

Centre left Label by the design company Bertsch & Cooper, Chicago, USA, *c.* 1915.

Bottom left Type display, Oswald Cooper's Cooper Black, from Barnhart Brothers & Spindler type specimen catalogue, 1922.

Right Poster for an exhibition of German posters, designed by Bertsch & Cooper, Chicago, USA, *c.* 1913.

Photography and illustration
With the launch of the Kodak 'Brownie' camera, photographs became a standard visual aid for illustrators and designers. Irregular pattern, caught mid-way between abstraction and objective representation, became a popular illustrative idiom (*top right*).

Walter A. Weisner was an illustrator who drew heavily on photographic reference. The reductive black-and-white style of illustration below (*top left*) became synonymous with the work of the professional illustrator or 'commercial artist'.

Foundries had been selling readymade illustrations to the letterpress printer in the form of stereotypes through much of the nineteenth century to enable them to compete with the engraver and the lithographer. Now it was also the commercial artist with whom they had to compete (*bottom*).

Top left Self-promotional advertisement for Walter A. Weisner, Chicago, USA, 1916.

Bottom Stereotypes from the catalogue of Schriftgießerei und Messinglinienfabrik Otto Weisert, Stuttgart, Germany, 1908.

Top right Cover, designed by the Faithorn Design Company for the Dunlap-Ward Advertising Company on behalf of the North White Pine Manufacturers' Association, letterpress, Chicago, USA, *c.* 1913.

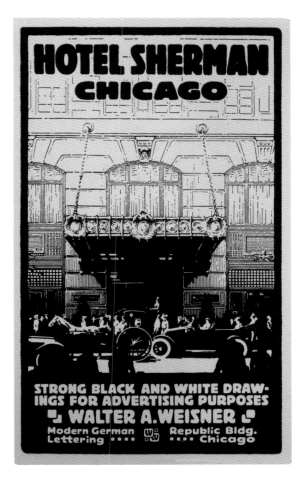

Formal and ceremonial documents
Documents relating to ceremonial events are, by their nature, generally traditional in design, often reflecting the predominant values and aesthetics at the time. In the poster (*top right*), the pomp of the annual event is captured in the elaborate yet formal design.

In the share certificate (*bottom right*) a standard range of engraved decorated borders and rubber-stamp effects, together with various security features, have been employed. The desired effect is better achieved in the safety certificate (*opposite*).

The receipt for lighthouse dues (*left*), paid by mariners for the maintenance of lighthouses, has incorporated bands to echo the red hoops commonly applied to lighthouses.

Left Receipt for lighthouse dues, letterpress printed with hand-stencilled bands in red, Istanbul, Turkey, July 1882.

Top right Poster for the Lord Mayor's Order of Procession, lithography, printed by Blades, East & Blades, London, 1892.

Bottom right Share certificate for the Chicago, Milwaukee, St Paul & Pacific Railroad Company, USA, 1935.

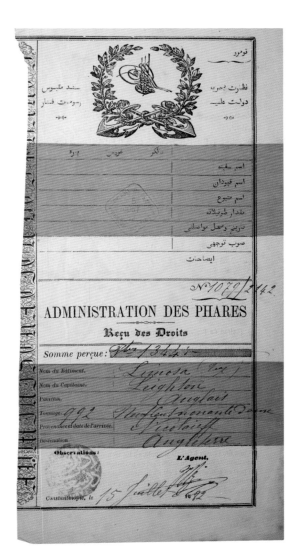

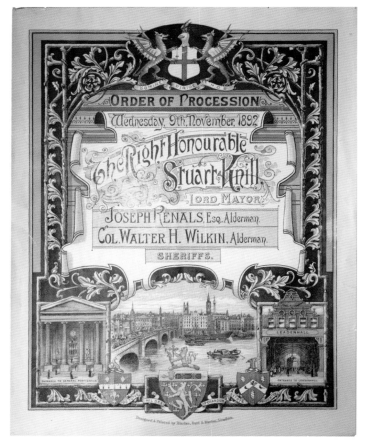

Below Safety certificate issued by
the Port of Montevideo, Uruguay, 1910.

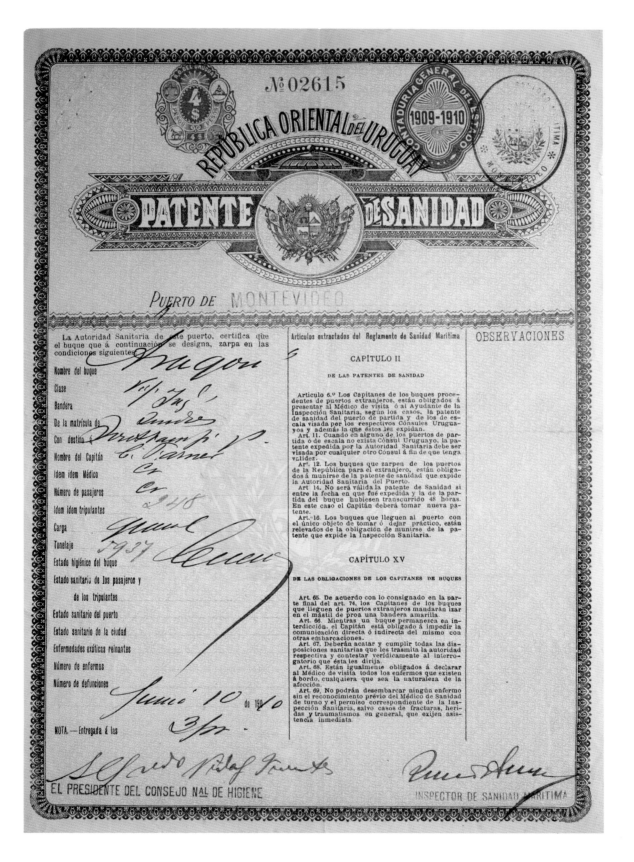

Artistic influences

Art movements such as Cubism, Futurism and Constructivism filtered into commercial printing and, eventually, dislodged Art Nouveau. Strong diagonals and simplified shapes were employed in the design of letterforms (*bottom*), while dynamic figures expressed the liberation of speed provided by technology (*centre left*).

Exaggerated perspective and emphasis on machine-like regularity are used in the poster (*opposite*) to present this hotel as a modern, efficient enterprise. The hand-drawn lettering is reminiscent of the 'Milano' example below.

Advertising stamps had no intrinsic monetary value and were generally glued to company letters, compliment slips and packaged goods deliveries. Smallness of scale encouraged strong, simple design (*top left*).

Magazine samples promoted upcoming magazine publications. The dual function of this sheet (*top right*) – a magazine cover adapted to act as a poster – gives it an uneasy but intriguing appearance.

Top left Advertising stamp for fur goods, Germany, date unknown.

Centre left Advertising stamp for travel goods company, Germany, date unknown.

Top right Magazine sample, letterpress, 1910.

Bottom Poster (detail), designed by Molteni Arti Grafiche, lithography, Milan, *c.* 1914.

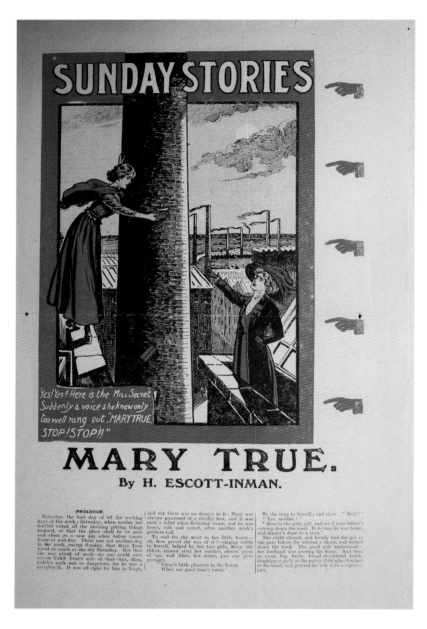

Below Poster for the Hôtel de Paris,
lithography, Paris, *c.* 1920s.

Modern advertising

Advertising agencies were keen to distance themselves from the stigma of the circus and theatre poster and what they saw as the undisciplined work of the printer. Instead, agencies opted for simple designs with minimal commentary. Isolation – even in the case of the humble steel nib, manufactured in the millions (*opposite, top right*) – could give the product a heroic aspect. In the remarkably pared-down poster below, however, the sparkling clarity of the image has been compromised by the fussy lettering at the bottom.

Decoration was considered acceptable as long as it maintained a modern (meaning simple and dynamic) appearance, as in the examples opposite (*top left* and *bottom right*), where it is used to suggest heat and energy respectively.

Below Poster for Vim, designer unknown, London, *c.* 1910s.

Top left Hotel baggage label, Rio de Janeiro, Brazil, early twentieth century.

Bottom left Point-of-sale item for Pelikan, Germany, early twentieth century.

Top right Poster for internal display, Soennecken nibs, Berlin, Germany, early twentieth century.

Bottom right Novelty advertisement for Bovril, die-cut interlay with a movable wheel, UK, 1910s.

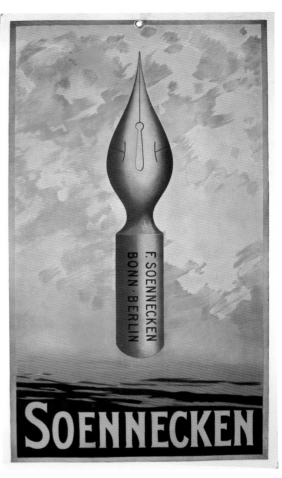

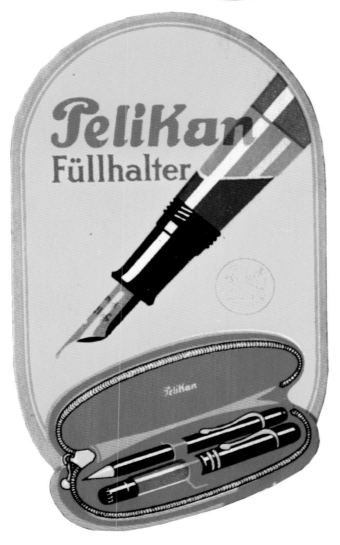

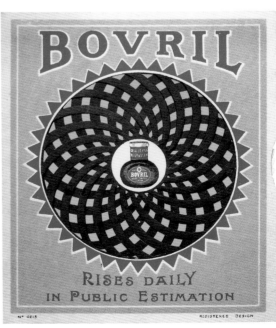

Advertising and typography

Despite the overpowering influence of modernist ideology, the first quarter of the twentieth century was a golden age for display types and the catalogues that showcased them (*top left* and *bottom left and right*). From 1900, typefoundries commissioned new fonts from artists and designers working outside the printing and typefounding industries. There was a remarkable strength and energy to these types, which were expressly designed to meet the particular needs of a maturing advertising industry; the catalogues opposite, using wood type, contain particularly good examples.

This development was increasingly echoed in the way the type itself was displayed. Instead of showing an entire font, catalogues began to display letterforms as they might appear in advertisements (*bottom right*).

Top left Cover of *Neue Schriften und Ornamente*, catalogue of Schriftgießerei Ludwig & Mayer, Frankfurt am Main, Germany, 1916.

Bottom left and right Cover and page from *Buchschmuck*, catalogue of Schriftguss A.G. (formerly Brüder Butter), Dresden, Germany, 1926.

Top right Cover of *Industria*, type specimen catalogue of Schriftgießerei Emil Gursch, Berlin, Germany, 1914.

Top left and right Page and cover
of the Acme Wood Type catalogue,
New York, 1937.

Bottom Cover of the Deberny & Peignot
catalogue, Paris, *c.* 1930s.

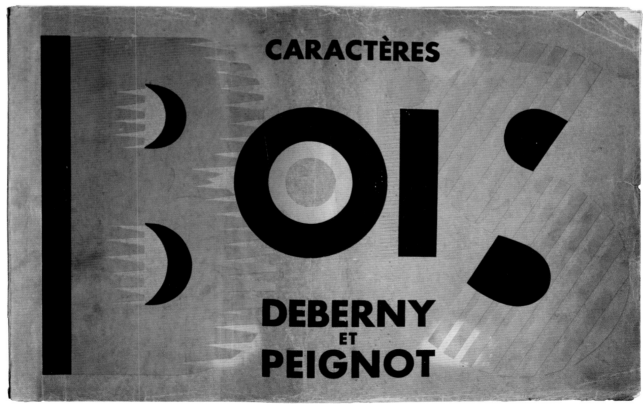

From billhead to letterhead
The first decades of the twentieth century saw a reduction in the weight and visual complexity of letterhead design. However, nineteenth-century curlicues, seen in the examples below, were slow to give way to modern design models. Medieval banners (*bottom*) were even used by manufacturers of modern products.

The methods and materials used to create these designs are similar enough to suggest that studio techniques and processes were becoming standardized as clients learnt what to expect from a designer or advertising agency. Meanwhile, it was rare for the average printer to have the skills to provide such a service.

Top Hand-drawn billhead design for a motor engineering company, designer unknown, London, *c.* 1920.

Bottom Billhead for Tubeless Pneumatic Tire and Capon Heaton Ltd, lithography, Birmingham, UK, 1902.

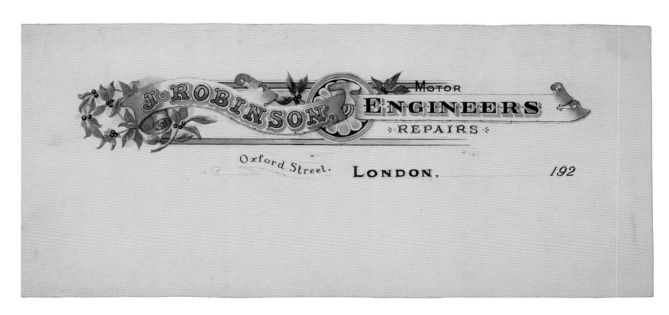

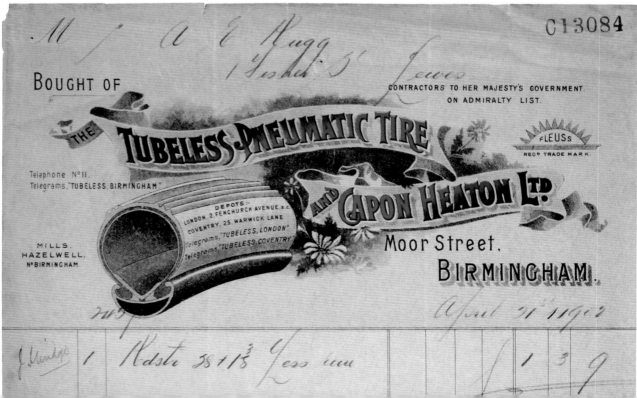

Aesthetics of clarity and order
The comfort of the familiar, which many enterprises thought essential to their business, was shared by a conservative printing trade. Designers, meanwhile, had a predilection for newness, characterized by uncluttered clarity and order, especially in Germany (*bottom*) where they had sufficient status to make changes.

The aesthetics of clarity and order were associated with information-driven items such as transport labels, tickets (*top right*) and timetables (*centre right*). In the carriage label (*top left*), the dominance of purpose over appearance brings with it a severe aesthetic. The red cross is a wood-letter 'X' on its side.

Top left Carriage label, Southern Railway, letterpress, UK, date unknown.

Bottom Letterhead for an express delivery letter from the Ministry of Justice, letterpress, Germany, *c.* 1930s.

Top right Public transport ticket, Chicago, USA, *c.* 1920s.

Centre right Railway timetable, UK, *c.* 1920s.

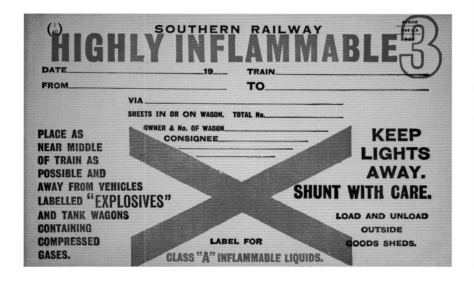

Art, advertising and print

This poster (*opposite*) for an ink manufacturer presents the printer as an artist, in a moment of deep concentration. Instead of a palette he holds a tin of green printing ink, and his press holds the same colour. The idea that the printer and the artist might share a common ideology was certainly one upheld by the Arts and Crafts movement and, even at this late date (1936), was still genuinely believed by some in the printing trade.

For the most part, however, printing was leaving concepts of Arts and Crafts behind in pursuit of something more tangible. Advertising executives argued that they did not need art to sell their products, although illustrators often came from an art-school background and had artistic aspirations. It is no surprise, therefore, that illustrative styles often reflected the various and eclectic movements associated with modernism, including Fauvism (*top left*), Art Deco (*top right*) and Futurism (*bottom*).

Opposite Poster for Hartmann inks and paints, Milan, Italy, 1936.

Top left Box-lid for Humphrey's chocolates, lithography with gold and embossing, UK, *c.* 1920s.

Top right Cover (detail) of a 'stylebook' for Hickey-Freeman Co., New York, illustrator Thomas H. Webb, full-colour lithography, date unknown.

Bottom Box-lid (detail) for glove manufacturer Gant Perrin, *c.* 1914.

Entertaining children

During the early twentieth century, 'disguised' or 'hidden' advertising aimed at children was common. The two board games below (*centre left and right*) are novelty advertising items, inserted free into magazines to promote Wood-Milne rubber heels.

The role of children's toys underwent a change during this period. Instead of being formative, toys might be bought purely for their entertainment value. The paper doll sheet (*top left*) required the costume cut-outs to be folded at the shoulder and placed over the head of the figure. The wardrobe promotes a positive if privileged representation of female social activities. More stereotypical gender roles are demonstrated on the lid of the printing set (*top right*).

Top left Paper doll sheet, three-colour lithography, USA, early twentieth century.

Centre left and right Two board games, lithography, Paris, *c.* early twentieth century.

Top right Toy printing kit with rubber letters, Italy, *c.* early twentieth century.

Bottom Pictorial alphabet, chromolithography, France, *c.* 1900.

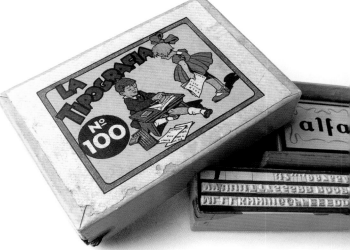

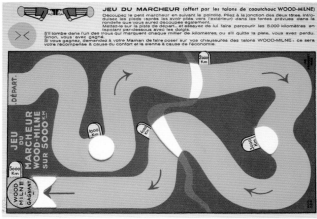

Advertising as art

Les Maîtres de l'Affiche (*top left*) was the first journal devoted to poster art. A number of miniature posters (usually eight) were reproduced in each issue, immaculately printed in colour on one side only of a page. Editorial content was minimal.

In this way *Les Maîtres de l'Affiche* was not a trade journal, but instead was aimed at the art-poster collector. The idea that printed advertising might be worthy – having a cultural value beyond its primary function – polarized attitudes.

Artists saw it as validation of a common intent: that they were, indeed, artists working on a commissioned project. But many in the business community (to whom the printer and, surprisingly, many in the advertising industry aligned themselves) considered poster artists self-serving and, therefore, thought that they did not address their main purpose – selling. Nevertheless, poster work maintained a high profile, with international exhibitions, reproductions in printing journals and fierce debate over national standards.

Top left Cover of the journal *Les Maîtres de l'Affiche*, Paris, 1895.

Bottom left Novelty advertisement (drink mat) for menswear company Hermann Scherrer, Switzerland, date unknown.

Right Poster for the North German Lloyd shipping company, printed by Munro & Hartford Co., New York, date unknown.

287

Rural values

Many posters promoting travel by bus or train were designed in Britain between the First and Second World Wars. They were united in their portrayal of values quite at odds with the modern high-speed service they advertised. Instead, these illustrations celebrate a more reflective, nostalgic notion of life.

In the colour sketch (*right*), the gouache has been applied in relatively flat areas of colour in preparation for the artwork.

Rather than reverting to full-colour lithography, these travel posters were produced by artists using a number of specially mixed colours, which could be overprinted to obtain more variations. But in contrast to the earlier chromolithographic work (in which overprinted sequences of dots would provide tones and hues), these poster artists kept the areas of colour flat. The results are modern (clean) in appearance, while their sentiments remain unapologetically romantic.

Below A preparatory pencil sketch and a rough colour visual for posters to promote rail travel, artists unknown, UK, *c.* 1920s.

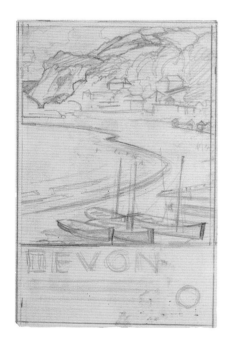

Urban values
These two cards focus firmly on the aspirations of the businessman and the environment in which he worked. The cityscape depicted in the first (*top*) – a hostile concrete jungle where steam, smoke and scaffolding blur the skyline and office lights glow red – is more akin to a science-fiction novel or comic. In the second example (*bottom right*), the company director is given the status of a statesman. Although modernism was wholeheartedly embraced in the United States (*bottom left*), working city life was often portrayed in a grittier, perhaps more realistic light.

Top and bottom right Two cards from a series promoting the use of writing pads, printed on thick, absorbent card (possibly for use as glass mats), Howard Printing Co., Chicago, USA, 1925.

Bottom left Illustration of a modern interior, reproduced in a catalogue by Munro & Hartford Co., New York, 1915.

Modern illustration
Type pictures (*right*) are simple illustrations made by compositors from rules and geometric ornaments. For a brief period in Germany, there was great interest in such work. The use of geometric ornaments appeared to combine scientific logic with something more playful, creating simple but attractive images. This example illustrates a travel diary.

Hand-drawn illustrations in the modern style could also be humorous, drawing on the short-hand narrative style of comics. The designs on the pen nib box (*top left*) and cigarette pack (*bottom left*) reflect the preference for clear, flat, bolder forms, depicting the businessman in a jocular yet dignified manner.

Top left Box of pen nibs, Milan, Italy, *c.* 1920s.

Bottom left Pack for Virginia Cigarettes, USA, date unknown.

Right Illustration, using letterpress ornaments, Germany, *c.* 1920s.

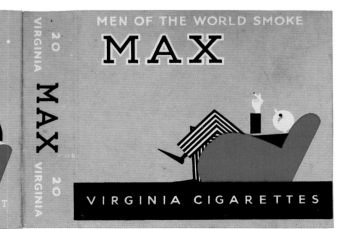

Trade journals
First published in 1903, *Typographische Mitteilungen* (*top left and bottom*) was the monthly journal of the German Printers' Association and set out to be rather conservative. When typographer Jan Tschichold was invited to be guest editor and designer of the October 1925 issue, he took the opportunity to transform its appearance and showcase work from the Bauhaus, De Stijl and Constructivism. The November issue

saw an immediate return to normality, but *Typographische Mitteilungen* was compelled to recognize that change was inevitable.

Meanwhile, other journals aimed specifically at advertising or design professionals had begun to appear. *Gebrauchsgraphik* (*top right*), founded in 1923, devoted considerable space to avant-garde-inspired design from the start, bringing these ideas more into the mainstream.

Top left and bottom Cover and spread from *Typographische Mitteilungen*, Berlin, Germany, July 1928.

Top right Cover of *Gebrauchsgraphik*, Berlin, Germany, September 1929.

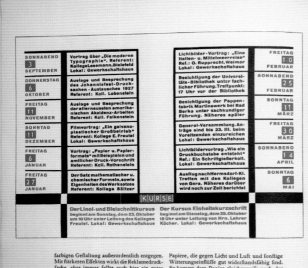

Point of sale and packaging
The point of sale (*top*) was the work of
an anonymous layout artist employed
in the art department of an advertising
agency and has clearly undergone a
number of changes. The next stage would
involve producing a 'client presentation'
model to simulate the printed item.
Usually working from a sketch provided
by the art director, the layout artist
provided an essential service by mocking
up the printed matter. Once this had been

accepted by the client, the advertising
agency then had to produce print-ready
artwork and commission a printer.
   An enterprising printer with print
finishing equipment (for cutting, creasing,
gluing and binding, for example) might
see the potential of setting up an office
in the city offering specialist expertise
in point-of-sale service to advertising
agencies (*bottom*).
   The so-called New Typography
advocated in Germany by Tschichold and

Top Hand-drawn point of sale for throat
mints, designer and date unknown.

Bottom Letterhead, hand-drawn layout
for a company specializing in point of
sale, London, early twentieth century.

others was resisted in France, where modernism could be made to look warm, amusing, even sensuous. Large bold areas of colour divided by gently curved lines and further softened by the use of cursive letterforms were typical of the French response to German angularity. Even everyday items such as these (*top* and *bottom*), while unmistakably modern, also have a joyful persona.

As the status of the designer grew, so the influence of the printer diminished. The only compensation – at least for those who had invested in industrialization – was a share of the spoils of a growing print-media market.

Top Packaging for chocolate, France, early twentieth century.

Bottom Packaging for gingerbread, France, early twentieth century.

Promoting design, relegating print
The initial production work on *Divertissements Typographiques* began in 1926, and the first issue was finally published in autumn 1928. It took the form of a folder that held a number of loose sheets of genuine graphic work chosen to show Deberny & Peignot's fonts at their best.

Peignot was scathing about the 'almost total lack of typographic culture and curiosity in the printing and publishing worlds'. Although *Divertissements Typographiques* was sent free of charge to printers who stocked Deberny & Peignot's fonts, it was also given to design consultancies in the knowledge that designers would be flattered to be included. Since it was the designer who now chose the typefaces, this created further demand for the fonts.

Below Cover, internal folder and open folder of *Divertissements Typographiques*, no. 1, art directed by Maximilien Vox, Deberny & Peignot typefoundry, Paris, 1928.

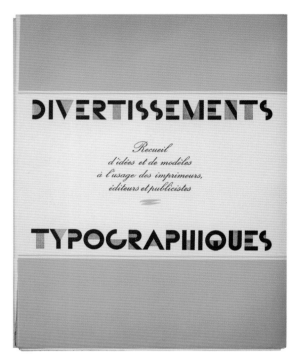

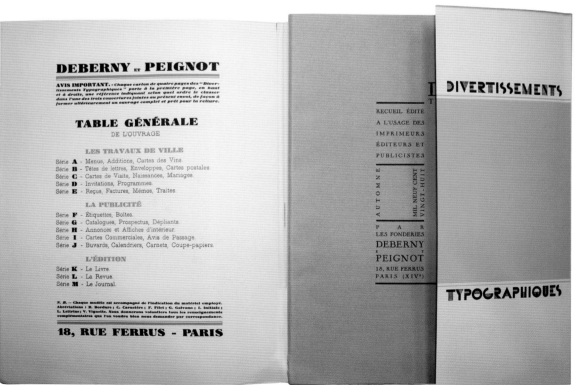

Designer journal
Despite its title, there is little evidence of the Arts and Crafts movement in either the design or editorial stance of *Arts et Métiers Graphiques Paris* (*bottom*). Consciously aimed at designers of print rather than the printing profession, the journal promoted modern design as well as Deberny & Peignot fonts.

Compare this cover with *The Printing Art* (*top*), renamed *Printed Salesmanship* in 1925, which had been one of the world's leading print trade journals at the beginning of the century (see page 219). As the design profession asserted itself, printing trade journals sought to align themselves with marketing rather than design.

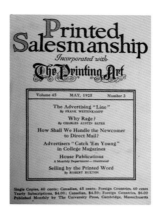

Top Cover of *Printed Salesmanship* (formerly *The Printing Art*), The University Press, Cambridge, Massachusetts, USA, May 1925.

Bottom Cover of *Arts et Métiers Graphiques Paris,* published by Charles Peignot, Paris, 1928.

Below Robert Hilton's complimentary copy of John Franklin Earhart's *The Color Printer: A Treatise on the Use of Colors in Typographic Printing*, 1892. Hilton was editor of *The British Printer* at the time, and this was probably offered as a review copy.

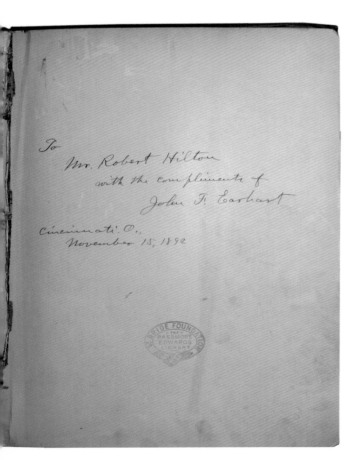

9 For a full description of the genuine master–apprentice relationship, see Steven R. Smith, 'The Ideal and Reality: Apprentice–Master Relationships in Seventeenth Century London', *History of Education Quarterly*, vol. 21, no. 4, 1981.
10 London Society of Compositors: report of the special committee on the apprenticeship question; appointed at the 117th quarterly delegate meeting, 28 February 1877.
11 T. K. Perry, 'Repeal of the apprenticeship clauses of the Statute of Apprentices', *Economic History Review*, 3, 1931–32, p. 67.
12 It has been well documented that the printer, and more specifically the compositor of bookwork, was a member of an elite 'aristocracy of labour', and certainly a literate craftsman. See Patrick Duffy, *The Skilled Compositor, 1850–1914*, 2000.
13 Graham Hudson, *The Design and Printing of Ephemera in Britain and America, 1720–1920*, 2008, p. 26.
14 Fred Smeijers, 'Typography versus Commercial Lettering', *TypoGraphic*, no. 54, 1999.
15 William Caxton in 1470 described his printing workshop as being 'at the sign of the reed pole'. See Richard Deacon, *William Caxton*, 1976, p. 118.
16 Nicolete Gray, *Lettering on Buildings*, 1960.
17 The transference of business signs to stationery is discussed in: David Jury, 'Corresponding to Form', *Baseline*, no. 41, 2003.
18 *The Universal Penman: A Survey of Western Calligraphy from the Roman Period to 1980*, p. 39. (Catalogue of an exhibition held at the Victoria & Albert Museum, London, 1980.)

Notes

Introduction

1 Huge resentment built up within the printing industry against the devastating role played by the designer, perceived as stealing the authority and pride of the printer and reducing the industry merely to that of mechanical reproduction: 'The printer had become the hod-carrier, and the designer, that flashy little stylist, the architect', from Beatrice Warde's essay 'The Crystal Goblet', *The Pencil Draws a Vicious Circle*, 1955.
2 Dr Jonathan Miller, *The Guardian* (Review section), 10 January 2009, p. 12.

Chapter One: Alternative Functions of the Black Art

1 The trade card of R. Wilson of Bidford refers to 'handbills at an hour's notice', 1825. From the John Johnson Collection (J J Booktrade Devonshire 1), Bodleian Library, Oxford, UK.
2 The metal frame is called a chase, which together with the arranged type locked into position is called a forme.
3 Here, De Vinne describes the 'improved' Willem Janszoon Blaeu wood press: 'Any intelligent mechanic [examining this press] must see in its shrinking nature of the wood framework; the sparsity of iron in the running movements; the fragility of the stone bed; and the general ramschackliness of its construction, abundant evidences of feebleness and unreliability. How then, it may be asked, could such a faulty press do even ordinary work? It did it by doing it very slowly.'
4 For instance, Charles Thomas Jacobi, *Some Notes on Books and Printing*, 1890, pp. 145–146.
5 Theodore Low De Vinne, *The Printer's Price List*, 1871, pp. 67–79.
6 Barry McKay, 'John Ware, Printer and Bookseller of Whitehaven: A Year from his Day-Books 1799–1800', in Peter Isaac and Barry McKay (eds), *The Mighty Engine*, 2000.
7 Michael Twyman, *Printing 1770–1970*, 1998.
8 *Erhebungen über die Lage des Kleingewerbes im Amtsbezirk Mannheim*, 1885. Quoted by Shulamit Volkov, *The Rise of Popular Antimodernism in Germany*, 1978, p. 25.

Chapter Two: Celebrating the Challenge of Change

1 T. A. Skingsley, 'Technical Training and Education in the English Printing Industry', *Journal of the Printing Historical Society*, no. 13, 1978/79, p. 3.
2 *Training for Tomorrow* (catalogue), IPEX, 1955, p. 3.
3 'The use of education to the workman', *Printers' Registrar*, 6 September 1880.
4 James Mosley, introduction to *Ornamented Types*, 1992, p. 15.
5 For example, in 1825 the London wood engraver Matthew Urlwin Sears produced his *Specimen of Stereotype Ornaments for the Use of Printers in General*, which included nineteen different varieties of decorated letters. In Paris, Pierre Durouchail added a specimen of *lettres ornées* to his series of stereotyped ornaments in 1827.
6 Rollo G. Silver, *Typefounding in America, 1787–1825*, 1965, p. 51.
7 Louis John Pouchée is a little documented figure in the history of typefounding. The relatively recent discovery of his *Specimens of Stereotype Casting*, which included all known examples of his company's original engraved wood blocks (now in the collection of the St Bride Printing Library, London) from which stereotypes had been made, provided the required attribution. In 1992 prints taken directly from these engraved wood blocks were published by I. M. Imprimit in association with the St Bride Printing Library in *Ornamented Types* (under Mosley, James, in the bibliography).
8 Nicolete Gray, *Nineteenth Century Ornamented Types and Title Pages*, 1938, p. 21.
9 Notably by William Cotterell (1766) and Edmund Fry (1788), but the general appearance of these types remained firmly based on roman characters, with fulsome bracketing on the serifs and graduated line-widths that are neither thick nor thin enough to be called a fat face.

10 Nicolete Gray, *Nineteenth Century Ornamented Types and Title Pages*, 1938, p. 29.

11 Confusingly, sans serif was also, initially, called Egyptian and Antique, as well as Gothic and Grotesque, or Grot.

12 Geoffrey Dowding, *An Introduction to the History of Printing Types*, 1998, p. 260.

13 Vincent Figgins used the term 'job-letter' (in two-line Great Primer Antique) to describe display types in his specimen book of 1823.

14 Walter Tracy, *Letters of Credit*, 1986, p. 82.

15 James Beattie, 'On Fable and Romance', *Dissertations Moral and Critical*, 1783, p. 374.

16 Henry Mayhew, quoting a pedlar, *London Labour and the London Poor*, vol. 1, p. 237.

17 William H. Bradley, 'Eighteenth Century Chap-Books and Broadsides', *The Chap-Book*, September 1904.

18 The railways exemplified the new power of machines. A train was described by Charles Dickens as a dragon, barely controllable, 'bubbling and trembling, making walls quake, as if they were dilating with the secret knowledge of great powers yet unsuspected in them'. In *Dombey and Son*, Dickens describes the inevitable progress of nineteenth-century industry in astronomical terms typical of the contemporary almanac: 'The earth was made for Dombey and Son to trade in, and the sun and moon were made to give them light. Rivers and seas were formed to float their ships … stars and planets circled their orbits, to preserve inviolate a system of which they were the centre.'

19 Francis D. Klingender, *Art and the Industrial Revolution*, 1968, pp. 122–123.

20 Although serious in intent, such 'medieval' musing was not beyond early Victorian humour. A hoax broadsheet, printed in 1837, intriguingly titled *Vortimer 448* and headed 'Most Remarkable Prophecy', described a stone coffin containing the sword of 'Vortimer, defender of Britons against the Saxons', supposedly discovered during the cutting of a railway tunnel on which these words were carved: 'In the year of eighteen hundred and thirty-seven, Strange signs and scourges will be sent from heaven: While under a stone I shall sleep, That year will make all Europe weep.'

21 Before daily or weekly newspapers began to be published, information concerning newsworthy events was, to some extent, covered by 'news-books', or, more appropriately, 'news-pamphlets'. In particular, the Anglo-Scottish wars of the 1540s produced numerous pamphlets containing eye-witness accounts. However, these were all ad-hoc publications. Between 1590 and 1610, some 450 English news-pamphlets were issued, of which some 250 have survived in at least one copy. S. H. Steinberg, *Five Hundred Years of Printing*, 1996, p. 121.

22 Joseph Addison, *Tatler*, 1710, also described the nature and content of early magazine and newspaper notices: 'It is my custom in a dearth of news to entertain myself with those Collections of Advertisements that appear at the end of all Publick Prints … [offering] everything that is necessary for life. If a man has Pains in his Head, Cholic in his Bowels or Spots on his Cloathes he may here meet with proper Cures and Remedies. If a man would recover a Wife or a Horse that is stolen or stray'd, if he wants Sermons, Electuaries, Asses' Milk or anything else, either for his body or his Mind, this is the place to look for them.'

23 Arthur Aspinall, 'The Circulation of Newspapers in the Nineteenth Century', *Review of English Studies*, vol. 22, January 1946, p. 29.

Chapter Three: Mechanization and International Ambition

1 Thomas MacKellar, *The American Printer*, 1866, pp. 103–105. The term 'print shop' was certainly not universally popular: see Wesley Washington Pasco's *American Dictionary of Printing and Bookmaking*, 1894, p. 463.

2 Thomas Shaw Houghton, *The Printers' Practical Every-Day-Book*, 1841, pp. 77–78.

3 Beatrice Warde would describe a similar situation one hundred years hence, when graphic designers were taking from the printing profession.

4 However, it should be noted that it was often difficult to distinguish between commercial and other announcements in newspapers before the 1870s.

5 E. S. Turner, *The Shocking History of Advertising!*, 1952. On p. 105, Turner describes an attempt to position a huge advertising display across the white cliffs of Dover, 'to extol the benefits of eating oats'.

6 Ian Maxted 'Single sheets from the country town: the example of Exeter', in Robin Myers and Michael Harris (eds), *Spreading the Word*, 1990, p. 114.

7 Eric J. Evans, *The Forging of the Modern State*, 1983, p. 278.

8 Michael Twyman, *Printing 1770–1970*, 1998, p. 26.

9 Anon., 'Technical Training for Printers', *The British Printer*, July–August 1895, p. 160.

10 Walter Gropius, in the pamphlet accompanying the 'Exhibition of Unknown Architects', 1919.

11 M. Guillotte, in evidence given to the Select Committee set up by the British government to look into the necessity of setting up a school of design. Quoted by Christopher Frayling, *The Royal College of Art*, 1987, p. 14.

12 T. A. Skingsley, 'Technical Training and Education in the English Printing Industry', *Journal of the Printing Historical Society*, no. 13, 1978/79, p. 5.

13 Alice Hamilton and Charles H. Verriel, *Hygiene of the Printing Trades*, Government Printing Office, US Department of Labor, Bureau of Labor Statistics Bulletin no. 209, 1917. Quoted by Walker Rumble, *The Swifts*, 2003, p. 178.

14 Michael Twyman, *Printing 1770–1970*, 1998, p. 95.

15 Edmund G. Gress, *Fashions in American Typography*, 1931.

16 Oscar Harpel, *Harpel's Typograph, or Book of Specimens*, introduction, 1870.

17 Oscar Harpel, *Harpel's Typograph, or Book of Specimens*, 1870, p. 48.

18 *Harpel's Typograph, or Book of Specimens* had evolved while Harpel was also working on *Poets and Poetry of Printerdom*. A third book, titled *Inside Glimpses; or Type, Press, and Sanctum*, was described as being 'in press', and scheduled for publication in 1875, but was never published. (See John F. Marthens, *Typographical Bibliography*, 1875, p. 18.)

Chapter Four: Artistic Aspirations for Mass Communication

1 Oscar Harpel, *Harpel's Typograph, or Book of Specimens*, 1870, p. 1.

2 Complex tabular work was typical of the kind of task for which a precise measuring system was necessary for type sizes. Previously, type sizes were entirely random and only given names that roughly coincided with their size, for example: 6 point, or thereabouts, was called Nonpareil; 7 Minion; 8 Brevier; 9 Bourgeois; 10 Long Primer; 11 Small Pica; and 12 Pica, etc.

3 'Foreign and English Manufacturers', *Printers' Registrar*, 6 December 1879.

4 Losing control of entry to the profession was a major concern because, the unions argued, the trade would find itself overwhelmed with applicants, which, in turn, would drive down wage claims. Added to this, of course, was the fact that women were generally paid less than men and so, potentially, put men's jobs at risk.

5 Sylvia Backemeyer (ed.), *Object Lessons*, 1996, p. 18.

6 L. T. Owens, *J. H. Mason, 1875–1951, Scholar-Printer*, 1976, p. 41.

7 'Illusionism' is the word chosen by Nicolete Gray and Ray Nash to describe what the compositors were attempting to achieve. *Nineteenth Century Ornamented Typefaces*, caption to colour plate opposite p. 115, Faber & Faber, 1976.

8 Howard Lyons, *American Art Printer* IV, June 1891, pp. 268–269.

9 George Joyner, in *Fine Printing*, 1895, p. 8, states that this process was invented by Samuel Reed Johnston, chief of the printing department of the company Eichbaum & Co., Pittsburgh, USA, who called it owltype. Chaostype (or owltype) was subsequently taken up by Anton Halauska of Hallein-Salzburg, Austria, who called it selenotype. This effect quickly became very popular throughout Europe, particularly between 1885 and 1890.

10 It was reported by Thomas Hailing in *Hailing's Circular* (no. 10, 1882) that only twelve copies of *Harpel's Typograph, or Book of Specimens* were made available in the UK.

11 Presumably William James Kelly (ed.), 'Our London Letter', *American Model Printer*, no. 2, 1879, pp. 30–31.

12 Quoted by Lawrence Wallis, *George W. Jones*, 2004, p. 14.

13 When Field died, in 1891, Tuer formed the Leadenhall Press Ltd.

14 Thomas Hailing, *American Model Printer*, January–February 1880, p. 32.

15 'Hailing's Specimen Book', *Hailing's Circular*, no. 10, 1888. Comparisons between Hailing's *Specimens of General Printing* and *Harpel's Typograph, or Book of Specimens* are inevitable if only because Hailing himself felt obliged to draw attention to the two publications in the pages of *Hailing's Circular*, no. 10, 1888. Such a comparison does Hailing few favours. The aim of Hailing's *Specimens of General Printing* was self-promotional, and the work (unlike *Hailing's Circular*) is mediocre. In contrast, *Harpel's Typograph* was more akin to a manifesto: a clarion-call for a radical realignment of printing and its function within the new consumer society.

16 *The Printers' International Specimen Exchange*, vol. 1, London, 1880.

17 Despite this, the importance of Ruskin's favour is explicit by the way George Joyner, in his book *Fine Printing*, 1895, draws Ruskin into support of the artistic printing movement: 'British typographers in course of time evolved a style whose fuller development renders it not an unworthy claimant for the occupancy of that "lovely field of design" which our great art critic, John Ruskin, considers open to the manipulators of decorative type.'

18 To many American printers, and certainly to the pages of *American Model Printer*, this obsession in England with 'Caxton' was cause for ridicule: 'I have not seen any of Caxton's own work, merely that of his imitators, and their name is legion. In fact, a stranger might think that Caxton was not dead, his name is bandied about so freely among printers. To an American, it seems strange that a style (which, to speak even with the greatest kindness, is crude, as compared with that of today) should be resurrected after so many years.' William James Kelly (ed.).

19 Andrew White Tuer: among his many remarkable publications is a collection of printers' jokes, *Quads Within Quads*, which has a miniature version of itself hidden in a hollowed-out cavity in the back of the book.

20 John Russell Taylor, *The Art Nouveau Book in Britain*, 1980, p. 49.

21 Tuer's books designed in collaboration with Joseph Crawhall were a major influence on Claud Lovat Fraser and his 'Flying Fame' chapbooks in the early 1900s. Another link between Tuer and twentieth-century printing is that his literary adviser in the 1800s was Wilfrid Meynell, whose son, Sir Francis Meynell, was to establish, among his many achievements, the Nonesuch Press.

22 See William H. Bradley, 'Eighteenth Century Chap-Books and Broadsides', *The Chap-Book*, vol. 1, no. 1, September 1904.

23 Hilton's introduction to the 1892 *Printers' International Specimen Exchange* referred to the term 'Leicester free style', adding: 'It is also gratifying to note, in looking through the current series, that a great majority of the contributors are not slavish imitators, but frequently produce decidedly fresh and original ideas of their own, a fact which tends to show that the new style is rightly named "free".'

24 Harry Whetton, 'On tour in the Land O' Cakes', *The British Printer*, no. 47, pp. 297–299.

25 Frank Luther Mott, *A History of American Magazines*, five volumes, vol. 4, 1968, p. 153.

26 This description is provided in Maurice Rickards, *The Encyclopedia of Ephemera*, 2000, p. 73.

27 Diana Korzenik, *Drawn to Art*, 1985, p. 215.

28 C. G. Zander, *Photo-trichromatic Printing*, 1896, p. 35. See also: W. D. Richmond, 'The Limitation of Three-colour Printing', *The Penrose Annual*, 1899, p. 25.

29 Blue [cyan], red [magenta], yellow and black, commonly referred to as CMYK. K stands for 'Key'.

Chapter Five: The Rise of Advertising and Design

1 Herbert W. Hess, Professor at the Wharton School of Finance and Commerce, University of Pennsylvania, dedicated his book, *Productive Advertising*, 'to those who dream, hope, think and work for a constantly improving world thru productive advertising.' Philadelphia and London: J. B. Lippincott, 1915.

2 J. Walter Thompson Company, *The J. Walter Thompson Book*, JWTCA, 1909, pp. 5–9.

3 Paul Nathan, *How to Make Money in the Printing Business*, 1900, p. 36.

4 Edmund G. Gress, *The Art & Practice of Typography* (second edition), 1917, pp. 36–37.

5 For example, Morris had his paper made for him, based on a north Italian pattern made wholly of linen using hand-woven wire moulds to provide a slightly irregular texture. The ink was made with linseed oil, freed from grease by the use of stale bread and raw onions rather than chemicals, then mixed with boiled turpentine and matured for six months before the organic, animal lampblack was ground into the mixture.

6 'Vulgarized' is the term used by Philip B. Meggs, *A History of Graphic Design*, 1983, p. 227.

7 The publisher's best engravers received annual salaries up to £2,000.

8 Gabriel P. Weisberg and Elizabeth Kolbinger Menon, *Art Nouveau*, 1998.

9 Quoted by Philip B. Meggs, *A History of Graphic Design*, 1983, p. 205.

10 Douglas C. McMurtrie (ed.), *Manual of Printing Office*, Ars Typographia Press, 1926, p. 51.

11 De Vinne disliked printed matter of any kind that self-consciously promoted itself. In a letter to Stanley Morrison, he made it clear that he was no more a fan of modernism than he had been of artistic printing.

12 George W. Jones, 'Craftsmanship and the Printer', *The Caxton Magazine*, May 1925.

13 The author was probably George W. Jones (see Lawrence Wallis, *George W. Jones*, 2004, p. 15).

14 Samuel E. Lesser, 'American Typography Largely Foreign', *The British Printer*, January/February 1929.

15 *The Monotype Recorder*, the Monotype Corporation's house journal sent free to all Monotype users, 1902, p. 1.

16 Christopher Burke, *The Monotype Recorder*, New Series, no. 10, Monotype Typography, 1997, p. 5.

17 Patrick Duffy, *The Skilled Compositor, 1850–1914*, 2000, p. 68.

18 Noax, 'Black and White Art for the Press', *The British Printer*, no. 47, 1893, p. 369.

19 Bitter descriptions of humiliating visits to art editors and the often excruciating experience of haggling over payment are found in Bruce St John (ed.), *John Sloan's New York Scene from the Diaries, Notes and Correspondence, 1906–1913*, 1965.

20 Quoted by Josep Renau, in *Signos del Siglo*, coordinating editor Irene Gil, Ministerio de Educación y Cultura, 2000.

21 'The Artistic Pictorial Poster', *Profitable Advertising*, 15 March 1895, p. 297.

22 The Grolier Club, New York, founded by printers and publishers, mounted an exhibition of art posters in 1890. There is no evidence that Penfield saw it.

Chapter Six: Printing at the Service of Design

1 There followed numerous other books, often published on an annual basis. *The Print User's Year Book* is a good example. It was first published in London in 1934 by Charles C. Knights, who invited printers to provide printed sections demonstrating their particular expertise.

2 Particularly Stanley Morrison and Beatrice Warde, in their roles as the Monotype Corporation's typographic adviser and head of publicity. Both produced prodigious amounts of material aimed at providing the trade printer with a sense of history and pride. However, they could not embrace the 'business' of advertising. The dilemma of the twentieth-century compositor can be discerned through the pages of *The Monotype Recorder*.

3 J. R. Riddell, 'Training the Printer of the Future', *The Monotype Recorder*, May–June 1928, p. 10.

4 Hower, Ralph M., *Advertising Agency*, pp. 378–382. Quoted by Pamela Walker Laird, *Advertising Progress*, 1998, p. 270.

5 The word 'printer' was equated with 'typographer' for much of the nineteenth century. Note Samuel Johnson's terse definition in the eighteenth century: 'Typographer: a printer'. This also explains why Mason's 'Printing' class is described as a 'class in typography'.

6 The Vale Press was founded by Charles Ricketts.

7 Lethaby considered teaching qualifications irrelevant.

8 Mason described the (ideal) experience of a young apprentice printer thus: 'The printer's need of verification will lead him to history and literature. Art and aesthetics will open wide and attractive fields before the youth who is interested in illustration. The inevitable interest in kindred or ancillary trades and activities will widen his range still further, and from the relations he will trace everywhere between the special activities in his own trade and that trade as a whole with other trades, will open the study of political economy – the chain is unbroken, it leads to ethics and philosophy. A trade is, or should be, the true university.'

9 W. R. Lethaby, 'Art and Workmanship', *The Imprint*, January 1913.

10 Anna Simons also translated Johnston's highly influential book, *Writing, Illuminating and Lettering*, into German in 1910.

11 For example, Johnston's calligraphic skills were incorporated into the design work of Cobden-Sanderson for the Doves Press. Johnston was also commissioned to design a font for the specific and exclusive use of Count Harry Kessler's Cranach Press in Weimar, Germany.

12 Quoted by Basil Ward, 'Symposium in Honour of Lethaby's Centenary', *RIBA Journal*, vol. 64, April 1956.

13 Jeremy Aynsley, *Graphic Design in Germany, 1890–1945*, 2000, p. 32.

14 Roger G. Sandoz and Jean Guiffrey, *Exposition française art decoratif de Copenhague, 1909*, Report to the Comité Français des Expositions à l'Étranger, 1912, p. 121. Quoted by Nancy Troy, *Modernism and the Decorative Arts in France*, 1991, p. 61.

15 Sylvia Backemeyer, *Object Lessons*, 1996, p. 18. These lectures were part of the syllabus for furniture salesmen. Similar lecture series followed for retail jewelers, the textile distributive trades and for book production.

16 It seems unlikely that during the previous five hundred years there had not been individuals who had broken through the vigorously defended 'closed shop' stance of the print trade. But one well-recorded example was William Pickering (1796–1854), a London antiquarian bookseller who also published books for which, importantly, he designed the typographic composition and commissioned the illustrations and printing.

17 Lawrence Wallis, *George W. Jones*, 2004, p. 22.

18 'Specimens', *The British Printer*, vol. 1, no. 4, 1888.

19 Joseph Blumenthal, *The Printed Book in America*, 1977, p. 64.

20 Any achievements of the Village Press were due to Bertha Goudy, Frederic Goudy's wife and co-worker. The Village Press continued until 1938.

21 'Mr Goudy, for instance … has designed a whole century of peculiar looking types.' Stanley Morison, letter of 15 September 1937, in David McKitterick (ed.), *Stanley Morison & D. B. Updike*, 1979, p. 185.

22 Burt H. Vernet, 'Artistic Advertising', *The British Printer*, vol. 5, no. 29, 1892, p. 7.

23 Editorial notes, *The Inland Printer*, vol. 38, no. 4, 1907, p. 531.

24 Sally Wyner, *A Literary Product: The Relationship of American Literature and Advertising Copy* (PhD dissertation, Harvard University, 1995).

25 Pamela Walker Laird, *Advertising Progess*, 1998, p. 293. Also, in 1910, *The Inland Printer* advised compositors on what was meant by 'clean' copy: 'The ad man wants simplicity. Rarely will he pass the florid effort. He especially dislikes fancy borders. They interfere with his direct-talk effort, for he depends more on his words to induce sales than on the art preservative. This may seem like a stunning blow to the pride of the "artist" at the case, but it is a lesson he will have to learn… It is not within his province to present the beauties of typography – rather the message he has to convey'. Louis F. Fuchs, 'Concerning Agency Composition', *The Inland Printer*, April 1910, pp. 61–63.

26 Harry S. Basford, *The Printing Art*, March 1914, pp. 120–22: 'Most printers know enough about their product to produce printed advertising that will make money for others, but many lack the broad view of the importance of printing as a selling force to talk intelligently about its use.'

27 *The Art of Typography* was originally published in 1910. The second edition, although begun in 1913, was not published until 1917.

28 Edmund G. Gress, *The Art and Practice of Typography*, 1917, pp. 38 – 39.

29 Jeremy Aynsley, *Graphic Design in Germany, 1890 – 1945*, 2000, p. 56.

30 *Printers' Ink, A Journal for Advertisers: Fifty Years 1888 – 1938*, section 2, p. 165. Quoted by Ellen Mazur Thomson, *The Origins of Graphic Design in America, 1870–1920*, 1997, p. 76.

31 George French, *The Art and Science of Advertising*, Books LLC, 2009, p. 17 (originally published 1909).

32 T. A. Skingsley, 'Technical Training and Education in the English Printing Industry', *Journal of Printing Historical Society*, no. 14, 1979/80, p. 58.

33 *The Printing Art*, January 1914, p. 361: 'The report of the Typothetae committee, 1912, records that of the 1,441 shops making reports, there were employed 2,353 apprentices. The dearth of apprentices was not the only surprising fact contained in the report. Of those that answered the committee's questions regarding instruction of apprentices, 764 reported that no attention whatever was given to them, while 304 gave some attention (given by journeymen, workmen, or foremen). If anyone has heretofore been in doubt as to what is the matter with the printing business, these figures should convince him that the trouble is due almost entirely to the manner in which apprentices are supposed to be trained.'

34 'Arts Club Warned of "Thought Trust"', *The New York Times*, 13 November 1913.

35 W. A. Dwiggins, *Layout in Advertising*, 1928, pp. 193 – 194.

36 W. A. Dwiggins, 'New Kinds of Printing Calls for New Design', *Boston Evening Transcript*, 29 August 1922, Graphic Arts Section, 3:6.

37 Walter Gropius, in the pamphlet accompanying the 'Exhibition of Unknown Architects', 1919.

38 Samuel E. Lesser, 'American Typography Largely Foreign', *The British Printer*, January/February 1929.

39 J. Horace McFarland, 'University Training for Printers', *The Printing Art*, May 1910, p. 181.

Selected Bibliography

Current Journals
Baseline
Economic History Review
Ephemerist
Eye
History of Education Quarterly
Journal of the Printing Historical Society
Matrix
TipoItalia
TypoGraphic
Typography Papers

Journals contemporary with the subject. (Those marked with an asterisk are still published.)
American Art Printer
The American Lithographer & Printer
American Model Printer
Art Age
Arts et Métiers Graphiques Paris
The Atlantic Monthly
The British Lithographer
*The British Printer**
The Caxton Magazine
Century
The Chap-Book
Commercial Art
Fleuron
The Futurists
Gebrauchsgraphik
The Graphic
Hailing's Circular
The Illustrated London News
L'Illustration
Illustrirte Zeitung
The Imprint
The Inland Printer
Journal de Paris
The Journal of Design
The Monotype Recorder
Motif

The Paper & Printing Trades Journal
The Penrose Annual
Prang's Chromo
Printed Salesmanship
Printer's Ink
The Printing Art
The Printing World
Profitable Advertising
Punch
Schweizer Graphische Mitteilungen
*Scientific American**
The Strand
The Studio
Superior Printer
Typographische Mitteilungen
Typographic Advertiser
The Yellow Book

Books

Adams, Marion (ed.), *The German Tradition: Aspects of Art and Thought in German-speaking Countries*, Sydney and London: Wiley, 1971.

Adamson, Glenn, *Thinking Through Craft*, Oxford and New York: Berg, 2007.

Annenberg, Maurice, *Type Foundries of America and their Catalogs*, New Castle, Del.: Oak Knoll Press, 1994.

Aynsley, Jeremy, *Graphic Design in Germany, 1890–1945*, London: Thames & Hudson, 2000.

Backemeyer, Sylvia (ed.), *Object Lessons: Central Saint Martins Art and Design Archive*, London: Lund Humphries in association with the Lethaby Press, Central Saint Martins College of Art and Design, 1996.

—— and Gronberg, Theresa (eds), *W. R. Lethaby, 1857–1931: Architecture, Design and Education*, London: Lund Humphries, 1984.

Beattie, James, *Dissertations Moral and Critical*, Dublin: Exshaw, Walker, Beatty, White, Byrne, Cash and McKenzie, 1783.

Beck, Robert Holmes, *A Social History of Education*, Foundations of Education Series, Englewood Cliffs, NJ: Prentice Hall, 1965.

Benson, Richard, *The Printed Picture*, New York: Museum of Modern Art, 2008.

Berra, Sandro, *A Story with Character: Ten Years of Tipoteca Italiana*, Cornuda, Treviso: Tipoteca Italiana Fondazione, 2006.

Berthold, Arthur B., *American Colonial Printing as Determined by Contemporary Cultural Forces*, New York: Lenox Hill Press, 1967.

Blumenthal, Joseph, *The Printed Book in America*, Boston: D. R. Godine, 1977.

Bradley, William H., *The Chap-Book*, vol. 1, no. 1, Jersey City, NJ: American Type Founders, September 1904.

Brooks, Chris, *The Gothic Revival*, London: Phaidon, 1999.

Burlingham, Cynthia, and Whiteman, Bruce (eds), *The World From Here: Treasures of the Great Libraries of Los Angeles*, Los Angeles: UCLA Grunwald Center for the Graphic Arts and Hammer Museum, 2001.

Chappell, Warren, and Bringhurst, Robert, *A Short History of the Printed Word* (revised edition), Vancouver: Hartley & Marks, 1999.

Clair, Colin, *A History of Printing in Britain*, London: Cassell, 1965.

——*Christopher Plantin*, London: Cassell, 1960.

(Anon.) *Composition: A Record of Seven Practical Shop Discussions Conducted by the Boston Club of Printing House Craftsmen, the Society of Printers and the Boston Typothetae*, Boston, Mass., 1927.

Consuegra, David, *American Type: Design and Designers*, New York: Allworth Press, 2004.

Corrigan, Andrew J., *A Printer and his World*, London: Faber & Faber, 1945.

Davis, Alec, *Package & Print: The Development of Container and Label Design*, London: Faber & Faber, 1967.

Day, Kenneth, *The Typography of Press Advertisement: A Practical Summary of Principles and their Application*, London: Ernest Benn, 1956.

De Vinne, Theodore Low, *The Printers' Price List: A Manual for the Use of Clerks and Book-keepers in Job Printing Offices*, 1870.

—— *The Practice of Typography: Correct Composition*, New York: Century Co., 1902.

—— *The Practice of Typography: A Treatise on Title Pages*, New York: Century Co., 1902.

Deacon, Richard, *William Caxton: The First English Editor*, London: Frederick Muller Ltd, 1976.

Dormer, Peter, *The Meanings of Modern Design: Towards the Twenty-first Century*, London: Thames & Hudson, 1990.

—— (ed.), *The Culture of Craft: Status and Future*, Manchester: Manchester University Press, 1997.

Dowding, Geoffrey, *An Introduction to the History of Printing Types*, London: British Libary and Oak Knoll Press, 1998.

Duffy, Patrick, *The Skilled Compositor, 1850–1914: An Aristocrat Among Working Men*, Aldershot: Ashgate, 2000.

Dwiggins, William A., *Layout in Advertising*, New York: Harper & Bros, 1948 (revised edition, originally published in 1928).

Dyson, Anthony, *Pictures to Print: The Nineteenth-Century Engraving Trade*, London: Farrand Press, 1984.

Eisenstein, Elizabeth L., *The Printing Revolution in Early Modern Europe*, Cambridge: Cambridge University Press, 1993.

Evans, Eric J., *The Forging of the Modern State: Early Industrial Britain, 1783–1870*, London: Longman, 1983.

Ferebee, Ann, *A History of Design from the Victorian Era to the Present*, New York: Van Nostrand Reinhold, 1992.

Frayling, Christopher, *The Royal College of Art: One Hundred and Fifty Years of Art and Design*, London: Barrie and Jenkins, 1987.

Grabar, Oleg, *The Mediation of Ornament*, Princeton, NJ: Princeton University Press, 1992.

Gray, Nicolete, *Nineteenth Century Ornamented Types and Title Pages*, London: Faber & Faber, 1938.

—— *Lettering on Buildings*, London: Architectural Press, 1960.

—— and Ray Nash, *Nineteenth Century Ornamented Typefaces*, London: Faber & Faber, 1976.

Gress, Edmund G., *The Art and Practice of Typography*, New York: Oswald Publishing, 1917.

—— *Fashions in American Typography, 1780 to 1930*, New York: Harper & Bros, 1931.

Harpel, Oscar, *Harpel's Typograph, or Book of Specimens*, Cincinnati, 1870.

—— *Poets and Poetry of Printerdom*, 1873.

Harris, Alexandra, *Romantic Moderns: English Writers, Artists and the Imagination from Virginia Woolf to John Piper*, London: Thames & Hudson, 2010.

Hartwell, R. M., *The Industrial Revolution and Economic Growth*, London: Methuen & Co., 1971.

Hilton, Roger (ed.), *The Printers' International Specimen Exchange*, volumes 9 to 16 (volumes 1 to 8 were edited by Andrew White Tuer). The complete series was published between 1880 and 1898.

Holtzberg-Call, Maggie, *The Lost World of the Craft Printer*, Urbana: University of Illinois Press, 1992.

Houghton, Thomas Shaw, *The Printers' Practical Every-Day-Book*, London (self-published), 1841.

Howe, Ellic (ed.), *The Trade: Passages from the Literature of the Printing Craft, 1550–1935*, London, Walter Hutchinson, published for the benefit of the Printers' Pension, Almshouse and Orphan Asylum Corporation, 1943.

—— *The London Compositor: Documents Relating to Wages, Working Conditions and Customs of the London Printing Trade, 1785–1900*, London: Bibliographic Society, 1947.

Hudson, Graham, *The Design and Printing of Ephemera in Britain and America, 1720–1920*, London and New Castle, Del.: The British Library and Oak Knoll Press, 2008.

Hutt, Allen, *Fournier, the Compleat Typographer*, London: Muller, 1972.

Isaac, Peter, and McKay, Barry (eds), *The Mighty Engine: The Printing Press and its Impact*, Winchester and New Castle, Del.: St Paul's Bibliographies and Oak Knoll Press, 2000.

Jacobi, Charles Thomas, *Some Notes on Books and Printing*, London: Charles Whittingham & Company, 1890.

James, Louis, *Print and the People, 1819–1851*, Harmondsworth: Penguin, 1978.

Joachim, Leo H., *Production Yearbook*, New York: Colton Press, 1948.

Joyner, George, *Fine Printing: Its Inception, Development, and Practice*, London: Cooper & Budd, 1895.

Jury, David (ed.), *TypoGraphic Writing*, International Society of Typographic Designers, 2001.

Karolevitz, Robert F., *Newspapering in the Old West: A Pictorial History of Journalism and Printing on the Frontier*, Seattle: Superior Publishing, 1965.

Kelly, Rob Roy, *American Wood Type, 1828–1900: Notes on the Evolution of Decorated and Large Types and Comments on Related Trades of the Period*, New York and London: Van Nostrand Reinhold, 1969.

Kinross, Robin, *Modern Typography: An Essay in Critical History*, London: Hyphen Press, 1992.

Klingender, Francis D., *Art and the Industrial Revolution*, New York: Augustus M. Kelley, 1968.

Knights, Charles C. (ed.), *Print User's Year Book*, London, 1934 and 1935.

Korzenik, Diana, *Drawn to Art: A Nineteenth-Century American Dream*, Hanover, NH: University Press of New England, 1985.

Laird, Pamela Walker, *Advertising Progress: American Business and the Rise of Consumer Marketing*, p. 270, Baltimore, MD, and London: John Hopkins University Press, 1998.

Lambert, Julie Anne, *A Nation of Shopkeepers: Trade Ephemera from 1654 to the 1860s in the John Johnson Collection* (exhibition catalogue, Bodleian Library), Oxford: Bodleian Library, 2001.

Lambourne, Lionel, *The Aesthetic Movement*, London: Phaidon, 1996.

Larkin, H. W., *Compositor's Work in Printing*, London: Staples, 1969.

Larson, Magali Sarfatti, *The Rise of Professionalism: A Sociological Analysis*, Berkeley, CA: University of California Press, 1979.

Last, Jay T., *The Color Explosion: Nineteenth-Century American Lithography*, Santa Ana, CA: Hillcrest Press, 2005.

Laver, James, *Victoriana*, London: Ward Lock, 1966.

Lawson, Alexander, *The Compositor as Artist, Craftsman and Tradesman*, Athens, Ga.: Press of the Nightowl, 1990.

Lewis, John, *Printed Ephemera: The Changing Use of Type and Letterforms in English and American Printing*, London: Faber & Faber, 1969.

—— *Anatomy of Printing: The Influences of Art and History on its Design*, London: Faber & Faber, 1970.

—— *Collecting Printed Ephemera: A Background to Social Habits and Social History, to Eating and Drinking, to Travel and Heritage, and just for Fun*, London: Studio Vista, 1976.

—— and Brinkley, John, *Graphic Design: With Special Reference to Lettering, Typography and Illustration*, London: Routledge & Kegan Paul, 1954.

Loos, Adolf, *Ornament and Crime: Selected Essays*, Riverside, CA: Ariadne Press, 1998.

Lucie-Smith, Edward, *The Story of Craft: The Craftsman's Role in Society*, Oxford: Phaidon, 1981.

McCullough, Malcolm, *Abstracting Craft: The Practiced Digital Hand*, Cambridge, Mass., and London: MIT Press, 1998.

MacKellar, Thomas, *The American Printer*, Philadelphia, 1866.

McKitterick (ed.), David, *Stanley Morison & D. B. Updike: Selected Correspondence*, London: Scolar Press, 1979.

McMurtrie, Douglas C. (ed.), *Manual of Printing Office Practice by Theodore L. De Vinne*, Ars Typographia Press, 1926.

Margolin, Victor, *The Struggle for Utopia: Rodchenko, Lissitzky, Moholy-Nagy, 1917–1946*, Chicago, Ill., and London: University of Chicago Press, 1997.

Marthens, John F., *Typographical Bibliography: A List of Books in the English Language on Printing and Its Accessories*, Pittsburgh, Pa.: Bakewell & Marthens, 1875.

Massin, *Letter and Image*, London: Studio Vista, 1970.

Mayhew, Henry, *London Labour and the London Poor*, 1851–64.

Meggs, Philip B., *A History of Graphic Design*, London: Allen Lane, 1983.

Meynell, Francis, and Herbert Simon (eds), *Fleuron Anthology*, London: Ernest Benn, 1973.

Moran, James, *Printing Presses: History & Development from the Fifteenth Century to Modern Times*, Berkeley, CA: University of California Press, 1978.

Mosley, James (introduction), *Ornamented Types: Twenty-three Alphabets from the Foundry of Louis John Pouchée*. Limited edition produced by I. M. Imprimit in association with the St Bride Printing Library, London, 1992.

Moxon, Joseph, *Mechanick Exercises*, The Typothetae of

the City of New York, 1896.

Myers, Robin, and Michael Harris (eds), *Spreading the Word: The Distribution Networks of Print 1550–1850*, Winchester: St Paul's Bibliographies, 1990.

Nathan, Paul, *How to Make Money in the Printing Business*, New York: Lotus Press, 1900.

Opie, Robert, *Packaging Source Book*, Secaucus, NJ: Chartwell Books, 1989.

Owens, L. T., *J. H. Mason, 1875–1951, Scholar-Printer*, London: Frederick Muller Ltd, 1976.

Pankow, David, *The Printer's Manual: An Illustrated History*, Rochester, NY: RIT Cary Graphic Arts Press, 2005.

Pye, David, *The Nature and Art of Workmanship*, Cambridge: Cambridge University Press, 1968.

—— *The Nature and Aesthetics of Design*, London: Barrie & Jenkins, 1978.

Raven, James (ed.), *Free Print and Non-Commercial Publishing since 1700*, Aldershot: Ashgate, 2000.

Reed, David, *The Popular Magazine in Britain and the United States, 1880–1960*, London: British Library, 1997.

Richmond, W. D., *The Grammar of Lithography: A Practical Guide for the Artist and Printer*, Cambridge: Cambridge University Press, 2010 (originally published in 1878).

Rickards, Maurice, *The Public Notice: An Illustrated History*, Newton Abbot: David & Charles, 1973.

—— (edited and completed by Michael Twyman), *The Encyclopedia of Ephemera: A Guide to the Fragmentary Documents of Everyday Life for the Collector, Curator, and Historian*, London: British Library, 2000.

Romans, Mervyn (ed.), *Histories of Art and Design Education: Collected Essays*, Bristol and Portland, Ore.: Intellect, 2005.

Rosner, Charles, *Printer's Progress: A Comparative Survey of the Craft of Printing, 1851–1951*, London: Sylvan Press, 1951.

Rumble, Walker, *The Swifts: Printers in the Age of Typesetting Races*, Charlottesville, VA: University of Virginia Press, 2003.

Rydell, Robert W., *World of Fairs: The Century-of-Progress Expositions*, Chicago, Ill., and London: University of Chicago Press, 1993.

St John, Bruce (ed.), *John Sloan's New York Scene from the Diaries, Notes and Correspondence, 1906–1913*, New York: Harper & Row, 1965.

Schmeckebier, Laurence F., *The Bureau of Engraving and Printing: Its History, Activities and Organization*, Baltimore, MD: John Hopkins Press, 1929.

Schwartz, Frederic J., *The Werkbund: Design Theory & Mass Culture before the First World War*, New Haven, Conn., and London: Yale University Press, 1996.

Sennett, Richard, *The Craftsman*, New Haven, Conn.: Yale University Press, 2008.

Shipcott, Grant, *Typographical Periodicals between the Wars: A Critique of The Fleuron, Signature and Typography*, Oxford: Oxford Polytechnic Press, 1980.

Silver, Rollo G., *Typefounding in America, 1787–1825*, Charlottesville, VA: published for the Bibliographical Society of the University of Virginia by the University Press of Virginia, 1965.

Simon, Herbert, *Song and Words: A History of the Curwen Press*, London: Allen & Unwin, 1973.

Simon, Oliver, *Printer and Playground*, London: Faber & Faber, 1956.

Sivulka, Juliann, *Soap, Sex, and Cigarettes: A Cultural History of American Advertising*, Belmont, CA, and London: Wadsworth, 1998.

Skingsley, T. A. 'Technical Training and Education in the English Printing Industry', *Journal of the Printing Historical Society* (printed in two parts), nos 13 and 14, 1978/79.

Southward, John, *Artistic Printing: A Supplement to the Author's Work on 'Practical Printing'*, London, 1892.

—— *Modern Printing: A Handbook* (two volumes), London: Raithby & Lawrence, 1924.

Steer, Vincent, *Printing, Design, and Layout*, London: Virtue & Co., 1934.

Steinberg, S. H., *Five Hundred Years of Printing* (new edition, revised by John Trevitt), London: British Library and Oak Knoll Press, 1996.

Tames, Richard, *The Printing Press: Turning Points in History*, Heinemann Library, 2001.

Taylor, John Russell, *The Art Nouveau Book in Britain*, Edinburgh: Paul Harris Publishing, 1980.

Thomas, Isaiah, *The History of Printing in America*, New York: Gramercy, 1988.

Thomson, Ellen Mazur, *The Origins of Graphic Design in America, 1870–1920*, New Haven, Conn., and London: Yale University Press, 1997.

Tracy, Walter, *Letters of Credit: A View of Type Design*, London: Gordon Fraser, 1986.

—— *The Typographic Scene*, London: Gordon Fraser, 1988.

Troy, Nancy, *Modernism and the Decorative Arts in France: Art Nouveau to Le Corbusier*, Yale University Press, 1991.

Tuer, Andrew White (ed.), *The Printers' International Specimen Exchange*, volumes 1 to 8 (volumes 9 to 16 were edited by Roger Hilton). The series was published between 1880 and 1898.

—— (ed.), *Old London Street Cries*, London: Field & Tuer, 1885.

Turner, E. S., *The Shocking History of Advertising!*, London: Michael Joseph, 1952.

Twyman, Michael, *Early Lithographed Books: A Study of the Design and Production of Improper Books in the Age of the Hand Press*, Farrand Press & Private Libraries Association, 1990.

—— *Printing 1770–1970: An Illustrated History of its Development and Uses in England*, London, Reading and New Castle, Del.: British Library, Reading University Press and Oak Knoll Press, 1998.

Updike, D. B., *Printing Types: Their History, Forms and Use*, two volumes, Oxford University Press, 1937 (second edition).

Volkov, Shulamit, *The Rise of Popular Antimodernism in Germany: The Urban Master Artisans, 1873–1896*, Princeton, NJ, and Guildford: Princeton University Press, 1978.

Wallis, Lawrence, *Typomania, Selected Essays on Typesetting and Related Subjects*, Upton-upon-Severn: Severnside Printers, 1993.

—— *George W. Jones: Printer Laureate*, Plough Press, 2004.

Warde, Beatrice, *The Pencil Draws a Vicious Circle*, London: Sylvan Press, 1955.

Weisberg, Gabriel P., and Elizabeth Kolbinger Menon, *Art Nouveau: A Research Guide for Design Reform in France, Belgium, England, and the United States*, Taylor and Francis, 1998.

Wlassikoff, Michel, *The Story of Graphic Design in France*, Gingko Press, 2005.

Young, Matthew McLennan, *Field & Tuer, The Leadenhall Press: A Checklist with an Appreciation of Andrew White Tuer*, New Castle, Del., and London: Oak Knoll Press and the British Library, 2010.

Zander, C. G., *Photo-trichromatic Printing, in Theory and Practice*, Leicester: Raithby & Lawrence, 1896.

Picture Credits

Photographs were taken by the author, with the exception of those credited to Tipoteca Italiana, which were taken by Fabio Zonta, and those credited to Richard Sheaff, which were taken by Richard Sheaff.

(T: top; C: centre; B: bottom; L: left; R: right)

Ephemera Collection, Department of Typography and Visual Communication, Reading University

7; 12R; 17R; 18L; 18R; 19L; 19TR; 19BR; 20L; 21BR; 22TL; 22BL; 22TR; 22BR; 23TL; 23BL; 25; 26; 27BL; 27TR; 27BR; 28; 29TL; 29B; 29TR; 30L; 30R; 31TL; 31BL; 31R; 32L; 32TR; 32BR; 33L; 33TR; 33BR; 34; 35TL; 35BL; 35TR; 35CR; 35BR; 40T; 40BL; 40BR; 41TL; 41CL; 41BL; 41TR; 41BR; 42TL; 42TR; 44TL; 44CL; 44BL; 44TR; 44BR; 45T; 45C; 45BL; 45BR; 49TR; 49CR; 49BR; 50TL; 50TR; 51TL; 51BL; 51TR; 51BR; 52TL; 52BR; 53TL; 53TR; 54BR; 55TR; 58TL; 61BR; 62; 63BL; 64R; 66L; 67BL; 68R; 69R; 70L; 70C; 72TL; 72BL; 75TC; 75BL; 75BR; 76BL; 77T; 78TC; 78TR; 78B; 80; 81TL; 81TR; 86TR; 87BR; 89TL; 89BL; 89R; 91T; 91BL; 91BR; 93TL; 93BL; 93BR; 94TL; 94BL; 94TR; 94BR; 95TL; 95BL; 95CR; 95BR; 99TR; 100TL; 100TR; 100BR; 101TL; 101BC; 101TR; 102TL; 102CL; 102BL; 102TR; 102CR; 102BR; 107L; 107TR; 109L; 109R; 111L; 111R; 112TL; 112BL; 112R; 121; 125TL; 125BL; 125R; 126TL; 127TR; 127CR; 128TL; 128BR; 128TR; 129; 130L; 130TR; 130BR; 131TL; 131CL; 131BL; 131TR; 131BR; 132B; 132R; 134TL; 134BL; 134TR; 135TL; 135B; 135TR; 136; 137TL; 137BL; 137TR; 138B; 140TL; 140BL; 140BR; 141TL; 141CL; 141BL; 141TR; 142TL; 143T; 143B; 144TL; 144BL; 144TR; 144CR; 144BR; 145TL; 145B; 145TR; 146TL; 146BL; 146R 147TL; 147BL; 147R; 149L; 149TR; 149CR; 149BCR; 154; 165L; 165TR; 165BR; 167TR; 168L; 176B; 187TL; 187BR; 188TR; 194BR; 195L; 195C; 195TR; 195BR; 203TR; 203BR; 214L; 214R; 222BR; 223T; 223B; 224BL; 224BC; 224BR; 226TL; 226TR; 227BL; 227BR; 228TL; 233CR; 233BR; 236TL; 236B; 236TR; 237TL; 237BL; 237BR; 239TL; 239TR; 240B; 241TL; 250L; 250R; 251TL; 251BL; 260R; 274L; 274BR; 275; 276TL; 276CL; 276R; 277; 279TL; 279BL; 279BR; 282TL; 282BL; 282TR; 282BR; 285TL; 285BL; 286TL; 286CL; 286B; 286CR; 288L; 288R; 289TL; 289BR; 290BL; 293T; 293B; 294T; 294B

St Bride Printing Library, London

12BL; 16; 46; 47TR; 48BR; 53B; 54BL; 55L; 59TR; 63TL; 65L; 65R; 66BR; 68TL; 71TR; 73; 76L; 82; 84; 85; 86L; 86–87; 87TL; 87TR; 87CR; 88CL; 88BL; 96BR; 97BL; 97BR; 98TL; 98BL; 98TR; 99TL;

99BL; 99BR; 100BL; 103L; 103TR; 103BR; 106; 108TL; 108BL; 108R; 114L; 115L; 116; 117L; 117BL; 119L; 119R; 120; 122L; 122B; 123TL; 123B; 126R; 132TL; 133TL; 133BL; 133TR; 133CR; 133BR; 137BR; 139R; 142BL; 150L; 150TR; 150BR; 151T; 151B; 155B; 156; 157L; 157C; 159C; 159R; 160L; 160R; 161L; 161R; 162L; 162R; 163T; 163B; 164L; 164R; 166L; 166R; 167L; 169; 170TL; 170B; 170TR; 171; 172; 173TL; 173B; 173TR; 174L; 174TR; 174BR; 175L; 175TR; 175CR; 176L; 177; 178TL; 178BL; 178TR; 178CR; 178BR; 179C; 179B; 180; 181BL; 181TR; 182TL; 182R; 183TR; 183BR; 184T; 184B; 185T; 185BL; 185BR; 186; 192TL; 192TR; 192B; 196CL; 196B; 196TR; 197T; 197B; 202TL; 202CT; 205TR; 207R; 208L; 208R; 210; 211L; 211R; 212TL; 213L; 213R; 216T; 216B; 217; 218; 219TL; 219BL; 219TR; 219BR; 220; 221BL; 221BR; 228TR; 232; 234; 238T; 238C; 238BL; 243; 245TR; 250C; 251R; 252TL; 252BL; 252R; 254L; 254C; 254R; 255L; 255R; 256C; 256TR; 256BR; 257; 258L; 258C; 258R; 259; 260L; 260C; 261R; 261BR; 262L; 263; 266BC; 267R; 268TL; 268B; 268R; 269TL; 269BL; 270BR; 270B; 271TL; 271BL; 271TR; 272TL; 272B; 272TR; 274TR; 276B; 280TL; 280BL; 280TR; 280BR; 281TL; 281TR; 285TR; 287L; 287R; 289BL; 290R; 291TL; 291TR; 291B; 294TL; 294B; 294TR; 295T; 295B; 296

John Hall

36; 37TL; 37BL; 37TR; 37BR; 38L; 38R; 39L; 39TR; 39CR; 39BR; 42B; 47B; 58L; 58BL; 76R; 77B; 79; 88TL; 88TR; 88CR; 88BR; 90TL; 90BL; 90BR; 117R; 138T; 139TL; 139BL; 142CL; 142R; 194TL; 194BL; 194TR; 221TL; 221TC; 221TR; 222TL; 222TR; 225; 239BL; 239BR; 240T; 242T; 242C; 244T; 244B; 248TL; 248BL; 248R; 249; 251; 267; 278

Richard Sheaff

90TR; 127L; 140TR; 157R; 159BL; 159TL; 168R; 175BR; 176TR; 179T; 181TL; 183L; 187BL; 187TR; 188L; 188BR; 189; 190; 191T; 191C; 191B; 196TL; 198T; 198B; 199TL; 199B; 199TR; 199CR; 199BR; 222BL; 224TL; 224TC; 224TR; 233TL; 233BL; 233TR; 235TL; 235BL; 238BR; 241BL; 241TR; 241BR; 242B; 245TL; 245TC; 256L

Tipoteca Italiana Fondazione, Cornuda

2; 8; 11TR; 13R; 14; 15L; 15C; 15BR; 21L; 43B; 54TL; 54TR; 55B; 56; 58BR; 61L; 61TR; 74; 81B; 104; 152; 167BR; 200; 205BR; 209L; 209R; 212BL; 250; 266R; 284; 286TR

Martin Andrew

21TR; 60L; 60TR; 60BR; 97TL; 97TR; 110L; 110R; 113L; 113R; 118L; 122; 123TR; 124T; 124B; 226B; 227TL; 227TR

Tony Cox

24BL; 48L; 48TR; 52BL; 52TR; 64L; 67TL; 92L; 92R; 96L; 181BR; 204L; 204R; 205L; 206L; 206R; 207L; 213C

John Ellis

134BR; 228BR; 229L; 229R; 230L; 230TR; 230BR; 231TL; 231BL; 231TR; 266BR

Central Saint Martins College of Art and Design, London

253L; 253R

Brian Webb

264C; 270TL; 270TR

David Wakefield

71BR; 118R; 281B

Michael Wood

279TR; 290TL

Joe Freedman

176CR; 235TR

George K Fox

182BL

Ian Mortimer

10R

V&A Picture Library, London

262TL

The generosity of individuals in providing access to their personal collections has also been essential in the research and writing of this book. Most significant of these has been Richard Sheaff, USA, a collector specializing in artistic printing and a member of the Board of Directors of the Ephemera Society of America. Access to his remarkable collection, as well as his knowledge of artistic printing, proved essential. His website address is sheaff-ephemera.com.

I would also like to express my gratitude to the following for their generous help, expertise and enthusiasm:
Clive Chizlett, ex-compositor and educator.
Tony Cox, Claude Cox Antiquarian Bookshop, Ipswich, UK.
John Hall, Treasurer to the Ephemera Society, UK, and ephemera collector.
Mikhail Karasik, Russia, book artist and collector of the Russian avant-garde book.
Ian Mortimor, UK, fine printer and proprietor of I. M. Imprimit, London.
David Wakefield, UK, collector specializing in wood type.
Michael Wood, UK, Writing Equipment Society.

My thanks also to:
James Clough, UK/Italy
John Ellis, UK
George K. Fox, USA
Joe Freedman, USA
Barry Hurd, UK
Professor Manuel Junco, Spain
Professor Jay Rutherford, Germany
Stephen O. Saxe, USA
Brian Webb, UK

Finally, my thanks to everyone at Thames & Hudson who contributed in so many ways to this book.

Acknowledgments
The following public collections and those responsible for them have provided invaluable access to essential material.
Sandro Berra, Coordinator of the Tipoteca Italiana Fondazione, Cornuda, near Treviso, Italy.
Diane Bilbey, Head of the Ephemera Collection, and Martin Andrew, Reading University, Reading, UK.
Nigel Roache, Head Librarian, St Bride Printing Library, London.

Tipoteca Italiana Fondazione is a working museum of typography and printing and holds a wonderful archive of printed material, metal and wood type and printing presses, all in working order and regularly in action. Fabio Zonta's poignant photographs of 'retired' Italian print shops (taken for their archive) were one of the inspirations for this book. Tipoteca Italiana Fondazione saved the equipment, restored it and now have it working in their workshops. As Silvio Antiga, prime motivator of the Tipoteca, said: 'What better way to save printers from oblivion than saving the tools, materials and equipment they used?' One of Fabio Zonta's photographs provides the frontispiece for this book.

Reading University's Department of Typography and Graphic Communication maintains and administers a remarkable collection of printed matter, including a substantial archive of print ephemera, the nucleus of which is made up of the Maurice Rickards's collection. Rickards was a founder member and original president of the Ephemera Society. The collection now consists of some 20,000 items stored by subject matter. Diane Bilbey is the first point of contact for the Centre and acts as its administrator.

Martin Andrew, lecturer at Reading University's Department of Typography and Graphic Communication, introduced me to the School's various collections and also provided several items from his personal collection of journals, wood blocks and copperplates. His generosity is very much appreciated.

I am also indebted to Nigel Roache at St Bride Printing Library, London, for his inestimable knowledge of print technology and history and, importantly, where to find it.